FINDING
Susan

FINDING
Susan

Molly Hurley Moran

Southern Illinois University Press
Carbondale

Library of Congress Cataloging-in-Publication Data

Moran, Molly Hurley, 1947–
  Finding Susan / Molly Hurley Moran.
        p. cm.
  Includes bibliographical references.
  1. Murder—Maryland—Case studies. I. Title.
HV6533 .M3 M67 2003
364.15'23'092—dc21
ISBN 0-8093-2519-5   2002151208

For Jonathan and Nicholas,
and in loving memory of Susan

Contents

Illustrations

Preface

The material in this book comes from my own memories, from letters and notes written by my sister and others, from conversations with my sister's friends and with police and other investigators involved in my sister's case, from public records such as police reports and open legal documents, and from newspaper and magazine articles published about the case. (Many of these articles can be found on my website: www.findingsusan.com.) There is no information in this book that is derived from documents protected by attorney-client privilege or from documents that have been sealed by a court. I did not sign the confidentiality agreement regarding the resolution of the civil suit my nephews brought against James Harrison.

I have reported events and conversations I witnessed and participated in as accurately as my memory allows. Any errors in detail or chronology are inadvertent and would not affect the substance of my narrative. When I refer to "we" or "the family" throughout the book, I mean the relatives of my sister who were most actively involved in trying to solve the case: my three brothers, my two nephews and their father (Susan's two sons and first husband), and myself. The generalizations I make about the family's collective attitudes and hypotheses concerning the case are based on my own inferences. I do not necessarily speak for every family member in every opinion I attribute to "the family." The only one of my blood relatives who has read and approved the manuscript of this book is my brother Bill Hurley.

James Harrison was never convicted of my sister's murder in a court of law; therefore, my statements in this book about his probable role in my sister's disappearance are presented as suspicions, speculations, and theories, not as confirmed facts.

In writing this book, I feel that I have found my sister. I understand her now in a way that I did not when she was alive. I wish I could tell her that she already possessed the beauty and the worth she thought she lacked and sought so desperately, and in such wrong places. *Finding Susan* is, finally, my way of telling her. It is my way of showing that my sister, and my sister's life, mattered.

Acknowledgments

I would first like to express my gratitude to the editors, reviewers, and staff at Southern Illinois University Press for seeing the value in this book and choosing to publish it. In particular, I want to thank Jennifer Williams, Carol Burns, Jane Carlson, Jonathan Haupt, and Barb Martin.

I would like to thank the many friends who have read my manuscript at various stages and offered suggestions and support, including Jackie Markham, Julie Checkoway, Judy Page, Carol Myers, Marianne Causey, Sherrie Nist, Pat McAlexander, Sally Randall, and Mayo Bulloch. Friends Sara Baker, Donna Maddock-Cowart, Rosemary Hathaway, Rosemarie Goodrum, Theresa Cullen, and Laura Ferguson aided in other ways, ranging from their ongoing interest and support to advice about the book's graphics and marketing. And I am deeply indebted to my new friend Anne Kosvanec, who designed and maintains the website for *Finding Susan*. Many other people helped me to check facts and hunt down sources, including Roger Cassell, Frank Napfel, Cary Woodward, Andra Whitworth, Chris Hayes, Mary Kelly, Mark Cooney, and Aisling Maguire. William Gignilliat provided excellent guidance concerning First Amendment issues, and I greatly appreciate his volunteering his time and expertise to do so.

I also want to thank family members for providing many of the photographs contained in the book. All the photos submitted either belong to me or were contributed by relatives (Hurley and Owsley family members). All the written documents, except for the strange postcard that was sent to our family, were found in Susan's cottage when we cleaned it out. Whenever known, the photographer who took the picture has been credited in the caption.

I am most indebted to my eldest brother, Bill Hurley, who read several drafts of the manuscript and spent innumerable hours on the phone with me over the past four years offering suggestions, filling in gaps in my memory about certain details, and giving me moral support. I could not have written this book without the knowledge that he was 100 percent behind my efforts.

This book also owes its existence to my sister's many wonderful friends, who in the years following her tragedy phoned and wrote me to offer emotional support and to share memories of Susan, memories that helped me in my "finding" of my sister and that have made their way into this book. These friends include Helen Lamberton, Lister Bradley, Carol Even, Connie Weeks, Mary Jo Gordon, Clare Hume, and, most especially, Terry MacMillan.

Finally, my deepest gratitude goes to my husband, Mike, and daughter, Alison, whose belief in the importance of this book and in me as a writer kept me going during periods of discouragement, when I would convince myself no one would ever want to publish or read a memoir about an unknown woman. Mike has also served as my best stylistic critic, offering astute editing suggestions that helped me to hone the manuscript into publishable form. I thank him for this, and both Alison and him for their love, which sustained me during the dark period following Susan's disappearance and which sustains me always.

FINDING
Susan

Prologue

My need to write this book began in the first weeks and months after my sister disappeared, in August of 1994. That autumn was surreal for me. One minute I would be involved in the quotidian world of grocery shopping, and the next I would be abandoning my half-filled cart and walking out of the store, disoriented by having spotted a fashionable middle-aged blond bearing an uncanny resemblance to Susan. One minute I would be driving in my car singing along with the radio, and the next I would be pulling off the road, reduced to tears by a golden oldie that had suddenly conjured up an image of my big sister as a teenager in the 1950s, playing 45s on her phonograph. One minute I would be convinced my sister was dead and would long for the phone call telling me her body had been found; the next minute I would be dreading that phone call and latching once again onto the tiny hope that Susan was alive and out there somewhere.

As an English professor, I have always found writing to be a way of making sense of experience, and so there grew in me the need to take this nightmare and shape it into words, thereby framing it and in a sense controlling it. But as time went on, my need became more complex. I found myself also wanting to write about Susan as a way to try to understand her, to figure out why her life had taken the tragic turn that it did; in particular, I wanted to come to terms with my bewilderment as to why she and I, so similar in so many ways and springing from the same roots, had met with such different fates. One night in early 1998, while I was taking a shower, the title *Finding Susan* suddenly came to me, and at that moment this book was born. I knew then and there that I wanted to write a book that at once described our family's nightmare, explored my sister's life, and ultimately paid tribute to my sister. *Finding Susan* would be about both the literal finding of Susan—the search for and discovery of her body—and the figurative finding of her, through my narration of her biography and analysis of her character.

But as I began to think about and write about my sister's life, an additional purpose began to emerge: I wanted to share her story with other women who are ensnared in violent relationships, particularly relationships in which alcohol is involved. Although Susan's background, psychology, and marital situation were, like everyone's, unique, I believe that many such women reading this book will see something of themselves in Susan and will consequently, I hope, be motivated to get out or to get help.

It was these multiple needs that motivated me as I worked on the book for the first year or so, beginning in February 1998. But by the fall of 1999, when it had become clear that a prosecution would never take place, I had an additional, burning motive: I wanted to show that justice had not been served for my sister. *Finding Susan* is thus also intended to open readers' eyes to the sad fact that in the United States of America, it is all too easy to get away with murder.

Part One

The Nightmare Begins

1   Susan Disappears, August 1994

August 10, 1994, dawned promisingly. I awoke early to another cloudless New Mexico day and, as was my habit on vacation, made myself a cup of coffee and prepared to settle into a peaceful hour of reading before my husband and daughter arose. No sooner had I become absorbed in my book, however, than I registered the crunching sound of a Jeep making its way up the dirt road that winds through the D. H. Lawrence Ranch. The vehicle came to an abrupt stop outside our cabin; a second later there was a brusque knock at the door. I opened it, and the burly caretaker of the ranch thrust a pink telephone memo slip at me, on which was scrawled, "Urgent—call one of your brothers." Beneath this terse message were listed the phone numbers of my three brothers in Massachusetts. Panicked, I asked the caretaker to drive me to his cabin, which contained the only phone on the ranch, and jumped into his Jeep, still wearing my bathrobe and slippers.

En route, while I made nervous small talk, my mind raced from one worst-case scenario to another: one of my teenage nieces had been critically hurt in a car wreck; my twenty-three-year-old nephew had been killed while vacationing in Europe; my sister-in-law's cancer had returned. Then another possibility struck me: something had happened to Susan, my older sister. This in a way was the most likely explanation, since the phone message had been from my brothers, with her name conspicuously absent, and since over the past several years the majority of the family crises my brothers had contacted me about had concerned Susan. But then I reminded myself that those crises were a thing of the past: Susan seemed to have her drinking under control and, since January, had been separated from Jim, her second husband, with whom she had endured a tempestuous relationship; we had had seven months uninterrupted by the hysterical phone calls from Susan that used to disrupt our lives periodically.

And so, I reasoned, the occasion for the urgent phone call probably wasn't anything to do with Susan. Besides, she had been scheduled to travel from Baltimore, where she lived, to Boston a few days earlier with Nicholas—her younger son from her first marriage—for a visit with my brothers, and therefore she wasn't even anywhere near Jim. No, it had to be something else. Reaching this conclusion, I resumed my frightening speculations concerning other family members and was in a cold sweat by the time I arrived at the caretaker's cabin.

Expecting the news to be a death in the family, I felt a certain amount of relief when I reached my eldest brother and learned that the urgent situation was Susan's disappearance, five days earlier. My brothers hadn't contacted me right away because they didn't want to disrupt my vacation until they were sure the situation was critical. Bill explained that on August 5, the night before Susan and Nick were to have flown to Boston, she had gone over to Jim's house and never returned. A missing person report had been filed the next day, and the police had questioned Jim, who claimed to know nothing of her whereabouts. He said that they had gotten into an argument that night, he had left her yelling at him in the living room and had gone upstairs to bed, and a few minutes later he had heard her leave in her car. Listening to my brother Bill's account, I thought that surely this was just another crazy episode in Susan and Jim's sick relationship. She had probably sought refuge at a friend's house and was reluctant to call the family because she knew we would be disappointed that she had been seeing Jim again. So why were my brothers so alarmed?

Despite my skepticism, I couldn't help but be preoccupied by this development, and therefore my husband and daughter and I decided to cut short our vacation and return home to Georgia. During the three-day drive, as I became increasingly acquainted with the facts through daily phone calls to my brothers, my sense of urgency began to match theirs. The first thing I would do each night when we stopped at a motel would be to telephone one of them for an update, and with each call I would learn that another hope had been eliminated: another friend of Susan's who turned out to know nothing, another credit card search that showed no transactions after August 5, another women's shelter contacted that had no Susan Harrison staying there. Somehow while on the road, I managed to keep the panic at bay, but once home, I could no longer deny the grim facts: it had now been a week since my sister had disappeared; there had been no activity in any of her bank accounts; she had had nothing with her but the clothes she was wearing, her wallet, and less than five dollars; her car had contained only a quarter of a tank of gas; she had never before not contacted one of us during a crisis; and— most importantly— it would be totally out of character for Susan to put her two sons, to whom she was devoted, through this kind of frightening ordeal. The evidence seemed to point to only one conclusion: Susan had been murdered.

This realization first fully struck me the night of our return from vacation, August 13. Attempting to divert my thoughts from the crisis, I was watching a television sitcom with my husband and daughter, a rerun of a *Designing Women* episode involving the wedding of one of the characters. Suddenly, just as the rest of my family burst into laughter at a humorous scene, I found myself convulsed with uncontrollable sobs. I had looked at the bride walking down the aisle and, instead of focusing on the intended comedy, was unexpectedly overcome by the memory of a young, happy Susan at her wedding to Tom Owsley, her first husband, twenty-seven years earlier. And that mental picture had been rapidly followed by an image of her lying dead and discarded somewhere. The contrast hit me like a punch in the stomach.

That moment marked the beginning of the nightmarish odyssey my life was to become. I grew obsessed with the search for my sister. The following week, I spent most of every day on the phone with my brothers and nephews—Nick and his older brother, Jonathan, who had been on vacation in Greece but had flown home as soon as he was informed of the situation—hungry for the facts about Susan's disappearance and about the incipient police investigation. By week's end, I had pieced together the following account.

Susan had planned to drive to Massachusetts on Friday, August 5, with nineteen-year-old Nick, who was home from Middlebury College for the summer and splitting his time between his dad Tom's house in Baltimore and the rented cottage in Ruxton where Susan had been living since moving out of Jim's. However, she wasn't feeling well Friday morning, so the two decided not to drive but instead to take an early flight to Boston the next day. Nick spent Friday afternoon packing and running errands. Shortly before 4:00, he took Susan's dog to the kennel, using her car so as to avoid getting white dog hairs in his brother's car, which he had driven over from his dad's house that day. He noticed that her car was down to a quarter of a tank of gas, and he made a mental note to remember to fill it that afternoon so they wouldn't have to stop on their way to the airport the next morning (he forgot). Returning to the cottage around 4:30, he spent about a half an hour talking with Susan. She was feeling depressed and said she thought she'd rest for a couple of hours while he went back to his father's house to finish packing. Checking her wallet and noting that she had only about five dollars in it, she gave Nick her ATM card and instructed him to get cash for the trip and to pick up some Chinese takeout for their supper. She told him not to be too long because they needed to get to bed early. When Nick said good-bye to Susan, assuring her he'd be back in a few hours, he had no idea that he would never see her again.

Nick returned around 8:30 p.m. Susan's car was gone. The front door of the cottage was ajar, as though Susan had been in such a hurry to leave that she had not taken the time to close it properly. Nick found her purse on the floor near the phone; it was open and the wallet was gone. There was a message on the phone machine from my brother John, which had been left at around 7:00, saying he'd be home for the rest of the evening if she wanted to call him back. Susan had phoned John (we would later learn) at his Cambridge, Massachusetts, home around 5:15 that afternoon, sounding depressed and anxious, but he'd been on his way out the door to play in a softball game and so had to cut the call short. He felt bad about putting her off but figured they would have plenty of opportunity to talk about what was troubling her when she was up in Boston over the next few days. Aware that Susan had been agitated after visiting Jim earlier that day—to discuss the divorce she was pursuing, Nick assumed—Nick interpreted all these signs to mean she had probably been on the phone with Jim some time before 7:00, had become upset or angered by something he'd said to her, and on impulse had jumped up, grabbed her wallet and car key—the only things she'd need for the short trip from Ruxton over to Lutherville, where Jim lived, and back—and dashed out the door. Nick's heart sank, but he was used to his mother and stepfather's rocky relationship. Both he and his brother abhorred Jim and tried to keep their distance from him, so Nick was not inclined to go over to Jim's house or to phone there.

Nick waited and waited. By 11:30, he was very worried and phoned his dad to ask if he'd heard from Susan. Tom hadn't. He instructed Nick to call the police, to see if there had been any car accidents in the area. The police knew of none but suggested that Nick call around to hospitals. These inquiries yielding nothing, at 2:00 A.M. Nick phoned Tom again and asked if he should go to Jim's. Tom said no, for he knew how upset Nick was and didn't want him to become further distressed by an encounter with Jim. Tom told Nick to leave Susan a note and come back to his house to wait to hear from her. Nick did so. By 6:00 A.M., there was still no word from Susan, so Nick called her house. There was no answer. Next he called my brother Bill in Hingham, Massachusetts, to alert him about the situation and have him pass the word on to John before John left for the airport to meet the flight Susan and Nick had been scheduled to arrive on.

Nick called Susan's house all morning and called Jim's house around 9:30 A.M. My brother Bill also called both Susan's and Jim's homes a few times. There was no answer at either place. Nick drove back to Susan's in the morning; there was no sign that she'd returned. He drove past Jim's house; Jim's car was there, so either he had gone out without his car or he was home but wasn't answering his phone. Midmorning, Tom went out to hit golf balls for about a half hour to try to relieve some of the stress that was building up inside him. When he finished, he phoned Nick from the club to ask if Nick wanted him to go by the police station on his way home. Nick said yes. Tom went to the Towson precinct, the one closest to Susan's house, to report her missing; the officers there also notified the Cockeysville precinct, the one closest to Jim's house, and asked Tom to bring them a photo of Susan. Tom went home to get one, driving by Jim's house on the way and noting that Jim's car was still in the driveway. After locating a photo of Susan, Tom returned to the police station, accompanied by Nick.

By this time, Nicholas was convinced Susan was dead. Nonetheless, police department protocol is such that the case had to be assigned to the missing person, not the homicide, division—a maddening situation, as any family who is convinced their loved one has been murdered and has not simply run off will attest, for it means that precious time and evidence are lost, and if a murder is not solved within the first several hours, its chances of ever being solved are greatly diminished. In the early afternoon, a couple of officers from the Cockeysville precinct drove over to Jim's house; his car was still there, but no one answered their knock. They taped a note to the door requesting that Jim phone the precinct as soon as he returned. At around 7:00 P.M., he phoned them. They asked him if he knew where Susan was, and he replied that she'd gone to Boston. When they informed him that she wasn't in Boston and that she had been reported missing, he seemed surprised and said he didn't know where she was.

Later that evening, Nicholas phoned Jim's house again; this time Jim picked up. Nick asked him if he knew where Susan was; Jim again expressed surprise, as though he hadn't been informed that she was missing. Then Nick asked him where he'd been all day, and Jim replied that he'd been home. Nick pointed out that people had been phoning his house all day but he hadn't answered, nor had he appeared to be home when the police stopped by in the afternoon. Jim then changed his story and began a garbled account of where he'd been, starting to say something about going to "the eastern" and then switching midphrase to "downtown." Nick hung up and immediately called the police to report this strange conversation, the first of many in which Jim appeared to be hiding his knowledge of and involvement in Susan's disappearance.

Another such conversation occurred the next day, Sunday, when Jim called Bill back in the afternoon in response to a message Bill had left that morning on Jim's answering machine saying that the family was very concerned about Susan's disappearance and asking Jim to call him. Jim's first comment was that he thought Susan was up there in Massachusetts with Bill. Bill reiterated what he had learned from the police, and after that Jim's conversation seemed inconsistent with his first comment: he proceeded to say that Susan's disappearance was terrible and that he was trying to contact her friends to see if he could locate her. Bill then asked him at least twice if he had any thoughts at all as to where we should be checking; Jim said no, he was baffled. However, Jim told the police officer who interviewed him only twenty or thirty minutes after his conversation with Bill that Susan had an old boyfriend in Boston named "Dave" (a nonexistent character, as far as any of us has ever been able to ascertain) and that she might be visiting him. When the officer phoned Bill after the interview with Jim to ask if Bill had any information about "Dave," Bill told the officer that Jim's story was nonsense and said he found it curious that Jim would not have mentioned "Dave" to him when Bill asked him at least twice where we should be checking for Susan.

Inconsistent accounts and unlikely explanations characterized Jim's responses to police queries during interviews conducted over the next few days. Jim acknowledged that Susan had come to his house at about 7:00 Friday night, a fact that was confirmed by his daughter Wendy, one of six grown children from his first marriage, who was leaving just as Susan arrived. Then in one version of the ensuing events, he said that after a couple of hours of their drinking wine and arguing off and on, he went upstairs to bed, leaving Susan downstairs in the living room yelling at him; in a subsequent version, he said she was asleep on the living room couch when he went upstairs. In both versions, he said that shortly after 10:00 he heard a car door slam, and he assumed she was leaving. He claimed that the next morning he awakened around 8:00, spent an hour or so cleaning the house, and around 10:00 decided to go back to bed and rest; he said nothing about hearing the phone ring, and yet Bill and Nick had both rung his house several times. Waking up a second time in the late morning and noting that it was a beautiful day, he decided to go for a jog. This scenario rang false to the police, as well as to our family, for Jim is an out-of-shape heavy drinker who, as far as we knew, was not a jogger. Jim went on to say that after jogging a short distance, he felt fatigued, slowed to a walk, and decided to take the Light Rail commuter train into downtown Baltimore. He got off at Pratt Street and spent the afternoon walking around the Harbor-place area. Two people he knew saw him and called out, "Hi, Jim," but he couldn't recollect who they were (making it impossible for the police to verify this story). In one version of this tale, he claimed to have eaten lunch at a restaurant but couldn't remember which one; in another version, he said he made a sandwich before setting off for jogging, put it in his shorts pocket, and ate that for lunch. After his alleged afternoon of wandering around the Harborplace, he took the Light Rail back to Lutherville and walked the rest of the way home, arriving there around 5:00 P.M. and finding the note from the police on the front door.

My brothers and nephews were skeptical of Jim's account. A more likely explanation, they thought, was that Jim had murdered Susan and driven her body somewhere in her car, dug a grave for the body, abandoned the car, and then taken various forms of transportation back home. This scenario would account for why his own car was at his house all day Saturday but he was not there and why he claimed to have gone jogging: he probably figured that if any neighbors had noticed him hiking home from the Light Rail stop in grubby athletic clothes, he could attribute his appearance to exercise, when in reality it had been incurred from lugging a body and digging a shallow grave.

My brothers' and nephews' suspicions increased when they learned that a utility company worker repairing a power line had seen a car leave Jim's driveway around 4:00 Saturday morning. There had been a bad storm in the area late Friday afternoon and a tree had gone down near Jim's house, destroying some electric lines and causing a power

outage in the neighborhood for a couple of hours. After a tree company removed the fallen branches and limbs blocking traffic on the
road, workers from Baltimore Gas and Electric came out to restore
a utility pole that had been knocked over. Then late in the evening,
workers from Bell Atlantic arrived to repair damaged cable. They
worked on and off throughout the night. At around 4:00 A.M., a
crewman situated in an aerial bucket high above and to the east of
Jim's house heard the sound of a car door being slammed loudly. His
first thought, he later told police, was, "Gee, somebody's coming
home really late." But then he realized the person was leaving, not
arriving: the car pulled out of the driveway and headed west, in the
opposite direction from where the aerial bucket was situated. The
crewman couldn't make out what kind of car it was but, in response
to the police officers' questioning, said that yes, it could have been a
dark green Saab convertible, the make of Susan's car. When Nicholas learned of the utility worker's testimony about the loud sound of
a car door being slammed, he was convinced the car was Susan's
because he knew that the door on the driver's side of the Saab had
been sprung for the past couple of weeks and would latch shut only
if slammed hard. Nick, as well as Jonathan and my brothers, suspected that what the worker had seen early that Saturday morning
was Jim driving off in Susan's car, intending to dispose of her body
somewhere.

These are the facts and theories I gathered from marathon phone
conversations with family members during the first week following
my return from New Mexico. Fortunately, I had no other pressing
obligations at the time and could devote all my energy to the Susan
case, as we soon began calling it. The research and writing activities
that as a college English professor I normally did during my summers paled in importance next to the urgent need to find my sister,
and I threw myself into this task. Part of me clung to the tiny hope
that she was alive, in hiding somewhere from Jim, and so I scoured
my memory for the names of friends and acquaintances she had
mentioned, besides those I knew the police had already interviewed,
tracked down their phone numbers, and called them to ask if they'd

seen or heard from her. I called women's shelters in the Baltimore area, national missing persons organizations, the Polly Klaas Foundation in California, and any other such source that popped into my head. Formerly frugal about making long-distance calls, I now thought nothing of picking up the phone at any time of day to call anywhere in the country if there was a remote chance I might obtain a lead. By week's end, I had filled the pages of several legal pads with phone numbers, names, notes, and ideas.

One of the reasons I hurled myself into this frenetic activity was that it was a way of staving off pain. While focused on the sleuth work, I would be temporarily distracted from the debilitating sadness that would otherwise overwhelm me. But it was impossible to avoid the pain entirely, for every day brought hundreds of reminders of my sister and of her sudden, eerie absence from the world. Getting through each day was like making my way across a field of land mines. I would take detours through my home to avoid walking through the living room, where Susan at various ages stared out at me from family photos on the mantel. These photos made me feel her presence palpably, in a way that they hadn't done when I knew she was alive, and each time I looked at them I experienced anew a sense of disorientation. That pigtailed eight-year-old playing on the Cape Cod beach in front of our childhood summer home; that suddenly sophisticated teenager, home from boarding school with talk of debutante parties and dances at Exeter; that glowing young mother holding her first baby in his christening dress—where had she gone? Similarly, thumbing through my recipe box, I would come across a card written in Susan's handwriting and would experience a jolting sensation: the backward-slanting 1950s prep-school girl penmanship; the characteristic misspellings—*raisons* for *raisins,* for example ("Geniuses are often poor spellers," she would retort when I, her jealous little sister, would delight in pointing out a spelling error she'd made— spelling being one of the few skills I could hold over Susan, whose artistic talent I could never hope to emulate); the recipe itself, always something elegant, something difficult, involving ingredients like *bouquets garni* and fresh herbs—these intensely concrete reminders would conjure her up so powerfully that I would gasp and sometimes have to grab on to a piece of furniture to steady myself.

At the end of that first, surreal week following our return from New Mexico, my husband went out to have our vacation photographs developed—one of the many routine tasks, along with cooking and grocery shopping and carpooling our thirteen-year-old, that we formerly shared but that he took over while I was preoccupied with the crisis. When he returned with the batch of prints, I began halfheartedly to riffle through them, my mind as always elsewhere, on the case. But then my attention was suddenly caught when I came upon a picture taken on what I now knew to be the same day my sister was probably murdered. Mike and Alison and I had spent the afternoon of August 5 hiking in the beautiful mountain range north of Taos. On our request, a passing hiker had snapped a shot of us—a picture that I had no way of knowing at the time would become an emblem of tragic irony: there stand the three of us, a happy family on a bright summer day, oblivious to the fact that two thousand miles away a tragedy was unfolding that would forever change our lives. Two weeks later, on August 19, I stared at that sunny photo superstitiously. I began to scrutinize it for some indication that all was not right in the universe, for some sign of the catastrophe that was happening offstage. How could I have felt so carefree? I yearned to step into the frozen time frame of the photograph and divert the course of the next few hours. I felt guilty that I hadn't even been thinking of my sister that day.

In fact, I had been keeping an emotional distance from Susan all summer because I suspected she might be slipping back into her relationship with Jim, and if that were the case, I didn't want to know about it. For the ten years that Susan had been involved with Jim, I'd witnessed her crying "wolf" innumerable times—claiming he abused her, working the family up into a state of alarm about her situation, and then retracting her claims—and I had grown cynical. Although for the first few months after she left Jim, I was sure she was going to stick with her decision, I began to have my doubts in the late spring when she stopped talking so persistently about the rightness of the decision in her phone conversations with me. Now I realized I should have pointedly asked her what was going on; I should have challenged her if she said anything that gave me the impression she might be seeing him again. I should have warned her that she was playing with fire. But I didn't fully realize, until it was too late, that she *had* been playing with fire. Looking back at Susan and Jim's relationship from the present vantage point, I deeply regretted not having taken more seriously the signs of trouble, signs that had been there from the beginning.

2 The Early Years of Susan and Jim's Relationship, Mid-1980s

Susan and Jim had been married for a little over five years when Susan moved out, in late December 1993. Before their marriage, they had lived together for four years, while they waited for their divorces from their first spouses to come through, and prior to living together they had carried on an affair, at first secretly but eventually known to their spouses, for about a year and a half. These behaviors on Susan's part—her becoming involved in an extramarital relationship, her "living in sin," her getting divorced—struck people who had known her all her life as being out of character.

When in 1984 Susan informed the family—my parents, who were still alive then, my three brothers, and me—that she and her first husband, Tom, had separated, we were stunned. In the seventeen years that they had been married, she had never indicated that there were any problems between them. In fact, we assumed she was completely contented, living just the kind of life she'd always wanted. Artistic and domestic (one of her friends has described her as having been "a Martha Stewart before anyone had heard of Martha Stewart"), she had created an elegant home and thrived in the role of housewife and mother. She adored her two young sons and was forever doing school projects with them, knitting them sweaters, baking them cookies, and, as they got older, regularly cheering them on in their athletic matches. An indication of how thoroughly ensconced in family and domesticity Susan seemed to be is that once in the 1970s, I had a nightmare that her life was falling apart—Tom had left her; her home and possessions were being destroyed by a violent hurricane; she was sobbing hysterically and trying to stay afloat on the rising flood waters—and when I awoke I thought how far-fetched the dream had been: how Susan's current life was the very opposite of the apocalyptic situation my subconscious had weirdly concocted.

I therefore experienced a guilty déjà vu sensation when, phoning Susan in early December 1984 to ask if my husband and daughter and I could stop to visit them on our way home to South Carolina, where we were living at the time, from Christmas at my parents' in New England, I was greeted not with the cheery response I'd expected but with an awkward silence followed by the grave statement, "Well, you can visit, but I need to explain first about something that's happened: Tom and I have separated." My far-fetched dream from a decade earlier immediately flew into my mind. For a fleeting, irrational second, I feared that maybe I, who at age thirty-seven was still subject to occasional twinges of jealousy toward my artistically accomplished older sister, had *willed* her perfect life to crack. Within minutes, however, I had revised my picture of the situation. I discovered that rather than the situation in my dream, in which Tom had left Susan, she had left him: she had become involved with someone else. This news was the next shocker, for Susan had always prided herself on her proper, ladylike behavior. Plus, she had a strong Catholic sense of guilt; we used to kid her about how as a child she would often return to the confession box after her confession was completed, having remembered yet another "sin" she wanted to mention. It therefore seemed unthinkable that Susan would enter into an extramarital affair.

The final shocker was that the man in question was Jim Harrison. I had heard Susan mention him as well as his wife, Molly, frequently over the course of the previous two years and had assumed that the Harrisons were just family friends. Tom and Jim had become acquainted through professional conferences—both were lawyers, although Jim also had an MBA and eventually moved from the job of general counsel to that of chief financial officer at McCormick

Spice Company. Many of these conferences were social occasions, held at resorts and with spouses included, and in this context the two couples became friendly. In 1982, when the Owsleys moved from Reston, Virginia, to Baltimore, where Tom had accepted the position of chief legal officer at Crown Central Petroleum Corporation and where the Harrisons lived, the Owsleys and the Harrisons began to see more of each other.

This was the extent of my knowledge of Jim Harrison prior to that phone conversation with Susan. Now I learned that he had been pursuing her almost from the beginning of their acquaintance. At cocktail and dinner parties, he would seek out her company, listen attentively to what she had to say, and praise her for her taste and artistic skills. She began to feel that he appreciated and understood her in a way that Tom didn't. His attentions gradually turned to wooing, as he confided that he had been smitten with her from the moment he'd first seen her and that she was the kind of woman he had always wanted. Eventually Susan succumbed, and in June of 1983 the two began an affair. Susan was forty-one, Jim almost forty-seven.[1]

The affair was conducted in secret for the first year. Then one night in the spring of 1984, after the two couples had gone to the theater together and were back at the Owsleys' having drinks, Jim suddenly stood up and announced to Tom and Molly that he was in love with Susan and wanted to marry her.[2] This kind of histrionic gesture was typical of Jim, I would later come to realize as I became acquainted with him. A scene ensued;[3] Tom demanded that Jim leave the house, and then Tom told Susan he wanted her to stop seeing Jim. But Susan put up an argument. Although she had continued to pretend to the rest of the family that she was happily married, in fact—I was to learn later—she and Tom had been growing apart as their sons got older, and they both felt that certain needs were not being met in the relationship. Tom, however, thought these dissatisfactions could be lived with, and he wanted to stick with the marriage for the sake of the children. But Susan begged him to give her some time to work out her feelings and argued that she could do so only if she spent some sustained time with Jim. Tom finally—and reluctantly—agreed to go along with this plan, with the understanding that Susan would come to a decision before the end of the summer. And so over the next couple of months, whenever Jonathan and Nicholas were away at camp or other out-of-town activities, Susan stayed with Jim in the house he had moved into after separating from Molly following the announcement of the affair. Susan also accompanied him on business trips to California and Ireland, experiences that she described to me in our phone conversation in glowing terms. By the end of the summer, she had pretty much arrived at the decision that she wanted to leave Tom for Jim.

The fact that Susan had been dissatisfied with Tom was news to me. She had never said a word about this to me in the past, and I suspected that she was exaggerating the problems in the marriage in order to rationalize her involvement with Jim and assuage her guilt about having committed adultery. I also suspected, knowing Susan's awe of upper-crust society, that a major attraction Jim held for her was his wealth and his preppy image. Although Jim was not from "old" Baltimore society, his experience as a student at the exclusive Gilman School had caused him to adopt some of the manners of that class, manners he had further honed during his tenure at the patrician firm McCormick. And when Susan first met him, before his years of heavy drinking had taken their toll, he was a fit and handsome young man, with the tanned, blond looks of an aristocrat. In fact, one time in a later phone conversation, Susan confessed to me that her head had initially been turned by Jim because he reminded her of "someone who would have gone to Exeter or Lawrenceville." Despite my skepticism of her reasons for being attracted to Jim, I wanted to give Susan the benefit of the doubt, so I tried to put a good spin on the situation in my own head: maybe she had begun to feel stultified in the marriage to Tom, as though she was nothing more than a "pretty little wife" in his eyes, and maybe Jim made her feel recognized and appreciated as a person. I'd always wished Susan had been more liberated. Five years younger than she, I had come of age during the height of the modern feminist movement, whereas Susan had been formed by the 1950s notions about women's roles. Hearing her describe her reasons for becoming involved with Jim, I tried to believe that they were healthy ones and that maybe she would be a stronger, more independent woman in this new relationship.

However, I still had one major reservation: the effect the breakup of their parents' marriage was having on Jonathan and Nicholas, who were only fourteen and nine at the time. Susan told me that this concern had been her main reason for stalling in her decision. But when it became apparent to Tom, by early fall, that the marriage was over, he confronted Susan and said they had to tell the boys. She reluctantly conceded—this was a task she dreaded. Being devoted parents, they agreed to spare the boys the facts about Susan's involvement with Jim, which would be confusing to them at their age, and to tell them instead that Susan and Tom had unfortunately stopped loving each other, as happens in some marriages, but that they still loved the boys very much and that Susan would still be spending a lot of time with them. They took it surprisingly well, Susan said.

Shortly after this conversation with the boys, in October, Susan moved in with Jim. However, she told her sons that she was staying with a female friend until she found a place of her own, and only gradually did she introduce them to the fact that she had begun "dating" Jim. Wanting to ease the trauma of the separation as much as possible, Susan continued to spend most of the boys' waking hours at Tom's house. She would be there every afternoon when they arrived home from school, help them with their homework, drive them to their athletic events, and do all the other motherly things she had formerly done. Then she would prepare supper for them and usually eat with them, leaving later in the evening when Tom arrived home. Tom, who also had the boys' best interest at heart, went along with this plan; he would either eat a takeout supper in his office or fix himself leftovers later in the evening after Susan left. Relations between the two of them, Susan told me, were cool but cordial. She wound up our phone conversation by asserting that as long as I understood the situation, there would be no problem with our stopping for a visit on our way home from Massachusetts. Still reeling from Susan's account, I said good-bye, telling her we'd see her in a month.

While in New England for the holidays, I found myself in the awkward position of having to tiptoe around the facts concerning Susan and Tom's separation in discussions with my parents, who were naturally distressed about it. Susan had been vague when she'd informed them of the situation, no doubt out of guilt and embarrassment. She had told them that she'd left Tom for Jim, but she didn't tell them she had moved in with Jim, instead giving them the same story about staying with "a friend" that she had given Jonathan and Nicholas. I could tell my parents suspected the truth, but they clearly felt uncomfortable addressing it; as was typical of Irish-Catholic parents of their generation, they avoided the topic of sex with their children. Thus began a pattern in which the family didn't talk openly about what was going on in Susan's life and didn't confront her about it—a pattern that was easy to maintain since none of us lived in Baltimore and since Susan preferred to be evasive about her relationship with Jim in phone conversations with us.

Despite my intention to regard this new relationship in a positive light, I was forced to revise my view of it the first time I met Jim. As planned, Mike and Alison and I stopped at the Owsleys' for the night on our drive back to South Carolina after the holidays. For the occasion of our visit, Susan and Tom made an exception to their usual arrangement, and all of us—the four Owsleys and the three Morans—sat down together to eat the dinner Susan had made. Things went pretty smoothly and seemed almost normal, although I did notice that Susan was drinking more wine than usual. Then just after the meal was finished and the three children had excused themselves to go play a game, I heard the sound of a car pulling into the driveway. Somewhat flustered, Susan jumped up and said it was time for her to go. She grabbed her coat and purse and then did something that unsettled me: she transferred the wine remaining in her wineglass to a plastic travel cup. This action made me uneasy because it was so at odds with the usual behavior of Susan, who had always placed a high priority on being ladylike and controlling her drinking. After saying good-bye to us and closing the door behind her, she suddenly popped her head back in and asked me if I would step outside for a minute. Not sure what to expect, I put on my coat and followed her out into the snowy night.

What I saw was a coatless, red-faced man standing in the driveway next to his car holding some sort of cocktail. Nervously, falling into schoolgirlish giggling, Susan introduced me to Jim Harrison, who walked toward me and cavalierly reached out to shake my hand, acting as if he were meeting me at a cocktail party rather than in the present absurd context. Feeling uncomfortable, I muttered a perfunctory response, and after a few lame attempts at small talk, we bid one another good night. I watched them make their way through the snow to Jim's car, laughing and holding their drinks carefully, in case they lost their footing. I shuddered, and not from the cold: the whole scene—the drinking, Susan's nervous laughter, Jim's inappropriate hail-fellow-well-met behavior—gave me a feeling of foreboding.

My reservations about the relationship were at first limited to the effect it seemed to be having on Susan's psychological health. Susan had always been unsure of herself. Although pretty—slim, blond, and stylish—and artistically talented, she suffered from feelings of inadequacy. Influenced like most women of my generation by the feminist movement, I thought that the solution to Susan's lack of confidence was a career outside the home and had often tried to persuade her to channel her talents into one. But she resisted, and as more and more women she knew began entering the workforce, she became defensive about her choice. From what I gathered from our phone conversations during the months after I learned of her affair, Tom too had been encouraging her to start a career—the boys were getting older and didn't need her every minute of the day—and this had contributed to her growing dissatisfaction with the marriage. Jim, however, made no such noises, a fact that she presented to me as something positive but that I saw as the opposite. Everything she told me about Jim's attitude toward her suggested that the relationship was increasing her dependency rather than liberating her. I recoiled at her descriptions of the flattering remarks he would make about her looks and her accomplishments, of the jewelry and other gifts he frequently surprised her with, of the lavish trips he took her on. Such sugar-daddy treatment was the last thing Susan needed, I thought.

However, I hesitated to voice my reservations because I wasn't sure they were legitimate. Maybe they really just boiled down to a difference between Susan's values and my values. Growing up, I'd tried to forge my own identity by being the opposite of Susan, steering away from the traditional female accomplishments she excelled in. In my twenties, I became involved in the hippie and feminist movements, and in my thirties, I became a career woman and a working mother. Although I had accomplished things Susan hadn't and although—I'm now ashamed to admit—I felt somewhat contemptuous of women who stayed home, I continued to harbor certain feelings of jealousy and inadequacy regarding my sister. Knowing, then, that my attitude toward Susan was complex and my motives sometimes murky, I usually refrained from preaching to her about her relationship with Jim. Even so, she seemed to sense my disapproval. It must have been for that reason, I assumed, that our relationship had been gradually cooling.

In the ensuing months, Susan's phone calls to me were infrequent and superficial, as they were to other family members. She would call to wish one of us happy birthday or to announce an accomplishment of one of her sons and avoided mention of her relationship with Jim, especially to my parents. I figured this was because she was embarrassed and ashamed; it didn't occur to me that there might be other reasons for her reticence. In keeping with this new pattern of secrecy, Susan opted not to make her annual summer visit to New England; in the past, she and Tom and the boys had usually spent a week or two with the rest of the family at my parents' summer home on Cape Cod. But my father died suddenly in late July, and so of course Susan went up to Massachusetts for the funeral.

During the five days she was there, she appeared highly emotional and agitated. I attributed her condition to the same grief we were all feeling, but I sensed that compounding Susan's was her paranoia that my father had died disappointed in her: she was no longer the good little Catholic girl that she had always been in his eyes. I didn't think there might be additional reasons for her distress. I didn't, until much later, think there might be a connection between it and the nasty gash on the bridge of her nose. When I questioned her about this injury, she said that she had bumped into the corner of the medicine cabinet door, which she hadn't realized was open, when raising her head up after washing her face in the bathroom sink. That sounded feasible enough to me; in fact, for months afterward I double-checked the latch of my own medicine cabinet door whenever I went to wash my face, picturing that painful-looking cut above my sister's nose.

Over the course of the following year, I began to receive intermittent, disturbing phone calls from Susan. She would be worked up and upset, often in tears. The alleged cause of her distress was always something to do with the slow progress being made toward her and Jim's respective divorces and the subsequent legitimization of their relationship in marriage. Often the trigger would be something Molly Harrison had allegedly done to hold up or complicate the works, and Susan would recount this tale to me hysterically. But I sensed that the reason for her hysteria was deeper and more psychological: that she was experiencing acute conflict about the way she was living. It wasn't just the identity clash between her current role of kept woman and her former one of respectable wife and mother; it was also the insecurity and lack of definition of the situation that so distressed her. Susan and I both placed a high value on order and clarity in our personal lives, having reacted against the emotionally chaotic family life we had experienced growing up. Our childhood had been punctuated with periodic dark episodes in which our mother would get drunk and go into rages; there would follow several days in which she neglected her household responsibilities, and our home would become physically messy and emotionally insecure, the confusion compounded by the fact that my repressed parents would not subsequently mention the episode. When we were older, Susan and I often talked about how traumatic this syndrome had been for us and how as a result we both felt driven to create orderly homes of our own. Knowing this need of Susan's, I inferred that the anomalous nature of her present domestic arrangement must be what was really upsetting her.

After awhile, I began to discern an additional contributor to her distress. At first I'd attributed her incoherence in some of our phone conversations to hysteria related to the conflict I've just described. But then I started to note her occasional slurred speech and the clinking sound of a glass being set down, and that's when I started to suspect that alcohol was also a factor. Jim, from what I understood, was a heavy drinker: the condition he was in when I met him, as well as Susan's descriptions of the cocktail-party context in which their relationship was formed, had given me this impression. Now I began to fear that he, along with the stress of the situation, was influencing Susan to drink more than she should. Because she associated alcoholic excess with the insecurity of our childhood, she had consciously reined in her appetite for alcohol, an appetite that all of us in the family share but that the rest of us control. In social situations, she had always tried to stick to a few glasses of wine and was upset with herself if she overindulged. The heavy drinking she was currently sliding into was no doubt contributing to her sense of losing control of her life. I therefore had yet another reason to be skeptical of Susan's involvement with Jim.

This skepticism grew even stronger the next time I saw the two of them. In June of 1986, my husband and daughter and I moved from South Carolina to Rhode Island, and we accepted Susan's invitation to stop for a visit with her en route. The plan was that we would have dinner with Susan and Jim at their house but would spend the night at Tom's. This way, Mike and I would get to visit with both Susan and Tom, and Alison could spend maximum time with her cousins. By now Jonathan and Nicholas knew that their mother was living with Jim, but they spent little time there; Susan still saw them mainly on their own turf. My exposure to Jim on this occasion confirmed my initial impression. He was never without a glass in his hand all evening and went at his drinking recklessly, moving back and forth between wine and hard liquor and exotic liqueurs and frequently pressing drinks on the rest of us as well. Although a generous host, he struck me as being motivated more by the need to impress others with his largesse than by any real interest in his guests. I had the impression he didn't really know how to interact with others on a one-on-one, equal footing. He would make jokes and sometimes shoot out questions at Mike or me, but more as though he were interviewing us than wanting to get to know us. He appeared uninterested in our answers and would deflect our attempts at real conversation. He seemed comfortable only in a kind of master-of-ceremonies role.

My fears about the effects the relationship was having on Susan also seemed to be borne out on this occasion. The kinds of attentions Jim paid her were just what I felt she didn't need: he treated her with ostentatious, patronizing affection—pulling out her chair for her, not letting her carry any heavy serving dishes, pointing out and praising every bit of interior decorating she'd done. Not only was this kind of treatment not helping her become more independent, it was pushing her even further into the dependent-female mentality than she'd been in during her marriage to Tom. The other thing that bothered me, of course, was Jim's influence on Susan's drinking. He was constantly jumping up to refill her wineglass, and she was clearly drinking more than she knew she ought to. Although she tried to act the cheery hostess, a certain giddiness and nervousness of manner betrayed the anxiety I suspected she was feeling about her drinking and her lifestyle.

About two months later, I saw Susan again, when she came up to Massachusetts to attend a memorial Mass for my father on the one-year anniversary of his death. She and Jim drove up together, and, except for the night following the Mass, which Susan spent at my mother's house in Taunton, stayed at the home of my middle brother, Bob, in Cambridge. Her plan was to have minimal contact with my mother so that she could avoid conversations about her relationship with Jim and her living arrangement; she didn't tell my mother that Jim had accompanied her, and she didn't have him attend the Mass. I didn't see Jim on this occasion, but my brothers and sisters-in-law in the Boston area did, and their impression of him coincided with my own. They witnessed the same kind of excessive, indiscriminate drinking, the same showy affection toward Susan, the same tendency to play the controlling, master-of-ceremonies role. One evening they all went out to dinner at an expensive restaurant and when the bill came, Jim pulled out a large wad of cash and began making a big show of insisting on paying it—another habit of his I would become familiar with over time. He was clearly uncomfortable when my brothers wouldn't let him do so.

Because of the brief time that Susan was at my mother's house and because of all the relatives milling about during the reception following the Mass, I didn't have much of a chance to talk with her. But one conversation we did have would come back to haunt me later. I'd noticed a scar on her arm, which must have been covered up by long sleeves when I'd seen her two months earlier, and when I asked her about it she explained that it was the result of the doctor's inserting a metal pin to help the bone set following a fracture she'd suffered in the spring. Laughing at herself—too merrily, I now realize—she regaled me with a tale about how she'd been riding her bike and, klutz that she was, had toppled over and broken her arm. Susan's athletic ineptness being well known in the family, I bought this explanation, and after being reassured by her that the bone had mended nicely, didn't give the matter any more thought—until years later.

3 The Search Begins, August–September 1994

$\mathscr{B}$y the time I learned of Susan's disappearance, the rest of the family (including Tom, who, as an old college friend of my brother Bill's and as the father of Susan's two children, had remained on good terms with the family after the divorce) had already embarked on the intense, hands-on activity that would characterize our involvement with the case for the duration. Almost certain that Susan had not run away but had been murdered, my brothers and Tom pressured the police to shorten the usual five-day waiting period it takes before a missing person case can be turned over to the homicide division, and their badgering proved successful: the wait was reduced to three days. Not content to leave everything to the police investigation, however, they decided we needed the additional services of a private detective. As a lawyer, Tom felt it would be wiser to have such services contracted through a law firm rather than through the family because that way the detective's work would be protected by attorney-client privilege and not subject to disclosure. Accordingly, early in the week he met with Carey Deeley, an attorney with the firm Venable, Baetjer and Howard, and arranged for him to represent the family in all matters related to the case; and at Tom's suggestion, Carey in turn contracted Frank Napfel, a private eye with Baltimore Security Systems.

Tom and my brothers also decided almost immediately to offer a reward for information leading to the discovery of Susan or to the arrest of the person responsible for her disappearance. Carey Deeley arranged for the phone calls responding to the offer to be screened by Metro Crime Stoppers, which supplemented the $5,000 the family put up with an additional $1,000. When Jonathan arrived home from Europe on Thursday, he and Nick, who had barely slept since the previous Friday, had the reward posters made up, with photos of Susan and her car printed on them, and they launched on an exhaustive flyer-distribution campaign all over Baltimore County. Nick had been working for a political candidate that summer, and the campaign manager allowed the entire crew to take Friday off from the campaign in order to spend the day helping Nick, Jonathan, and several of Jonathan's friends put up the posters.

The grassroots efforts continued the following week. Tom and Nicholas rode the Light Rail from Lutherville to downtown Baltimore and back—the route Jim allegedly took on August 6. Their hope was that they could identify individuals who were regularly on that line, such as passengers, conductors, and vendors, and question them about the events of Saturday, August 6. They were also hoping they might discover some kind of physical or factual evidence that would put the lie to Jim's story. But nothing useful came of this effort. On Frank Napfel's suggestion that a public parking area was the most logical place to abandon a car, Jonathan combed the lots of shopping centers and office buildings all over the county. He also went to gas stations and liquor stores throughout the county and along part of the route to the eastern shore, questioning clerks as to whether someone driving a car resembling Susan's had stopped there in the early hours of August 6. His thinking was that if Susan's murderer had driven her body any distance, he would have had to stop to fill up the car, since it had contained only a quarter of a tank of gas. And if, as Jonathan suspected, Jim was her murderer, there was a good chance, given his alcoholic tendencies and the worked-up state he was probably in, that he would have stopped to purchase liquor.

For the rest of us—my three brothers in Massachusetts and me in Georgia—it was frustrating not to be there on the scene. Never having been involved in a missing person situation before, we naively believed that our brainstorming and searching and prodding of the police would of course yield Susan's body; a body had to be *someplace.* And so we were itching to participate in the process. On Sunday, August 14, Bill and John flew to Baltimore for two days to meet with the police and to look things over at Susan's cottage. On his return to Massachusetts, Bill phoned me in a somewhat optimistic mood: the police had reassured him that the majority of cases like this handled by their department were solved within a few months. *"Months?"* I groaned. That seemed like an eternity to me. For the past week, the first words out of my mouth every time I'd received a phone call from a family member had been an impatient "Did they find her?" Now I saw that I would have to readjust my expectations. But I still believed that if we expended enough energy and effort, we would find Susan sooner rather than later.

Although I would have liked to put the rest of my life on hold and go to Baltimore to devote all my time to helping solve the case, this was not feasible, and so I had to settle for whatever contributions I could make from a distance. One thing I could do, I soon realized, was work on the media, for the police had told us that in missing person cases, appeals to the public were one of the most effective investigative strategies. At first I, along with the other members of the family, had qualms about involving the media because we knew how easy it would be for them to sensationalize the situation. Indeed, they had already discovered that the case had the ingredients for a headline-grabbing story. Shortly after news of the disappearance first broke in the *Baltimore Sun* on August 11, reporters began delving into Susan and Jim's marriage, and within a couple of weeks a lengthy article appeared—"Missing Ruxton Woman's Marriage Was Troubled"—playing up Jim's wealth, Susan's beauty, and the dark hints of domestic violence and rumors about the couple's heavy drinking.[1] We winced at the idea that our tragedy could be turned into the stuff of pulp journalism, and yet we also realized that our best hope for solving the case might lie in media exposure. We therefore decided to steer clear of tabloid journalists—for example, we turned down a request from a reporter from the TV program *A Current Affair* who had gotten wind of the case and wanted to do a segment about it on that show—but to respond to and seek out mainstream-news reporters and urge them to emphasize in their coverage the kinds of details about the case that might trigger someone's memory or inspire someone to help us.

By late August, I was dialing the phone numbers of Baltimore television stations and newspapers so frequently that I had some of them memorized, and I was on a first-name basis with a number of reporters whom I spoke with regularly. Interesting them in the case was easy to do at this stage; it was hot news. In fact, reporters contacted me as much as I contacted them. A few weeks after Susan's disappearance, Beverly Epstein of television station WJZ asked me if I would agree to be interviewed via satellite camera for the next night's local Baltimore news. I readily consented and the following afternoon drove from Athens to Atlanta, where arrangements had been made for the interview to be filmed at CNN. As the makeup people and technicians were prepping me—patting powder on my face, attaching the miniature microphone to the neckline of my dress, instructing me about where to focus my eyes and at what volume to speak during the interview—I reflected on the sad irony that my long-ago little-girl dream of being on TV was being realized in the present circumstances.

Although I had envisioned the television appearance as an opportunity to reiterate the facts surrounding Susan's disappearance and to suggest explicit ways the public could help us, the reporter clearly had in mind more of a Barbara Walters–style "tell-me-how-you-really-feel" type of interview. The last thing I wanted was for my private emotions to become public entertainment, and yet I couldn't help but break down when the reporter asked me what the last few weeks had been like for me, Susan's only sister. The tears rolled, and I found myself spilling out what was hardest for me: the thought that my sister was lying out there somewhere, her body discarded and uncared for, exposed to the elements and possibly to wild animals. I wanted to cover her with a blanket, I sobbed; the family wanted to give her a funeral and to bury her, to have a place where we knew she was. This was the first time I had said the word "body" out loud when referring to the search for Susan—I had winced whenever the police had used it in phone conversations—and hearing the word come out of my own mouth drove home to me more strongly than ever the reality that my sister was most likely dead. I then began to list, pleadingly, the things we would like the public to do: comb fields and woods near their homes, check out abandoned wells and sheds in their area (we had figured that if Jim was the murderer, he might have known of some out-of-the-way spot like one of these where a body could be effectively hidden, since he'd lived virtually his whole life in Baltimore County and owned rental properties in various parts of it), rack their brains to recall if they'd seen someone driving a dark-green 1992 Saab convertible with Maryland tags, number 043-AVF, any time after August 5. I begged gas station and convenience store owners to search through their receipts from the early hours of August 6; maybe they would come upon one that would jog their memory of a person driving such a car who stopped at their establishment to purchase gas. Or if they still had the tapes of any security camera filming done in their store on that date, I asked them to please review them. As the reporter tried to bring the interview to a close, I rushed to finish up my list of far-fetched requests. It wasn't until I was driving home that I realized, in sudden despair, how remote was the chance that someone watching the interview on the news that night was going to get up, go outside, and start walking through their neighborhood looking for my sister's body.

Despite the occasional sense of futility, I couldn't help but continue to brainstorm for new angles, new strategies, new sources of possible leads. And I would become naively hopeful all over again whenever I would hit upon one. Such was the case when I suddenly remembered Lonnie Marquand. Susan had been briefly engaged to him in her early twenties, and from time to time since then he had telephoned her from the Northwest, where he'd been living for years. Lonnie had been a troubled young man, subject to depression, and it occurred to me that, although Susan hadn't said anything about this to me, maybe he had offered a sympathetic ear when she was going through her own difficult times during the last few years. I allowed myself to entertain the tiny, irrational hope that Susan was alive and taking refuge with Lonnie on the other side of the country.

I subsequently launched upon an obsessive, two-week mission to track him down. I asked Tom to look through Susan's old address books, but the addresses and phone numbers he found for Lonnie all proved to be outdated. I called Susan's best friend since boarding school, Terry MacMillan, who lived in San Francisco, but she knew nothing about Lonnie other than that she thought he was living somewhere in Oregon. There being no way, at least that I was aware of, to locate the phone number of a person on the basis of state, I randomly tried information for any Oregon city that popped into my mind—to no avail. Then I suddenly recalled having read a review a few years earlier of a biography of Lonnie's father, the late novelist John P. Marquand. I went to the library, checked out the book, read the blurb about the author, Millicent Fenwick, to find out where she lived, obtained her phone number through Boston information, and called her. Although no doubt taken aback by the bizarre explanation I gave for calling, Ms. Fenwick was most gracious and sympathetic, saying she would love to be of help but had lost touch with Lonnie; she could, however, give me his brother Timmie's phone number in New York. I became excited: now I was finally getting somewhere! It was so easy to fixate on secondary goals, forgetting in the midst of this pursuit that the primary goal, finding Susan, remained doubtful. I phoned Timmie, only to receive a recording saying he was at his vacation house in Colorado. That launched me on another series of long-distance-information attempts, calling every Colorado resort town I'd ever heard of. Amazingly, I finally located his number, but when I rang it I received no answer and no machine picked up. So I resorted to dialing the New York number every day until one day, to my elation, Timmie answered and, after hearing my tale and expressing his sympathy, gave me his brother's address. But as always happened, my frenzied hopefulness was ultimately deflated: Lonnie, when finally reached, had no information about Susan. He was shocked and saddened to learn of her disappearance but said he hadn't heard from her in years.

Another such wild goose chase consumed me a short time after this one. In response to the reward offered for information concerning the case, many so-called leads were phoned in to Metro Crime Stoppers. The police dismissed most of these as outlandish and didn't bother to inform us of many of them, but we, in our desperation, were eager to follow up on any that we learned of that contained the slightest trace of feasibility. One such call came from a self-proclaimed psychic who said she'd had a vision of Susan riding a bicycle in Colorado. Hearing the mention of Colorado, I felt a click of recognition. There was some connection Susan had had with Colorado. Then I remembered what it was. When my daughter was around four, Susan had started a collection for her of small doll-like angels, the creator of which, I seemed to recall Susan telling me, was a Colorado artist she had met through a mutual friend she visited in that state. My daughter now being too old to play with the dolls, they had been converted to Christmas tree ornaments, so I hunted through our boxes of holiday decorations and found them. Scrutinizing the faded tag attached to one, I could make out the words "Simpich Creations" on it and beneath that the name of a city in Colorado. Irrationally excited yet again, I obtained the phone number of the designer and called her to tell her my story and ask who the mutual friend might have been who introduced my sister to her and how I could locate this woman, whom Susan might be seeking refuge with. Ms. Simpich was sympathetic but bewildered. She couldn't recall ever having met either a Susan Harrison or a Susan Owsley, and so she couldn't begin to think who the mutual friend could be. Defeated, and suddenly realizing the absurdity of the notion that Susan was alive and pedaling along the roads of Colorado, I thanked her and said good-bye.

But without a body, it was impossible to squelch entirely the recurring, teasing notion that Susan might not be dead. Often this notion would arrive as a kind of godsend in the midst of unbearable sadness I was experiencing. For example, about three weeks after Susan disappeared, I was in a supermarket, and, my eye alighting on two elderly sisters helping each other with their shopping, I found myself weeping at the thought that I would not have a sister to share old age with. But just when my grief was about to overwhelm me, a tiny hope began to stir: maybe Susan wasn't dead. I suddenly pictured her days hence, sheepishly explaining what had happened and trying to turn the whole thing into one of those high-jinks episodes she had always girlishly delighted in. Soon I was smiling, shaking my head and muttering endearingly, "Typical Susan!"

This trick of the mind, and sometimes of the eye, was something that others in the family also reported experiencing. In late August, my brother Bob and his wife were going to dinner at the Chart Room, a favorite restaurant of our family's near our former summer home on Cape Cod, and as they drove into the parking lot they saw a green Saab just like Susan's with Maryland plates. Feeling a surge of anticipation, Bob rushed into the restaurant, only to be disillusioned when his hasty survey of the guests turned up nothing. Similarly, walking along a crowded street in downtown Boston, Bill caught a glimpse in the distance of a stylishly dressed, slender blond, and his heart began to race. But as he hastened toward her, there came into focus the face of a stranger, and, deflated and feeling suddenly foolish, Bill slackened his pace and passed her by.

Just when I thought I couldn't stand another day of living with this kind of uncertainty, a break of sorts occurred in the case, which, while it didn't resolve it, pointed more strongly to the conclusion that Susan was dead. On September 1, the police informed us that Susan's Saab had been reported discovered at Washington National Airport in northern Virginia. The car had first been noticed during a routine airport parking lot inventory in the predawn hours of August 7. However, since news of Susan's disappearance had not spread beyond the Baltimore area at that point, the lot attendants were not aware that Baltimore County police were looking for such a car. And in the early days of the investigation when police were pursuing the possibility that Susan had flown off somewhere, they'd contacted only Dulles Airport and Baltimore-Washington International; it hadn't occurred to them to check Washington National. After more than three weeks had passed and no one had come to claim the car, though, airport personnel at Washington National became suspicious, especially since the lot it was in was for short-term parking. They noted the tag number and called local police, who in turn contacted Baltimore County police, who had the car towed to their headquarters in Towson.

Examination of the car indicated no signs of foul play, but three things about its condition helped the police fill in more details in the hypothesis they were building about the case: the car contained a half a tank of gas, whereas it had had only a quarter of a tank when Susan left for Jim's house the night she disappeared; the keys were in the ignition; and the battery was dead. The amount of fuel in the tank gave more weight to the police's hunch that Susan's murderer had probably stopped for gas, either before or after disposing of her body. If he had filled the tank up completely, or filled it up more than once, he could have driven quite some distance, and therefore Susan's body could be anywhere within a day's drive between Lutherville and northern Virginia—perhaps in Delaware or in southern Pennsylvania, for example. The police theorized that the murderer had figured a good way to cover his tracks would be to abandon Susan's car at an airport—but not at BWI, since the murderer probably assumed that that would be one of the first places the police would look, and he obviously wanted to buy time. If the car were found at an airport, the impression would be furthered that Susan had run away rather than been murdered, and more time would elapse while the police busied themselves with pursuing this red herring. But even better, the murderer no doubt calculated, would be if the car were stolen, and so he left the keys in the ignition, making the Saab an easy target. An expensive car like that would be picked up in a snap. At the very least, this would get the car out of the area in a hurry and, if it were tracked down, make the person who stole the car the murder suspect. Better still would be if the thief took the car to a chop shop to sell the parts, and then it could never be traced. One of these theft scenarios probably would have been played out had the battery not failed and rendered the car unable to be started. Nicholas said Susan had been having problems with the battery, and so it most likely had gone dead shortly after the car was abandoned. There was one additional reason that Jim, if he was the murderer, would have left the car at Washington National: there was much less chance he would run into someone he knew there than at BWI, and he could easily and anonymously make his way home from Washington National. He could take the subway that runs directly from the airport to Union Station in Washington, D.C., transfer to the Amtrak train that runs from Union Station to Penn Station in downtown Baltimore, take the Light Rail from Penn Station to Lutherville, and walk the two miles from the Light Rail stop back to his home.

Learning of the discovery of Susan's car on September 1, I was both relieved and saddened. Although this new development gave a little more definition to the situation and put an end to my exhausting pursuit of false hopes, it also forced me to confront more fully the wrenching thought that my sister was most likely dead. I now moved into a new phase of mental torment, in which I would picture in morbid detail the possible fates Susan had met. I often envisioned her lying in a remote wooded area, silent except for the rustle of animals, the sharpening winds whipping about her—I'd heard that the weather in the Baltimore area had turned cool unusually early that fall—and not a soul aware that she was there. This thought would cut into me like a knife. That Susan, who was so physically frail and domestic, whom I pictured happiest when ensconced in a snug family scene, enjoying the sensual and social pleasures of living, food and drink and laughter—that she would end her time on earth in this condition struck me as the cruelest of ironies.

Alternative gruesome scenarios would sometimes pop into my head. I went to see *The Piano*—a movie that, ironically, Susan had recommended to me the winter before—and found myself panicking during the drowning scene, picturing *that* as being Susan's fate: she had been weighted down and hurled into a deep lake. This notion had been planted in my head when I'd heard through the rumor mill that the wife of one of Jim's former McCormick colleagues had said something to the effect of "Susan's no doubt lying at the bottom of Loch Raven," a local reservoir. Always these morbid visions announced themselves unexpectedly, in the most unlikely of contexts. Another such moment occurred a month after Susan's disappearance, when my husband and I were at a Toyota dealership shopping for a new car. Trying to decide whether to go with the Camry or the Corolla, we asked the salesman if we could check out the trunk space of the latter. Just as he lifted the lid, I had a sudden vision of Susan's body being stuffed into the trunk of her car and being driven by her murderer to the spot where he disposed of her, and I had to struggle to keep from gasping audibly.

What made all these scenarios doubly horrifying was that they involved the very things that Susan, whose physical timidity had been the butt of frequent teasing by her more robust siblings, was most afraid of. Fast upon my visions of Susan's gruesome fate would come emblematic scenes from her life that threw her fearfulness into sharp relief. I would suddenly picture, for example, Susan on one of the rare occasions when she would concede to going sailing, frightened that the high winds were going to capsize the boat in choppy waters far from shore, or Susan trying to maneuver the car down a mountain road through a raging blizzard—she and I were returning from a ski trip, and I was too young to drive—terrified at the possibility of the car's breaking down and our freezing to death in some remote spot. Or sometimes I would recollect the way she would shiver at sensational murder or torture stories that were in the news, such as the Manson murders, the burying alive of heiress Barbara Jane Mackle, and—more recently and ironically—the brutal killing of Nicole Brown Simpson.

Another morbid vein of thought that obsessed me was the craving to find Susan's body before she deteriorated beyond recognition: I longed to see my sister one more time. And so I would find myself experiencing the perverse emotion of envying families of conventional murder victims, as opposed to missing-and-presumed-murdered victims. The Simpson-Goldman double homicide, which occurred a month and a half before Susan disappeared, was much in the news at this time, and while most viewers recoiled at the sight of the bloody murder-scene footage that was frequently replayed on television, I would be pierced with a pang of jealousy, musing to myself, "At least *they* [the Browns and the Goldmans] have the bodies." One day in mid-September, I was running errands downtown and happened to park my car across the street from a church where a funeral was just ending. As I watched the coffin being carried out by pallbearers, my eyes filled with tears of yearning; all I could think of was how lucky the family was to know that their loved one was there in that casket.

Although we were sure Susan was dead, without a body her death was not official, and so we were barred from the usual rituals of closure—funeral, burial, expressions of condolences from others—that help mitigate the pain of bereavement. Figuring out what to tell people posed a problem. I had immediately informed my close friends, of course, of the situation. But with others, I was in an awkward position. As the school year began and I was forced to go back into circulation, I would encounter acquaintances—colleagues at work, people I knew from church, the parents of my child's school friends— who would cheerily ask how my summer had been, expecting the perfunctory response of "Fine, and yours?" It seemed inappropriate to unload my tragedy on them in that context, so I would utter an ambivalent "Oh, okay" and quickly excuse myself, fabricating some errand I had to run. Then, the more time that went on, the harder it became to break the news to such people; it would seem odd that I hadn't told them earlier, and it would make them feel bad that they had been treating me as though everything was fine in my life when I had been suffering such anguish. My hope was that the news would just spread by word of mouth, and for the most part it did, but there remained many acquaintances who never learned of the tragedy and with whom I continued, awkwardly, to skirt the topic when I found myself in conversation with them.

Any lingering notion I had that Susan might be alive was banished on September 27, Jonathan's birthday. I had secretly held out a tiny hope—and I suspect other family members probably did too— that, miraculously, Jonathan would receive a phone call from her that day. Susan's children meant everything to her, and she had always been extremely sentimental about their birthdays. No matter what the circumstances she was in, I figured, if she was alive there was no way she would fail to contact Jonathan on the occasion of his twenty-fourth birthday. All day long that day, I tried to ignore the way my heart would start to beat faster each time the phone rang and tried to pretend I wasn't disappointed each time I answered it and discovered the call to be inconsequential. I finally went to bed at midnight: September 27 had come and gone. My sister's silence on that day was the most powerful testimony yet that she was dead. The despair I felt when I laid my head on the pillow that night was the deepest I had ever experienced.

4 Mounting Suspicions about Jim, Autumn 1994

$\mathcal{J}$im Harrison was the main, but unofficial, suspect in Susan's disappearance from the beginning. Strongly pointing toward his guilt was an abundance of circumstantial evidence: the fact that he was the last person to see Susan before she disappeared; the stormy relationship the two had had, including a lengthy record of calls Susan had made to the police accusing him of physical violence against her; and the implausible and conflicting accounts he gave concerning events of August 5 and 6.

In addition, much of his behavior over the next few days seemed suspicious. For example, a few days after Susan disappeared, Jim's next-door neighbor spotted Jim vigorously cleaning the trunk of his car and examining it at length. She called the police, who immediately went to the house and discovered a strong smell of gasoline in the trunk. Jim asserted that he had spilled gasoline there and was simply cleaning up the mess. But maybe, my brothers and I speculated when we heard this account, Jim had murdered Susan, put her body into the trunk of his car, and then changed his mind and decided it made more sense to drive the body away in her own car. If that were the case, what he may have been doing when the neighbor spotted him cleaning the trunk was trying to rid it of all vestiges of Susan's body, hoping the smell of gasoline would mask any lingering olfactory evidence.

Then, about a week or two after Susan disappeared, Jim's cleaning woman came to clean his house and noted two unusual things, although she had no reason at the time to regard them as suspicious because she had not yet heard the news about Susan's disappearance. One of these notable things was that the downstairs bathroom, which was not heavily used and ordinarily required only light cleaning, was unusually filthy, with loose dirt and soil on the floor, and Jim pressed her to do a thorough cleaning of it. The other notable thing was that after she finished her work, Jim asked her how often she emptied out her vacuum cleaner bag (she brought her own vacuum cleaner to her jobs). This question stuck in her mind, simply because none of her clients had ever posed it to her before. Unfortunately, by the time she learned of Susan's disappearance and gave the police this account, she had already disposed of the contents of the bag, contents that could possibly have led us to Susan's body—that is, if, as one of our theories posited, Jim had returned home on August 6 with a lot of dirt on him from having dug a shallow grave and had used the downstairs bathroom to clean himself up hastily. If such were the case and the contents of the bag had still been available, the police could have sent the soil in the bag to a forensic lab for analysis, and the results might have pointed to the specific geological area where Susan's body was. But it was too late for that now.

Jim appeared to be drinking excessively in the weeks and months after Susan disappeared. If one knew nothing of his other behavior, one might interpret this drinking to be his way of dealing with his grief and see Jim as an innocent man distressed by his wife's disappearance. But casting doubt on this interpretation were not only his suspicious actions and conflicting accounts but also the glaring fact that he did nothing—nothing—to try to find Susan, alive or dead, unless, that is, one counts as an attempt his overture, which he related to a reporter, of sending in fifty dollars to the 1-800-SEARCH outfit advertised on television that claims to help people locate lost loved ones. If he were really innocent and, as he histrionically claimed to various reporters who interviewed him, desperate to have Susan return, one would think he would have gone to great lengths to find her. A wealthy man, he could have paid to take out newspaper ads all over the country or could have hired an expensive, full-service private investigative firm. He could have flown to Ireland—a place he almost immediately suggested to the police Susan had probably gone to, pointing out that it was a country she loved—and checked out the villages and bed-and-breakfast establishments they had stayed in on their trips there. At the very least, one would think he would have hurled himself into the kinds of grassroots efforts Susan's children and siblings and first husband were making. But he did virtually nothing, except claim that he prayed for Susan's safe return.[1]

The police had advised my brothers and nephews and me to keep our dealings with Jim to a minimum and not to accuse him publicly. We complied with this advice and did not talk to Jim directly, that is, subsequent to Nicholas's and my brother Bill's phone conversations with him that first weekend. But we kept a close watch on his doings via accounts provided to us by Frank Napfel, the police, and reporters. Although in the exposures I'd had to Jim during Susan's years with him, I'd been put off by his showy, often drunken behavior, and although I had suspected and had gradually become convinced that he had physically assaulted Susan, it had never crossed my mind that he was capable of murder. After all, who ever thinks someone they know, or are related to, could commit murder? But now that I was learning more about Jim's character and behavior, I was forming a darker view of him, and I berated myself for not having sufficiently recognized the danger my sister was in and for not having insisted more vociferously that she get out of this potentially fatal relationship.

One of the biggest eye-openers was the lengthy record of visits Baltimore County police had paid to Susan and Jim's house in response to reports of domestic violence; my brother Bill obtained a copy of this record and shared it with me. Susan had called me in hysterics about some of these incidents at the time they occurred; but often she was drunk and incoherent, and she nearly always eventually retracted her claims, and so I had relegated them to a sort of gray area of reality. Now, however, with the police reports in front of me, as well as copies of some of Susan's medical records that my brother John had obtained, I realized with a shock that these incidents had been very real. There in black and white and dating back to 1987 were descriptions of clumps of hair having been pulled out of Susan's head, of abrasions, bruises, cut tongues, twisted wrists, black eyes, and fractured ribs—all allegedly caused by Jim. Susan and Jim's violent relationship, it turns out, was well known to all the officers at the Cockeysville precinct: Tom informed me that when he reported Susan missing at the Towson precinct, the officer who called over to the Cockeysville precinct told Tom that the officer there taking the call responded, "Oh, we know all about those two."

I spoke at length on the phone one time with one of the Cockeysville officers, a Lieutenant Jody Bentham, who had repeatedly responded to domestic violence calls at Susan and Jim's house. She told me that although by the time she arrived at the house, Susan would usually have begun to retract her story and Jim would insist Susan's injuries were the result of her falling down the stairs or tripping over the coffee table, Lieutenant Bentham was convinced, from her years of handling domestic violence cases, that Susan's cuts and bruises had been inflicted by Jim. Having herself been a victim of spousal abuse, and having finally summoned the courage to leave the marriage, she went out of her way to encourage Susan to leave Jim and to press charges. But, sighed Lieutenant Bentham to me over the phone, Susan always ended up dropping the charges. If *only*, I moaned to myself as I hung up after this conversation, I'd been exposed to these graphic police accounts when Susan was alive, if *only* I'd fully understood what was going on, maybe I could have saved her.

From what I gathered from both the police reports and articles in the newspaper, Jim routinely denied physically hurting Susan, despite evidence to the contrary. Indeed, he sometimes turned the tables and claimed she had abused him. For example, one time in 1992 Jim was arrested following police verification of injuries Susan had complained he'd inflicted on her; however, once in custody, Jim declared that he himself had injuries inflicted by Susan that he had not mentioned when the officer came to the house. Susan had scratched him on the back, he complained; however, examination by police revealed no signs of injuries. Then he stated that approximately two hours before the police officer's arrival, she had bruised his foot by stomping on it with her shoe. Susan countered that the bruise had been caused by his doctor during a physical examination four days earlier. When the police looked at the bruise, they noticed that it was dark purple with signs of yellowing on the outer edge, suggesting that

Jim had had it for several days and hence contradicting his claim that Susan had caused it a few hours earlier. Increasing the police's skepticism was the fact that Jim refused to allow them to photograph the bruise. They therefore contacted Jim's doctor, who corroborated Susan's story. Then after Jim was released on his own recognizance, he counted his money and claimed the arresting officer had stolen a $100 bill. But when he re-counted his money with the officer, he discovered he had the "missing" bill.[2]

Such evidence that Jim was prone to mendacity and that he had probably physically abused Susan made the Baltimore County police assigned to the investigation strongly suspect that he was lying about having played no role in Susan's disappearance. However, they felt they could not charge him with her murder without either a body or any physical evidence linking him to her disappearance. And the more time that passed, the colder the trail became. The police therefore thought their best hope lay in trying to get a confession out of Jim. Lieutenant Sam Bowerman, an FBI-trained criminal profiler who worked with Baltimore County police on the case, was convinced that he could effect this. His plan was to build a counseling type of relationship with Jim in which he would gradually work on the latter's conscience. Establishing a relationship was easy because Jim had few friends and seemed hungry for social contact. Sam began to drop by Jim's house regularly. Jim would offer him drinks, press him to stay for dinner, suggest they go out to a bar or restaurant; he even invited Sam to accompany him to Florida when he visited his two sons living there in early September (Sam declined). Jim knew that Sam regarded him as a suspect, but he ignored this fact and acted as though Sam was just his buddy. Whenever Sam, a religious man, would sound his recurring theme that God would forgive Jim if he confessed now rather than prolonging the agony for Susan's sons and siblings, Jim would let the accusation roll off his back. He would either look away and change the subject or raise his eyes to the heavens and moan something like, "Oh, I hope and pray nothing bad has happened to Susan."

Despite Jim's maddening way of deflecting Sam's questions and accusations, Sam persisted in his efforts. In October, he suggested that Jim attend a bereavement service with him for families of missing persons in the Baltimore area. Sam's fiancée's sister had disappeared eight years earlier—a suspected victim of spousal murder—and her mother had started a support group for families in similar situations. Every year her mother had a Mass held for these families; it was this service to which Sam invited Jim. Sam's notion was that the sight of the grieving family members might move Jim's conscience, so he felt optimistic when Jim agreed to accompany him. During the first half of the Mass, Sam began to believe his strategy might be working, for Jim kept chewing gum loudly and darting looks around the congregation at the weeping relatives—indications of his mounting nervousness, Sam inferred. Then suddenly Jim stood up, walked to the front of the church, and interrupted the priest in the middle of a ritual by tapping him on the shoulder and whispering something in his ear. The priest, in some confusion, nodded his head and then announced to the congregation, "This man has something he wants to say to you." Sam's heart was thumping. Surely, he thought, the moment had come! But no, instead of making a confession, Jim told the congregation he wanted them to pray for his wife, who was missing and whom he loved so much. He then began to lead them in prayer, oblivious to the inappropriateness of having interrupted the ritual of the Mass. After a couple of minutes, the priest tactfully got him to stop and return to his seat. Sam's plan had failed. Having this scenario described to me over the phone by my brother Bill that evening, I lost any hope I'd had that an appeal to Jim's conscience would be effective.

Jim's performance at the Mass was in keeping with his characteristic pattern of flamboyant, self-aggrandizing behavior, a tendency that seemed to be growing more pronounced in the months after Susan disappeared. Reports came to us periodically of his showing up, usually drunk, and making a spectacle of himself at places he associated with his former importance: the exclusive Green Spring Valley Hunt Club, where he was still a member but no longer a welcome one; his prep school alma mater, Gilman, which he had donated a lot of money to and hence seemed to feel he could throw his weight around at; and McCormick Spice Company, where he had once been known as a brilliant businessman but from which he'd taken early retirement after being passed over for his expected appointment to the position of chief executive officer. On these occasions, he would inappropriately insert himself into whatever event was going on, acting as though he had some sort of official role to play in it. For example, at a student Christmas concert at Gilman, he walked up to the front of the auditorium and, acting like the master of ceremonies, began saying to the audience something like, "Isn't this great?" Another time, he went to a shareholders' meeting at McCormick and stationed himself at the doorway, shaking hands with members as they were leaving. Just as he had tried to take over the Mass, despite not even being Catholic nor a member of the support group the service was primarily intended for, so he tried to assume a role of importance in many other events that he was only peripherally connected to.

Another increasingly prominent oddity of behavior on Jim's part was a psychological dissociation of sorts. One form this took was his habit of referring to himself in the third person when interviewed by police and reporters. He would say things like, "Jim loves Susan; he would never hurt her."[3] Another form it took was his persistence in acting as though the police and reporters were his pals, not his accusers. When they would show up at the house, he would heartily welcome them, offer them drinks, and ignore or deflect their accusations and their pointed questions about Susan's disappearance. One reporter described how, following his interview with Jim, the latter kept pressing him to stay longer and began pulling out photographs of his new grandchild from his wallet for the reporter to admire.

Particularly strange was Jim's behavior during the police search of his home in October. This search had to be conducted at night because the police planned to smear a glow-in-the-dark blood-detecting solution on the walls and floor of the family room, where Susan had spent the last evening before she disappeared. Accordingly, they arrived unannounced late one evening, presenting Jim with a search warrant. Jim acted delighted, as though he thought they were dropping by for a social visit. Playing the jolly host, he absurdly offered to grill hamburgers for all of them. Then later, while the police were fanning through his house, combing its contents, he was outside mowing the lawn in the pitch-black night, occasionally stopping to wave merrily at them through a window.

What was this loony behavior all about? How did it square with the facts that Jim was a wealthy, well-educated man with an undergraduate degree in engineering from Cornell, an MBA from Loyola, and a law degree from the University of Baltimore; that he'd held a powerful position in a major company; and that he had a reputation for being a super-smart businessman who had closed multimillion-dollar deals? One theory my brothers and I entertained was that Jim was a kind of Raskolnikov figure, losing his mind—with the aid of alcohol—in the effort to blot out the memory of the crime he'd committed. Another theory was that he was "crazy like a fox": putting on an act so as to pave the way for an eventual insanity defense. The more we learned about Jim's character and reputation from police and investigative reporters, the more weight we gave to the latter theory. Jim, we began to put together from reputed statements by former colleagues and acquaintances, fancied himself smarter than others and sometimes enjoyed manipulating his business competitors. At McCormick, he had been known as a brilliant, crafty businessman who often hoodwinked those he was negotiating a deal with by lulling them into thinking he was naive. (I always pictured the television detective Columbo when I heard one of these anecdotes.) One observer said that when Jim was plotting an acquisition, "He'd play this 'Oh, I'm just a poor old country boy' shtick. The next thing you know, McCormick owns the company, and he's rocking in his chair like Grandpa."[4]

The more we learned about Jim's enjoyment of play-acting and manipulating people for his own ends, the more we suspected that he might be toying with the police and the media when he behaved so oddly. We also suspected that his confidence in his own smartness and in his ability to outwit others was the reason he agreed to take a polygraph test, three months after Susan disappeared: he probably thought he could outwit the test as well. He was wrong. According to the officer who reported the results to us, Jim failed it "in spades," although Jim later argued that he was sure the test was faulty.[5] We were told that the graph registered the most extreme peak—that is, the strongest indication Jim was lying—when he responded negatively to the question of whether he knew where Susan was. The examiner who administered the test reputedly commented later that the only reason the peak wasn't higher was that the needle would have been off the page. Unfortunately, of course, the results of a polygraph cannot be used as evidence; they can only be used as an investigative tool. Had Jim passed the test, the police would have shifted their focus from trying to get a confession out of him to trying to unearth other suspects. His failing the test gave them confidence that they were on the right path.

The polygraph was only one of the indications that Jim may have played a role in Susan's disappearance. There were additional signs, betrayals in Jim's behavior. Tom taped all the local news interviews with Jim, and when my brothers and I would review them we would scrutinize his facial behavior and body language. We noted how when reporters asked him whether he was responsible for Susan's disappearance, often his jaw would pulse, perspiration would appear on his forehead, and he would avert his eyes and respond with a non sequitur. Sometimes he would slip into talking about Susan in the past tense, the way one does about the deceased, a seeming contradiction to his claim that he thought she was alive and had run off somewhere. An investigative reporter named Frank Mann, who interviewed Jim for a segment on a local television news series entitled "Missing Pieces," told me over the phone that he'd never been so convinced of the guilt of a suspect he'd interviewed as he was of Jim's guilt. When he asked Jim whether he'd heard the door close, indicating that Susan was leaving his house on the night of August 5, Jim looked trapped, as though he couldn't remember whether he'd said that before and was worried he might not get his story straight. But what mainly struck Frank was the way Jim kept dwelling, bemusedly, on the fact that Susan fell asleep on the sofa of the family room after they'd been fighting. Frank speculated that what may have happened was that after assaulting Susan into unconsciousness and inadvertently killing her, Jim tried to convince himself she had merely gone to sleep. According to Frank's theory, Jim's fixating on this scene suggested how deeply imprinted it was in his memory and how desperate had been his need to believe Susan was asleep, not dead.

The theory about Jim's behavior that my family more and more gravitated to was that although alcohol and denial were taking a toll on his mind and memory, Jim was more in control and more sane than he let on. We noticed in the newspaper and television interviews the way he calculatedly—we thought—kept bringing up Susan's "manic depression," hinting that this might have had something to do with her disappearance. The recurrent theme he sounded—that Susan would, as he put it, "go manic depressive"[6] and start behaving crazily—was intended, we believed, to create the impression that she was capable of running off, either on her own or with one of the "boyfriends" that he darkly hinted at but whose existence, as far as any of us knew, had no basis in fact and has never been confirmed. Jim's other motive in implying that Susan often behaved in a tempestuous or immoral way, we suspected, was to make the police and the public more sympathetic to him in the event he should ever be charged with her murder. Adding to our outrage at this strategy of Jim's was the knowledge that he was willfully distorting the truth about Susan. In asserting that she had a mental disease and that this disease had been the cause of their fights and her injuries (she would run into a coffee table in a rage and trip over it, he claimed), he was ignoring both his own role in Susan's emotional difficulties and the fact that her "manic depression" had turned out to be a misdiagnosis, made several years earlier.

In July of 1988, Susan had telephoned my brother Bill in distress because of a fight she and Jim had had. She claimed that he had locked her out of the house, and she didn't know where to go or what to do. Alarmed, Bill urged her to fly up to Boston to stay with him. These were the days when she was still keeping Jim's later-alleged abusiveness a secret from the family; we knew the two of them fought, but we didn't know the fights were physical, and Susan always ended up claiming that she'd instigated them or had exaggerated Jim's role in them. Therefore, we tended to focus more on getting her to seek psychological help than on getting her to leave Jim; besides, we knew from experience that she wasn't going to leave him no matter how much we advised her to do so. Bill's plan was to persuade Susan to undergo a psychiatric workup while in Massachusetts in order to uncover the reasons why she was unable to extricate herself from a dysfunctional relationship. In the distressed state she was in when she arrived at Bill's house, she agreed to do this. Bill arranged for her first to have a medical exam by a friend of his who was an internal medicine specialist, to rule out any physical bases to her problems; this doctor would then refer her to a psychiatrist. The internist did blood work on Susan, and his analysis of the results suggested she might have a chemical imbalance that was causing her to be manic depressive; he therefore recommended a course of lithium treatment to see if that was the answer, and he referred her to a psychiatrist at MacLean Hospital, a psychiatric institution outside Boston. But Susan went to only one or two sessions with the psychiatrist before she started itching to get back to Jim. As always happened a few days after one of their violent episodes, Susan began to revise her memory about the incident and to blame herself. Now that she had the tentative diagnosis of manic depression, she grabbed on to it and convinced herself that once she started taking lithium, everything would be fine in her relationship with Jim. All she wanted to do was to get her prescription filled and fly home to him. Bill and the rest of us warned her that things probably weren't that simple: that while her manic depression may have been a contributing factor, Jim and the relationship itself were no doubt other factors. Nonetheless, Susan gave the impression as she brightly boarded the plane to return to Baltimore that she thought she'd found the perfect panacea.

On the diagnosing doctor's advice, she continued to have her blood monitored when she was back in Baltimore and to have her dosages of lithium adjusted accordingly. However, after a couple of months of clinging to the hope that the lithium was going to turn her life around, she realized that it was not the answer: the fights began to flare up again. Subsequent physicians and psychiatrists who treated Susan disputed the manic depressive diagnosis, and even the original doctor conceded it probably had not been accurate. The various psychologists and counselors Susan sought out over the years felt the cause of her problems lay at least as much in the relationship and in Jim as they did in Susan herself. The only person to continue to put any stock in the manic depressive diagnosis was Jim. When the police would be called to the house during an argument, Jim would assert to them that his wife was manic depressive and had become violent.[7] Once in the summer of 1990 when Susan and Jim were spending a weekend on Martha's Vineyard, Bill and his wife, who had arranged to have dinner with them, arrived at the Harrisons' rented condominium during what was evidently the aftermath of a fight. Susan had been drinking, and Jim, seemingly for the benefit of Bill and his wife, fished an empty wine bottle out of the waste-basket and started waving it in front of Susan, sternly reminding her that she wasn't supposed to drink because of the lithium she was taking for her manic depression. Sometimes when Susan called me during or just after a fight with Jim—before she'd begun to soften her account—she would talk about this obsession he had with her "manic depression." He even, she told me several times, photocop-ied a letter I had written to her referring to her manic depression, back before this diagnosis had been dismissed, and stored it in his files. When I asked her why he would do that, she said, "He keeps a file of things he might want to use against me someday."

In the months after she disappeared, when I would hear of Jim Harrison's floating the red herring about his wife's "manic depres-sion," I would recall that explanation of Susan's and would picture Jim calculatedly filing away the photocopy of my letter. This picture was very much at odds with the image of an innocent, grieving hus-band that Jim was now trying to project.

5 Frustrations with the Investigation, Autumn 1994

$\mathcal{L}$ike most Americans, my brothers and I had derived our knowledge of murder investigations primarily from movies and television dramas in which savvy cops doggedly pursue a case until it is solved. Now that we were exposed firsthand to such an investigation, however, we were discovering that these fictional portrayals are usually highly idealized.

We had started off in good faith, encouraged by the Baltimore County Police Department's reassurance that they were usually successful at solving cases like ours within a year. But very soon we became dismayed with what seemed to us to be a less than committed attitude on the part of the officer heading the investigation, Detective Mike Paraguay. On the phone with him for an update two weeks after Susan disappeared, I expressed my frustration that her body had still not been found, and he responded, "Well, no news is good news." I was taken aback: I had believed the police were operating on the theory that Susan had been murdered, but Paraguay gave the impression he thought that her body's not having turned up meant she might be alive and had just run off. If that was his attitude, I felt, perhaps he wasn't really regarding this as a murder case and hence wasn't pursuing it as effectively as he otherwise would. Maybe Jim's innuendos about Susan's craziness and unpredictability were affecting Paraguay's approach to the case. Then about a week after my phone conversation with him, the family was informed that Paraguay was retiring imminently—a fact he'd never mentioned to us. In angry hindsight, we speculated that what appeared to us to have been Paraguay's blasé attitude may have been due to his being preoccupied with his impending retirement. Later, we often wondered whether crucial opportunities to solve the case had been lost because of the lack of consistent, committed leadership in the early days of the investigation.

The lead position was reassigned to Detective Bill Ramsey, a kindly cop who was very sympathetic to the family's feelings. He seemed committed to the case and kept in frequent contact with us, informing us of leads the police were pursuing, listening to our suggestions and concerns, and urging us to try to keep the story alive in the media. He devised some good strategies, but bunglings, mistimings, and other factors—many of them beyond his control—kept them from being efficacious. For example, when Susan's car was discovered at Washington National Airport, Ramsey decided he would release this information to the press but would withhold the fact that the key had been left in the ignition. Then in subsequent interviews with Jim, under the pretense of enlisting the latter's help in solving the mystery of who drove the car to the airport and abandoned it there, he would try to get Jim to let slip his knowledge about the key. This being information that only the police and the driver of the car would possess, Jim would implicate himself. The strategy was never tested, however, because someone in the police department let the key-in-the-ignition information leak to the press before Ramsey had a chance to meet with Jim.

At the time the car was found, we were still in the naive stage of trusting that the police were totally in control of the investigation and were doing their best to solve the case. The blown opportunity about the key was our first eye-opener to their limitations. As time went on, we discovered more oversights and missed opportunities regarding evidence the car possibly held. About two weeks after the car was found, my brother Bill received a phone call from a man in Nebraska named Sam Cooper, a former prosecutor who had had experience with cases like ours. He was a friend of our cousin Kate Dodge, who lives in Omaha, and Kate had told him about the situation. Cooper wanted to know whether the police had noted the position the driver's seat was in when they found the car. This was the first thing they should have checked, he said, for if the seat was pushed back rather than forward, this fact would suggest that a large man, rather than a slightly built woman like Susan, had been the last person driving the car. Even if the seat was in the forward position, a fingerprint analysis of the lever that adjusts the seat would indicate who had most recently handled it; that is, the driver could have pulled the seat forward before getting out, to make it look like Susan had been the last one to drive it. Bill didn't know whether the police had checked into these things; if they had, they hadn't shared their findings with us. So he phoned Detective Ramsey to ask him. Ramsey was a bit vague in his response; he didn't seem to think, as Cooper did, that the condition of the seat or the lever was all that significant. He told Bill he recalled that the seat had been in the forward position, and he assured him the car had been looked over thoroughly. But, he pointed out, a fingerprint analysis would have been meaningless since Jim's fingerprints would be in the car anyway, from all the times he'd driven it when he and Susan were living together and since the crime lab's technology did not allow for a distinction to be made between the most recent fingerprints and earlier ones. Even so, we couldn't help but think that the car contained potential critical evidence and that an investigative team with more scientific resources, including access to a more state-of-the-art forensic lab, would have taken advantage of this evidence.

This hunch seemed to be confirmed by an article I came across about a year later in the Annals of Crime series in the *New Yorker.* Author John McPhee described how the perplexing case of the disappearance several years ago of Colorado brewery magnate Adolph Coors III was solved by FBI-lab scrutiny of his murderer's car. After dumping Coors's body in a ravine in Colorado, the murderer drove the car across the country and abandoned it in a junk lot in New Jersey. When the car was discovered, and suspected to belong to Coors's murderer, the FBI assigned it to a forensic geologist, who analyzed the layers of soil that had accumulated in the tires and was thereby able to pinpoint the area of Colorado where the murderer had driven the car to dispose of the body. The result was that Coors's body was found.[1] This article strengthened our belief that with FBI resources, our case could be solved.

We had been pressuring the police to enlist the help of the FBI ever since Susan's car had been discovered abandoned in a state (Virginia) other than the state (Maryland) where her abduction or murder had most likely been committed, for we knew that the across-state-lines nature of the crime could justify FBI involvement. The FBI's response to the police requests, however, had been token: an FBI agent, John Barry, was assigned to the case, but he never did anything more—or so it appeared to us—than sit in aloofly on a couple of our discussions with the police. For months we were promised that the case was going to be presented before a team of forensic psychologists at FBI headquarters in Quantico, Virginia, who would piece together a criminal profile that would help the police hone their strategies for ensnaring the killer. But this session was continually postponed and eventually canceled.

It was maddening to us to realize that the resources were there, but we just didn't have access to them or couldn't convince authorities to use them. We would work ourselves into a pitch of frustration thinking about possibilities and missed opportunities. For example, the location where Susan's car had been found was closer to Quantico, Virginia, than to Towson, Maryland, so why hadn't the car been taken to the FBI's forensic laboratory, where it would have received expert analysis, rather than to the relatively primitive lab at the Towson police headquarters? Why didn't the FBI see if they could access any satellite photographs that had been taken over the Baltimore-Washington area on August 5 or 6? Wasn't there some way the FBI or the police could obtain a list of travelers who had parked their cars on August 6 in the airport lot where Susan's car was abandoned and question them about what they remembered seeing? What about locating and interviewing people who had ridden the train that day from Washington National to Union Station or from Union Station to Baltimore?

Granted, some of our notions and requests may not have been feasible, and, granted, we were no doubt somewhat monomaniacal in our obsession, forgetting that the police could not concentrate exclusively on our case. Even so, many of our suggestions were reasonable and our frustrations legitimate. For example, we kept urging the police to search the dump Jim used, for Tom had surmised that Jim was probably very familiar with the dump, having raised a large family and probably over the years having had to haul off a lot of household trash on a regular basis. If he murdered Susan, the dump may have been one of the first places it would have occurred to him to take the body. But the police dismissed this theory, pointing out that the dump was locked every night and so Jim couldn't have gained entry during the time frame when, they hypothesized, Susan's body was disposed of. However, a family friend of the Owsleys drove to the dump one night to see if there was any way one could enter it after hours, and he discovered that in fact there was a back entrance open. When we apprised the police of this fact, they switched to another excuse, claiming it would be virtually impossible to detect a decaying body in the midst of all the other decaying matter.

I don't mean to imply that the police were lazy or negligent. They were assiduous about questioning people, looking into Susan's credit cards and bank accounts, screening calls to Metro Crime Stoppers, pursuing leads that seemed promising, and so on. It's just that I think the investigation was probably hampered by the criminal psychology theory they were operating under. Had they not been so sure that the case was going to be cracked by Jim's giving a confession, they probably would have put more effort into trying to collect hard evidence or trying to find Susan's body. For example, they might have pressed harder to obtain a search warrant so that they could have searched Jim's house when any evidence it may have contained was fresh rather than at the belated date they did, in mid-October.

Becoming more and more aware of the limitations of the police investigation, we grew increasingly active in our own attempts. I intensified my campaign to keep the case alive in the media. In September and October, I wrote several letters to Baltimore newspapers—the *Baltimore Sun,* the *Towson Times,* the *Baltimore Messenger*—reminding area residents about Susan's disappearance, describing my family's pain, and imploring readers to ransack their memories for anything that might help us, to call in tips to Metro Crime Stoppers, and to search the fields and woods near their homes. Not all but some of these letters were published. Then I expanded to writing articles intended to reach a wider audience. I composed a poignant piece, initially entitled "Someone Out There Can Help Me Find My Sister," which I continued to revise and send out for the next several months, tailoring it to particular audiences. For example, for the *Washington Post* and for *Newsweek*'s "My Turn" column, I drew attention to the plight of the 21,000 American families like ours who had a loved one missing and presumed murdered (a statistic I obtained from the *ABA Journal*);[2] for women's magazines like *Redbook* and *Ladies' Home Journal*, I emphasized the probable role of domestic violence in my sister's tragedy; and for *Parade*, I played up the sensational aspects of the case (blond socialite wife of wealthy executive disappears; husband is prime suspect). But all of these publications turned my article down. Although as a scholar, I know how difficult it is to get published and have developed a thick skin concerning the endeavor, with the emotions I had vested in this effort, I couldn't help but be crushed by the rejections. The perfunctory phrase "does not meet our editorial needs" that appeared in many of the rejection letters seemed like such an unfeeling response to the heartbreaking tale I had sent them. I had a more promising response from some of the journalists and television producers I wrote to trying to interest them in doing some kind of coverage of the case: *People* magazine and the shows *America's Most Wanted* and *Unsolved Mysteries* were interested and said they might be able to do something on it eventually, encouraging me to get back in touch with them in a few months or to contact them if there were any dramatic new developments.

Another way I tried to enlist my skills in the service of the investigation was through reading and research. I read anything and everything I could lay my hands on that pertained to missing persons, abused wives, and unsolved murders—ranging from human-interest stories in newspapers and women's magazines to scholarly articles in law journals, from the gritty true-life crime books of Ann Rule to the feminist novel *Waverly Place*, Susan Brownmiller's fictionalized account of the domestic battery inflicted by infamous New York lawyer Joel Steinberg on his common-law wife, Hedda Nussbaum, and their adopted daughter. I also was constantly on the lookout for television shows on these topics, and I discovered, in the same way one does when one is pregnant and suddenly notices other expectant mothers everywhere, that there is an abundance of such programs. It was amazing how many times I would be skimming through the weekly television program guide and phrases like "missing person" and "unsolved murder" would jump out at me, and, as with my reading, I was indiscriminate, watching anything from respectable news-magazine shows to sensational Sunday-night dramas to what I formerly would have dismissed as "flaky" programs about psychics claiming success at helping locate missing persons.

Parapsychology, in fact, was an avenue my family and I became increasingly willing to consider, much like a terminally ill patient who turns to alternative treatments when conventional medicine is not proving successful. Although at first we had been skeptical about psychics who offered help, by mid-September we were receptive. And so when Connie Weeks, an old friend of Susan's living in Bermuda, contacted Tom with the information that a psychic on the island had become interested in the case after learning about it through a friend of Connie's, Tom told Connie we'd be interested in hearing what the woman had to say. Thus began a two-month-long involvement with this psychic, who obtained a map of Baltimore County and made pronouncements, which Connie relayed to us, about intuitions she had concerning the whereabouts of Susan's body. She said that in order to be more definite, though, she would need to come to Baltimore and spend some time in the house where Susan had last lived. She was planning to visit her daughter in Connecticut in November, and so we arranged to have her flown to Baltimore at the end of that visit.

It was difficult to suppress the mounting eagerness with which we awaited the psychic's trip to Baltimore. We tried to pretend we weren't pinning our hopes on her, but I suspect that secretly many of us were. Finally the day arrived; one of the men working for Frank Napfel, our private investigator, met the woman at the airport and drove her immediately out to Susan's cottage in Ruxton. She said she would need to sit in a chair Susan had frequently sat in; the rocking chair by the fireplace was selected. Then she said she would need to handle an object Susan had been in close contact with; they scouted around and found Susan's reading glasses. For a long time, the psychic sat there with her eyes closed, trance-like, running her fingers over Susan's glasses. She was attempting to "see" the spot where Susan's body had been buried. Suddenly she began to describe the spot: a wooded area, with a stream running through it, adjacent to a farmer's field. Coming out of the trance, she asked to be driven to this place, saying she could intuitively direct the driver to it. She and Frank's man got into the latter's car and drove out into the country; she had him stop when she sensed they'd arrived at the place she had envisioned. The two of them spent the next couple of hours traipsing through the fields and adjacent woods, but to no avail. She claimed that the layering of snow on the ground—there had been an early snowstorm that year—was making it difficult for her to find the spot that coincided with her vision, and she urged the investigator to bring a team back in a few days, after the snow had melted, to search again (she herself would not be able to participate because she had to return to Bermuda the next day). The psychic seemed convinced Susan's body was somewhere in that area.

The fact that we still gave the psychic's visions some credence even after this disappointment is a measure of how desperate we were. Although Tom—ordinarily a skeptical, rational person—felt somewhat foolish, as soon as the snow had melted he accompanied Frank Napfel to the area and combed the fields and woods for several more hours. Finally, with heavy hearts, they gave up. Tom called me later to report the results of their search, and after I hung up the phone, a chilling irony struck me: in the early years of their marriage, when Susan used to kid Tom about being such a Boy Scout—he had attained Eagle status and remained active in scouting as an adult—she never imagined that he would one day be using his outdoorsman's skills in the gruesome task of searching for her body.

Despite our disappointment, we were not ready to give up on psychics and soon found ourselves depending on another one. I happened to tune into National Public Radio one morning when an interview was being conducted with a Canadian psychic who had helped anthropologists pinpoint ancient Indian massacre sites in the Northwest. With mounting excitement, I listened to the old man describe how his ability to "hear" the cries of the Indians being slaughtered enabled him to lead the anthropologists to the sites. My hopes rising again, I started thinking that maybe this psychic would be able to "hear" Susan's cries the night she was being murdered and "see" her murderer disposing of her body. As soon as the show was over, I picked up the phone and called the Montana NPR affiliate that had aired it. I told the producer why I was calling, and he said he would contact George McMullen, the psychic, and ask if it was okay for me to get in touch with him. A couple of days later, the producer called me back and said that Mr. McMullen had requested that I write him a letter—in longhand, he specified—providing a detailed description of the facts surrounding Susan's disappearance. I promptly sat down and produced an eleven-page letter and mailed it out immediately. Then began another anxious, anticipatory wait.

About two weeks later, I received a reply. Mr. McMullen described where he envisioned Susan's body—"There is a very little used road going into a treed and brush area. It is a shallow grave and there is some moisture in the soil. There is a small pond or lake nearby"— but he spent most of the letter describing what the police ought to have done and urging me to have them do so if they hadn't. Had they compared the soil from Susan's car to soil from Jim's shoes, the rugs in his house, and perhaps any shovels or garden tools in his garage? A positive comparison could provide physical evidence linking him to her murder. Had the police done a proper analysis of the soil on the tires? This would help them determine where her body had been driven: "Soil from a farm would have insecticide residue or fertilizer traces. There would also be pollen samples to indicate the vegetation of the area. If the soil showed samples of humus or leaf mold it would indicate a forest or bush location." Had they calculated how far her car had been driven? Such a calculation could be made by factoring in how much gas the tank had in it when Susan left for Jim's and when the car was found, what capacity the fuel tank was, and what the car's mileage per gallon was. The police should then be able to "draw a circle around the husband's house to the miles indicated to see where she could have been buried. If there were areas that corresponded with the soil samples, this would further indicate where she was buried."[3]

I experienced both sinking and hopeful feelings as I read this letter—sinking because I knew the police had not done all these things, and hopeful because I thought it might not be too late for

them to do them now; for example, they still might be able to retrieve significant soil from the tires and from Jim's shoes and house.
I therefore made a copy of the letter and sent it off to Detective
Ramsey. But his reaction was similar to the one he'd had to Sam
Cooper's suggestions about the seat position and lever: the police
lacked the necessary technology; a coincidence of the soil on the
tires and of the soil in Jim's house would be meaningless; the murderer could have filled up Susan's car more than once; and so on.
While Ramsey's reasons no doubt held some validity, we were dis-
heartened by his response. By the end of the autumn, the family had
become very pessimistic about the prospect of the case's ever being
solved by the police.

I think the two main things that sustained us that fall and prevented
us from giving in to despair were the energy we threw into our own
efforts at pushing the case forward—it gave us the illusion we were
getting somewhere—and having each other. The latter was particularly crucial for Jonathan and Nicholas. It goes without saying that
they were devastated by the tragedy. They suffered not only the pain
of having lost the mother they adored and considered their best friend
but also the agony of wondering whether they could have done something to save her. Nicholas berated himself for not having driven over
to Jim's when he returned to Susan's cottage and found her gone that
last night—maybe he could have talked her into coming home, or
stopped the fatal blow, or called an ambulance in time to save her life.
Jonathan regretted that he'd been in Europe, away from her in her
last days of life. Both boys kept pondering what they could have done
differently to protect their mother from Jim.

At first, Jonathan and Nicholas had considered taking the fall
semester off from school, thinking they would be incapable of con-
centrating on their studies, but then they and their dad decided they
might be better off having something else besides the crisis to focus
on. So, reasoning that they could always withdraw if their schoolwork suffered too much, they headed, in some disorientation, off to
school in early September: Nicholas back to Middlebury College in
Vermont and Jonathan to his first year at Cornell University Law
School in New York State.

It was a rough autumn. Jonathan knew no one at Cornell, save a law professor who was a friend of Tom's, and so had no friends there to sustain his spirits. Socially, he was in an awkward position, never being sure what point in a developing acquaintanceship was the right time to open up about his personal tragedy. As a result, he had very little social life at Cornell and turned instead, via long-distance phone calls, to old friends who already knew about his situation. Nicholas was in a somewhat better position, since he'd already been at Middlebury a year and had formed some good friendships there. These young men and women, as well as the college's counseling program, helped him get through some of his particularly low periods. But mostly the boys turned to each other—they had always been very close and grew even closer as a result of their mother's tragedy—and to their dad, their uncles, and their aunt. Because my relationship with Susan had been strained during her marriage to Jim, I hadn't seen much of her sons in the last few years; but now I felt a deep need to be close to them. To the extent that I could, I tried to do the kinds of things Susan used to do for them. I baked them cookies, sent care packages, and asked them about their girlfriends. At first I was afraid they might resent my taking over the mom role, but I was wrong; they seemed to appreciate my gestures, just as they did the supportive attentions of Bill, Bob, and John.

My nephews and brothers and I spent much of that autumn on the phone with one another, as well as with the police and with our lawyer. We also began the pattern, which we would sustain for the duration of the investigation, of periodically convening in Baltimore. Every few months our frustration with the pace of the investigation and our need to be together would reach a crescendo, and we—or as many of us as could manage it—would descend upon Tom's house for a weekend of brainstorming, meetings with the police and our lawyer, and interviews with newspaper and television reporters. I came to think of these as family "powwows." The first one occurred in early October 1994.

6 Visit to Baltimore, October 1994: Flashbacks to Susan's First Marriage

On Thursday, October 6, I flew to Baltimore for the first gathering of Hurley siblings since Susan's disappearance. Although I would eventually become used to encountering reminders of Susan in my numerous visits to Baltimore, this first time the encounters were unnerving. As the plane descended into Baltimore-Washington International Airport that cold autumn afternoon, I gazed out at the fields and woods below and suddenly thought, "My sister is lying out there somewhere." And once again I was seized by an almost maternal urge to cover her with a protective blanket.

I was met at the gate by Bill and John—Bob would be flying in first thing Friday morning—and the three of us, after an emotional embrace, packed into the car my brothers had rented and headed off to the offices of the *Baltimore Sun,* for the first of a series of newspaper and television interviews we had arranged in advance. The following two days were a whirlwind of media interviews, in which we implored the public to help us find Susan, and meetings with the police, the private investigator, and our lawyer for updating on the case. This busy-ness and sense of purpose kept our spirits up, but any time there was a lull in activity, I think all our minds turned to the same morose thought: how strange it was for us Hurley siblings to be gathered together and for Susan not to be there. Our sense of disorientation would be intensified each time we encountered her face on one of the many missing person flyers that were posted all over the county or on the billboard looming surreally above the Timonium Road exit off Interstate 83. But the most difficult part of the weekend was the visit to Susan's house.

Following her separation from Jim the previous winter, Susan had moved into the guest cottage of a large estate in Ruxton, an affluent, semi-rural township in Baltimore County adjacent to Lutherville, where Jim lived. After her disappearance, her landlords, the Lanahans, a wealthy elderly couple who lived in the main house on the grounds, had agreed to allow the police and Susan's family to have access to the cottage for investigatory purposes for as long as needed. Since Susan had been living there only a short time, I had never been to her new house. But one of the items on the agenda for that first family gathering in Baltimore was a visit to it, partly for sentimental reasons and partly to see if it yielded any clues that the police had overlooked but the family might pick up on.

Accordingly, after dinner Thursday night, Bill and John and I piled into the rental car and drove to Ruxton, about ten minutes from Tom's house in the Homeland section of Baltimore. My heart beat rapidly in anticipation of the ghostly encounters the evening was sure to bring. Arriving at 1803 Ruxton Road—the address I'd scrawled on so many envelopes the previous winter and spring, when I was sending Susan frequent supportive letters—we turned into the tree-lined driveway of the secluded Lanahan estate. As we wound our way through the gracious grounds, I began to experience a sensation of déjà vu: the setting put me strongly in mind of the Connecticut estate on which Susan and Tom had rented a guest house in the early days of their marriage. I found myself simultaneously smiling at the thought of how typical it was of Susan, ever enamored of class and style, to situate herself in a place like this, and sadly noting the irony of the similarity in settings. When we rounded the final bend of the drive and I caught my first glimpse of Susan's house, the déjà vu and sense of irony intensified. This guest house, like the earlier one, was an old-fashioned clapboard cottage surrounded by meadows and woods; but whereas the Connecticut cottage had been pervaded with an atmosphere of coziness, security, and happy anticipation (Susan and Tom were expecting their first child the year they lived there), this cottage resonated with chilliness, despair, and death. Approaching the former on a nippy autumn evening like this one, I would have felt drawn to the warmth and life inside; in contrast, the present cottage appeared austere, its windows darkened and the only light that of the moon in the cold night sky.

Nonetheless, so overpowering was the association that as we walked up the path to the house, I half expected to be greeted by a smiling Susan, with the door opening on to an inviting domestic scene, perhaps a fire burning in the fireplace and the smell of beef bourguignon or apple pie wafting into the living room from the kitchen. But of course the door opened on to stillness and emptiness. Reminiscent of Miss Havisham's house in *Great Expectations,* the interior had a frozen-time quality about it, with signs of suspended daily activity everywhere: dirty dishes in the kitchen sink waiting to be washed, a cookbook open to the spaghetti bolognese recipe Susan had made a couple of days before she vanished, a sweater-in-progress spilling from her knitting bag on the living room couch. Strewn about the coffee table were sections of the *Baltimore Sun.* I shuddered when I glanced at their date: Friday, August 5, 1994. The most chilling of all the artifacts I encountered in our survey of Susan's house was the note Nick had left for his mother that last, fateful night. It was still propped up on the table in the front hall, its message now laden with poignant irony: "8/6, 2:00 A.M. Mom— I waited and waited for you. I couldn't sleep so I went to Dad's. Call me when you get in—*anytime!* Love, Nick."

Those words echoed in my ears as we drove in sad silence back to Tom's house. Later that night, I lay in bed awake for hours, pondering how this unbelievable turn of events had occurred in Susan's life. I kept recalling her as a happy young wife and protective mother, who never in her wildest imaginings would have predicted she would one day be the cause of such forlornness for her children.

Susan's engagement to Tom Owsley in the summer of 1967, when she was twenty-five, was something of a *deus ex machina* conclusion to the insecurity she had suffered from for much of her life, which had reached a head in a destructive relationship during her early twenties. Following her graduation from Manhattanville College, where she'd majored in art history, Susan had taken a job at the Boston Museum of Fine Arts. This position introduced her to the world of Boston bluebloods and art patrons, and she was soon dating a member of this set: Lonnie Marquand, whose father was the late novelist John P. Marquand and whose mother was related to the Rockefellers. Susan's head was turned by Lonnie—ever since boarding school she'd been in awe of Social Register types and ashamed of what she regarded as her inferior Irish-Catholic arriviste status— and so when he eventually proposed to her, she accepted. But Lonnie's lack of direction, bouts with depression, and heavy drinking increasingly disturbed Susan; if she married him, she began to realize, she would be re-creating for herself the same kind of insecure, alcoholic home life that she had longed to escape from as a child. She therefore broke off the engagement about a month before their intended wedding. It wasn't a clean break, though, and they soon drifted back into dating in an on-again-off-again fashion. This unsatisfying, undefined state of affairs went on for about a year. Susan was upset with herself for being so weak and so afraid of being alone, and she was also scared by the fact that she often drank heavily when she was with Lonnie. She used to confide all these fears in me because she knew that I, having grown up in the same home as she, could relate to them.

In the summer of 1967, between my sophomore and junior years in college, I went to Europe to work for a month at a camp in France and then to hitchhike through the British Isles with a friend from Brown. While in France, I received a number of distressed letters from Susan. She was feeling panicky, she said: she knew the involvement with Lonnie was bad for her, but she didn't have the courage to be on her own. When she would attempt to be apart from him for a few days by going home to my parents' house, her insecurity only increased because the weekend often turned into one of those chaotic, drunken episodes of my mother's. She had to get away, she said. Could she come join me in England in August, when she had some vacation time from her job? I said of course.

I was alarmed about Susan's condition. I was beginning to suspect that her inability to break with Lonnie and be on her own was due to more than the unliberated behavior typical of her generation of women; rather, it seemed to me to stem from a lack of a basic sense of self and self-worth. It felt strange for the tables suddenly to be turned: *I* was going to be the one giving advice and support to my big sister. For the first time, I realized that I possessed an emotional fortitude that Susan lacked, and, despite my concern about her, this insight gave me a small, guilty thrill, so used was I to being the little sister. With my new sense of authority, I began mentally to prepare for the counseling role I would play for Susan later in the summer.

When I arrived in England in early August, I was expecting a letter from her to be awaiting me, informing me of her planned arrival time. Sure enough, a letter was there, but its contents were not what I had anticipated—she would not be coming to England after all—and the tone was completely different from that of the letters earlier in the summer. Gone was the desperate Susan who felt doomed to insecurity; in her place was a confident, ecstatic Susan, bubbling over with an account of how she'd met a wonderful man, fallen in love, and felt that her life had taken a 180-degree turn. The relationship with Lonnie was a thing of the past. Tom Owsley, I learned, had been a friend of my brother Bill at Harvard and was spending the summer working in Boston, between his first and second years of law school at the University of North Carolina. Susan had been fixed up with him on a blind date, and the two had immediately hit it off, staying up all night talking. This was too good to be true, I thought. But it was for real: when I met Tom on my return home from Europe, I became convinced that Susan had found the answer to her insecurity. He possessed the Ivy League credentials and gentleman's manners that satisfied Susan's desire for class, but unlike Lonnie, he was ambitious and directed.

They became engaged at the end of the summer and planned to marry at Christmastime. Tom returned to law school, and Susan moved back into my parents' house in Taunton and commuted an hour to her job in Boston. She had had reservations about this arrangement, but she didn't have much choice, being unable to renew the lease on her Boston apartment for only a few months; besides, she figured that her blissful state of mind and the prospect of the secure life that lay ahead would insulate her against the emotional devastation my mother's episodes usually caused her. Susan spent most of her non-working hours that fall planning the wedding, sewing outfits for her honeymoon, and talking on the phone to Tom. When I would occasionally come home from college for the weekend, I would be astonished at how buoyant and confident she seemed. The weak, pathetic Susan of the Lonnie days was gone for good, I assumed.

Following the wedding, which took place in Taunton on December 16, 1967, Susan and Tom honeymooned in Canada and then moved into an apartment in Chapel Hill. Susan got a job at UNC's Ackland Art Museum, as assistant curator, but she poured most of her energy into her domestic life, having finally found herself in a position to create the kind of elegant home she had always wanted. She prepared gourmet meals, sewed Williamsburg-style curtains and drapes, refinished and re-upholstered antique furniture, made needlepoint covers for the dining room chairs, and generally transformed what would otherwise have been a modest young-marrieds' apartment into a showplace. She also strove to cultivate an appearance that was in direct contrast to that of my mother, whose dishevelment and lack of style had embarrassed Susan when she would bring friends home from prep school and college. She carefully watched her diet so as to maintain a slim figure, she wore her blond hair in a shoulder-length Joan Kennedy style, and she always had on just the right outfit for the occasion—and almost always one she had made, sometimes even designed, herself: rust-colored corduroy slacks and a nubby wool turtleneck for a fall football game, a Herringbone-tweed suit for a winter afternoon art gallery opening, an A-line linen "Jackie Kennedy" dress for a summer cocktail party. When I would visit, I would fall back into my childhood awe of her talent and would feel inadequate and shabby beside her.

But I knew that it wasn't just the superficial, cosmetic aspects of her life that Susan was striving to perfect; the driving force behind all her efforts was the desire for a snug, secure nest, with none of the physical or emotional chaos of the home life she had grown up in. Her main way of trying to achieve this goal was to work vigilantly at being the opposite of my mother. Accordingly, she never let herself or her home become sloppy, she never fought with her husband, and—most importantly—she tried to keep her drinking under control. But the true litmus test, I think she felt, would occur when she had children: she wanted to prove that she could give them the kind of cozy, stable home she herself had lacked as a child. And so she looked forward to starting a family, which she and Tom planned to do after he finished law school.

Tom received his law degree in the spring of 1969 and took a position at a small law firm in Danbury, Connecticut. Susan and he found a wonderful little guest cottage to rent—Susan dubbed it her "Hansel and Gretel" cottage—on an estate in nearby Newtown. I frequently took the train out from Philadelphia, where I had my first post-college job teaching, to visit them, and that year they spent in Connecticut stands out in my memory as a kind of Currier and Ives idyll. The wooded grounds of the estate they lived on contained a small pond, in which their new puppy, Gretel (aptly named by Susan), splashed in the summer and on which Susan and Tom and their friends ice-skated in the winter, and there were blueberry and blackberry bushes everywhere, whose bounty Susan would turn into pies and preserves.

With no museum work available in this rural area, Susan took a job as a substitute art teacher in the local public school system. However, her real focus was on starting a family, and she was ecstatic when she learned that winter that she was pregnant. Now she had another outlet for her creative skills: she threw herself into making baby clothes, quilts, stuffed animals, and nursery accoutrements. She read avidly about pregnancy and became an authority on prenatal care and nutrition, scrupulously avoiding alcohol, aspirin, second-hand smoke, and salt. Always a finicky eater, she forced herself to consume liver and spinach and all the other foods that the wisdom of the day held were important for developing fetuses. And she was adamant about the superiority of breast-feeding over bottle-feeding. I marveled at the way my once-squeamish, social-climbing sister had been transformed into an earth mother.

There is one memory in particular that became for me an icon of this happy, secure period of Susan's life: I was spending the weekend at Susan and Tom's, seeking temporary refuge from messy boyfriend problems in Philadelphia. Ensconced with Susan in the parlor of her "Hansel and Gretel" cottage, I gazed enviously across the room at my sister, who was in the early stage of pregnancy and blissfully radiant. She sat on a loveseat knitting a baby sweater; the window behind her looked out onto the snowy night. I noted the contrast between the warm, safe atmosphere of the room and the wild elements raging outside, a contrast that suddenly struck me as symbolic of the way Susan had succeeded finally in removing herself from the insecurity and chaos of her prior life.

That memory came back to me the first time I met Jim Harrison, when I stood in the doorway of the Baltimore home Susan had shared with Tom and watched her walk off into the dark, snowy night with Jim. I was struck once again by a symbolic contrast, this time between that snowy evening fifteen years earlier and the present portentous one.

After a year at the small law firm in Danbury, Tom applied for a more challenging position that he learned had opened up in the Securities and Exchange Commission in Washington, D.C. He was made an offer, and he and Susan decided he should accept it. They loved where they lived in Connecticut, but there were few young families in the area, and they were eager to move to a more child-oriented setting. The newly developed community of Reston, Virginia, within commuting distance from Tom's job in D.C., would be a perfect place to raise children, they thought. And so in May of 1970, they moved into a townhouse in Reston. Four months later, Jonathan was born.

Because her interests and talents lay in domestic arts, and because the feminist notion that women should have careers outside the home had not yet become widespread, it didn't occur to Susan to be anything other than a full-time, stay-at-home mother. She loved this role and was totally devoted to Jonathan and, a few years later, to Nicholas, who was born in June of 1975. The period when the boys were babies and toddlers was probably the happiest of Susan's life. She created the sunny, structured home life overseen by a gracious, dependable mother that she had craved as a child. The importance she placed on this achievement was driven home to me one time when she related an anecdote over the phone about how on a recent morning, at around 10:00, five-year-old Jonathan had expressed astonishment at the fact that the beds were not made yet. He wanted to know why. Susan's supposed reason for telling me this story was simply that it was amusing that a little boy would notice such a thing, but I sensed that her real reason was to prove how orderly and stable her home life was—so much so that any lapse in routine was noticed even by a small child. It must have validated Susan's achievement in her own mind to have it witnessed by me, who had also grown up associating household messiness with emotional insecurity.

When I think about this period of Susan's life, I tend to visualize it in a kaleidoscope of emblematic scenes. I see tow-headed Jonathan and Nicholas, wearing matching Tyrolean sweaters Susan had knit for them, leaning over to feed the ducks at the duck pond on a bright fall morning. I see Susan at the kitchen table patiently helping Jonathan put together a model airplane or Nicholas fashion animals out of Play-Doh. The most vivid scenes are of Christmastime. Susan had always loved Christmas and tradition and had always tried to turn our family Christmases into perfect Christmas-card-image ones. She would inevitably be disappointed, though, either because of my mother's unpredictable behavior or because of my brothers' balking at the rituals she proposed. Now with her own family, however, she could achieve the Christmases of her imagination. And that she did: her house would resemble a scene out of a Victorian Christmas tale, with ropes of fresh greenery festooning banisters and mantels, a towering balsam tree decorated with homemade ornaments, and plum puddings and gingerbread men cooling on the kitchen counters. The heart of this scene in my memory is a tableau in front of a blazing fire in the living room fireplace: Susan on the couch flanked by two pajama-clad little boys, snuggled up against her as she reads "'Twas the Night Before Christmas" in a hushed, magical voice.

How could the woman in that snug scene have ended up the woman whose face stared tragically out from missing person flyers posted on lonely telephone poles and seedy convenience store windows all over Baltimore County? This question first posed itself to me that October night as I lay awake in Tom's house—the house that would have

been Tom and *Susan's* if the script implied by the cozy Christmas Eve
tableau had not gone awry. I would return again and again to this
question over the next few months, especially during my visits to
Baltimore when I would come into contact with potent reminders
of Susan.

The half hour spent in Susan's cottage on that first visit had rendered me emotionally raw. I couldn't bring myself to return to it for
the rest of the weekend. The thought that in six weeks I was going
to have to spend sustained time inside the cottage—I had agreed to
come back at Thanksgiving to help pack up Susan's belongings for
storage—filled me with dread. I hoped I would have developed a
thicker skin by then.

7 Cleaning Out Susan's Cottage, November 1994

One of the pieces of business my brothers and I had conducted in the October visit to Baltimore was a meeting with Carey Deeley to begin the legal procedures for appointing a family member guardian of Susan's estate. Following the meeting, we conferred with one another and, over the phone, with Jonathan and Nicholas regarding the question of who should serve as guardian. Jonathan expressed a desire to do so. This choice made sense, despite his youthful age of twenty-four, because he was a mature, responsible, and extremely intelligent young man; more importantly, this was a way he could express his strong devotion to his mother. The law school training he had embarked on further qualified him for the role. We presented our choice to Carey, who concurred and said he would begin making the arrangements for the guardianship hearing.

The hearing was scheduled for two days before Thanksgiving; this was a date when Jonathan and most of the rest of us would be free to be in Baltimore. Although Jim planned to contest the appointment and to argue that he, as Susan's husband, should be guardian, Carey was confident the judge would rule for Jonathan; we therefore assumed we would be able to move Susan's belongings out of the cottage and into storage over the long holiday weekend. My brother John and I volunteered to do this, being the only two of the siblings who could be free at that time. Bill and Bob had family and in-law obligations for the holidays, but John is not married and so had no competing plans, and my husband had to go to North Carolina to attend to some matters for his elderly parents and would be tied up with that business for the whole Thanksgiving week.

My daughter and I flew to Baltimore the Sunday before Thanksgiving, as did John; Jonathan and Nicholas arrived on Monday; and Bill flew in early Tuesday, stopping just for the day before continuing on to Florida to join his family for Thanksgiving at his mother-in-law's. On Tuesday morning, we all drove over to the courthouse in Towson together, feeling apprehensive. This would be our first face-to-face encounter with Jim since Susan's disappearance, and, aware of his recent erratic behavior, we weren't sure what to expect. Perhaps he would be very cool or hostile toward us: he knew we suspected him, although we had not publicly declared so. Or perhaps he would play the histrionic grieving husband role he sometimes played for reporters. What we hadn't been prepared for was the hail-fellow-well-met manner he displayed. The first thing he did when he spotted us in the courtroom was to walk over, pat me on the back, and heartily congratulate me on the "wonderful letters" I had been writing to the newspapers, much the way one would congratulate an aspiring writer on getting a short story published. I was taken aback by his inappropriate manner and instinctively recoiled. He then moved on to my brothers, jocularly greeting each of them and behaving as though he were catching up with old pals at a class reunion.

Jim's behavior throughout the hearing continued in this outrageous vein. When called to be sworn in, he sauntered up to the stand, suddenly stopping dramatically to pick up a paper clip he spotted on the floor and handing it with a flourish to one of the female clerks, whom he proceeded to flirt with and chat up during breaks. Under questioning, he alternated between arrogant and eccentric. The judge moved from astonishment to impatience to anger as Jim, who was trained as a lawyer, continually failed to abide by courtroom rules and decorum—not answering questions, changing the subject, getting up and walking around. At one point, the judge even had to call a recess to instruct Jim's lawyer, Dana White, to advise his client on required courtroom behavior.

The hearing took up most of the morning, as Jim and Dana White attempted to convince the judge that Jim, with his experience as chief financial officer of a major corporation, was far more sophisticated about financial matters than Jonathan and hence more qualified to serve as guardian of Susan's estate. Carey Deeley, however, did a masterful job of undermining Jim's qualifications by focusing on Jim's alleged mistreatment of Susan and on her plans to divorce him. Not only did Carey succeed in convincing the judge to rule for Jonathan, but he also accomplished two other coups: (1) Through skillful questioning about certain dates Jim kept mentioning, Carey got him to pull out his diary to confirm that Susan had done such-and-such on a particular date, whereupon Carey requested and was granted by the judge permission to make a photocopy of the diary. Leafing through the diary in front of the court, Carey observed that it was interesting that Jim kept a record of and running commentary on his relationship with Susan over the past year, and yet there was no mention of her after August 5, a fact that seemed inconsistent with the behavior of an innocent husband baffled and distressed by his wife's disappearance. (2) Carey got Jim to deny under oath and as part of the public record that he had ever physically harmed Susan, providing Carey with evidence that could possibly be used in a perjury case against Jim at some future point.

We left the court after the hearing in some bewilderment, pondering the meaning of Jim's strange behavior. It was at that point that we began to formulate our theory about its being due in part to the mental stress created by guilt and denial and in part to a contingency plan to plead insanity if he were ever charged. But his confidence in his own cleverness and in his ability to manipulate situations must have been dealt a blow by the outcome of the guardianship hearing, we thought with some satisfaction. Jonathan's probity and courteousness on the stand had undone Jim and his lawyer's attempts to paint Jonathan as too young, inexperienced, and spiteful of his stepfather to act as a responsible guardian.

The legal obstacles taken care of, my brother John and I were now free to begin inventorying Susan's belongings and packing them up for storage. We decided to wait until the next morning when we would feel more rested and spent the remainder of Tuesday afternoon collecting boxes and purchasing labels, tags, markers, and other supplies we would need. Wednesday morning, we got up early and, steeling ourselves for the emotional ordeal that lay ahead, drove over to Ruxton. Armed with bracing cups of coffee, we let ourselves into the cottage.

I breathed a sigh of relief: this time it wasn't so bad. As I'd hoped would be the case, my earlier exposure to Susan's house had apparently served as a vaccination against the rawest kind of pain. Or so I thought at first. John and I busied ourselves with devising an elaborate coding system for categorizing and inventorying Susan's possessions. We decided I would be in charge of the more "female" categories—clothes, linens, dishware, and so on—and he would handle furniture, tools, and other things. We wrote up a timetable for each day's tasks, in order to ensure that we completed everything by Sunday, when we had to leave. And then, with our yellow legal pads, pens, and labels in hand, we embarked on the job.

Within minutes, I realized that it was going to be impossible to maintain a businesslike approach to this activity. No sooner had I begun to itemize the contents of Susan's kitchen cupboards than I was catapulted into the first of the many Proustian time shifts I would experience over the course of the next four days. Picking up a piece of the French peasant-style cookware Susan had received as a wedding present, in the earthy rust color that was popular during the mid-1960s, I was suddenly back in the kitchen of Tom and Susan's first apartment, in Chapel Hill, sipping a glass of wine while watching Susan prepare one of her impressive gourmet meals. These kinds of flashbacks occurred again and again. As I took down the Wedgewood plates and Waterford goblets from her china cabinet, there paraded before my eyes the many elegant dinner parties I had seen Susan create over the years. Each of the mental pictures would cause the emotions of old to arise—once again I was the shabby little sister, envious of my big sister's superior taste and lifestyle—to be replaced quickly by those of sadness and guilt when I would realize how ironic that jealousy seemed now. I would gladly have smashed every one of those once-envied objects if I could have had my sister back.

Inventorying the contents of the bedrooms was equally distressing. In the room where Jonathan and Nicholas slept when they stayed with her, Susan had stored articles from their earlier bedrooms. Unearthing the homemade mobiles, fabric pictures, quilts, and curtains, featuring such little-boy motifs as Superman and cowboys, I conjured up the colorful nurseries and bedrooms Susan had created for her boys, and I was once again disoriented by the thought that

that creative, protective young mother would one day unwittingly put her children through the emotional devastation they were experiencing now. Susan's own bedroom was an even more potent trigger of memory. The scent of her characteristic perfume—I don't know its name, but it was one she wore for years—overwhelmed me when I entered the room and made her presence feel more palpable here than anywhere else in the house. Opening her closet door for the first time, I experienced yet another Proustian moment: the sight of her beautiful wardrobe, containing many of her own creations, gave me the same delicious rush of anticipation I used to experience as an adolescent when Susan would be home on vacation from college but out of the house for an hour or two and I'd sneak into her room to try on her clothes. I would stand in front of her floor-length mirror gazing at the new me, suddenly transformed by a sleek silk cocktail dress or an Irish-tweed skirt and wool fisherman's sweater, and fantasize about what my life would be like if I could possess such a wardrobe. Now, ironically, I could, for the clothes would otherwise just sit in storage until the case was resolved, and then anything that family members didn't want would be given to Goodwill—but the thought filled me with despair. I could not face trying on any of the clothes; at this stage of the mourning process, having them would have been more upsetting than comforting, and so I decided to put off until a later date the decision about which items to take. I hurried through the clothes inventory, trying to be as businesslike as possible. Occasionally, though, I would be seized by the urge to hold a garment to my cheek, as if doing so would mystically connect me to Susan.

Throughout the days that we were engaged in this macabre task, John and I experienced the same cycles of moods, ranging from brisk efficiency to crippling sadness. We would start each day on an energetic note, ready to tote off items on our to-do lists. But as the day wore on, our steely resolve would crumble, and we would increasingly be felled by emotion. Often I would go in search of John with a question about inventorying and, rounding the corner to the room where he was supposedly working, would come upon him sitting utterly still, staring dejectedly at some item he held in his hand—a photograph, a china figurine, a scrap of paper covered with Susan's handwriting. Or we would be sitting at the kitchen table taking a coffee break when suddenly there would come into my head a ka-leidoscopic parade of all the long-morning and late-night sisterly coffee klatches I'd had with Susan at a series of kitchen tables over the years—and I would crumple.

The painfulness of our days in Susan's cottage would be allevi-ated every evening when John and I returned to Tom's house. Tom would have a fire going, wine poured, and a meal cooking; Jonathan and Nicholas and often some of their close friends would be there. The warmth and conviviality presented a marked contrast to the chill and gloom of Susan's house. But as welcome as this changed atmo-sphere was to me, it also served to heighten my disorientation by underscoring Susan's absence. This was just the kind of scene Susan loved, just the kind of evening we had had so many times when the extended family got together. But she was not here. What made the situation doubly disorienting was that this was the first time I had spent any length of time with Tom since he and Susan had split up, ten years earlier. I felt as though I was suddenly slotted back into my twenties when I used to escape my hippie life for the weekend by visiting the Owsleys and wallowing in their comfortable, upscale lifestyle. I kept expecting Susan to breeze into the room, carrying a tray of hors d'oeuvres and laughingly embarking on some funny anecdote about one of the kids or the dog. That kind of image would be followed by one of how things *should* be now, of what Susan's life would have been at this point if she hadn't been pursued by Jim and hadn't succumbed to him. I pictured a gracious, matronly, fifty-some-thing Susan, basking in the security of a stable marriage and the ful-fillment of having raised two accomplished, handsome sons; I imag-ined her delighting in the friends and girlfriends and eventually wives her sons brought home; I saw her, five or ten years hence, knitting baby booties and sewing little outfits for her grandchildren. This vision of what Susan's destiny *should* have been was so compelling that for a second or two, I would almost believe that the tragedy we were experiencing was a weird nightmare. Then as the vision faded, I would ache at the thought of the future Susan could have had but, because of deluded thinking, threw away.

In the process of combing through the contents of her cottage, I gained a fuller understanding of what she had traded this future for, and my horror at the mistake she had made intensified. Like an archaeologist on a dig, I unearthed artifact after artifact that allowed me to piece together a fuller picture of Susan and Jim's profoundly unhealthy relationship, which Susan had given me only glimpses of when she was alive. One category of artifacts consisted of sentimental possessions of Susan's that Jim had allegedly destroyed in various fits of rage. Susan had related many of these incidents to me, often using the metaphor of a volcano erupting to describe the way Jim's mood would suddenly turn violent; but since it was her habit to retract or modify her tales a few days later, I was never 100 percent sure they were true. In the cottage, though, we uncovered what I considered to be definitive evidence. There was the silver candelabra that had been in our family for years and that Susan had inherited, now badly dented and disfigured. There were the shredded pieces of photographs taken at the 1990 ceremony in our hometown in which we Hurley children had a library at the local historical society dedicated in the name of our late parents. And—the most heinous act of destruction, in my opinion—there was the smashed remains of the framed block print Nicholas had made for Susan for Mother's Day when he was in preschool: an imprint of his tiny hands, a memento of his childhood that Susan had cherished. I recalled her heartrending sobs as she described this act of destruction to me over the phone shortly after it occurred.

Another category of artifacts was photographs. We came across a picture album on the cover of which Susan had written "Ireland 1984 to Cherry Blossoms 1986," chronicling the trips she and Jim had taken in their first years together. But to me, what it was really a chronicle of was their attempts to mask the violent undercurrent of their relationship by pretending they were a carefree couple living a honeymoon-like life. In recent years, as Susan's complaints about abuse had become more frequent and her retractions less convincing, I had begun to suspect that she was caught up in the classic battered wife syndrome of always taking her husband back after he had beaten her because his lavish displays of affection and showering of gifts convinced her that she must have provoked and deserved his outburst or that she must have exaggerated the episode in her own mind. Now these photographs seemed to confirm that theory. There was something unnatural and forced about the blissfulness the snap-shots were intended to portray. Every one of them was taken in an exotic setting—in front of a sublime Irish castle, on a craggy cliff overlooking the Pacific, in the bedroom of a five-star European ho-tel—and in every one, Susan and Jim look like the perfect couple: she is beautiful, dressed in some appropriate fashion for the setting, such as Irish tweeds or a linen sundress, and he holds a protective arm around her shoulder or gazes adoringly at her. But there are tell-tale signs of the truth about their relationship: in many of the snap-shots, a sad, lost look in Susan's eyes undercuts the cheerful image she is trying to project, and in all of the "cherry blossom" photos, taken during their spring 1986 trip to Washington, D.C., Susan has her arm in a sling. Gazing at the pictures of her in this condition, I suddenly realized that this was the injury she had attributed to a bicycle accident when I questioned her about the scar on her arm in the summer of 1986. At a later point, in one of her distraught phone calls, she had confessed to me that the real story was that Jim had broken her arm on that occasion; but still later, when she'd made up with Jim, she had retracted that claim. The result had been my usual bewilderment about where the truth lay. Now, though, with these concrete pictures spread before me, I felt certain that her allegations had been true.

Additional artifacts we came across suggested the extent to which Jim both degraded and controlled Susan, manipulating her into thinking the relationship's problems were her fault. Susan hadn't kept a diary, but tucked away in her desk and nightstand drawers we found various sheets of paper on which she had in distressed moments scribbled notes describing degradations Jim had subjected her to. Some of these were incidents I'd gotten glimpses of in her phone calls to me when she was upset; others were new to me. Together they painted a picture of a relationship that made George and Martha's of *Who's Afraid of Virginia Woolf?* seem tame in comparison. There were references to Jim's calling her "whore," "slut," "bitch"; to his leaving her stranded in bars and by the side of the road; to his punch-ing her, pulling out her hair, locking her in rooms. At the end of one such litany of degradations, she had written, "[A]ll meant to render his power over me and the situation—very sick . . . I really should remove myself from this intolerable situation once and for all."

We also found a copy of a letter Jim had apparently forced Susan to write "confessing" that she had slept with a black man. Dated November 16, 1991, the letter begins, "Dear Jim, First of all, I love you very, very much and I am sorry at my drunken behavior on Sunday, Nov. 10, 1991." She goes on to write, "Here is what I did," and proceeds to describe sitting down at the bar of the restaurant where Jim had left her following an argument at dinner, striking up a conversation with a black man, proceeding to drink and talk with him until around midnight, accepting the man's offer of a ride home, and then, the next thing she knew, waking up around 3:00 A.M. in bed with the man at his apartment, not recalling how she had gotten there because she had been drunk and had apparently passed out. She then asked the man to drive her home, and he did. Her final paragraph reads, revealingly, "I am writing this *of my own free will* [italics mine]. I am mortified and sorry. Love, Susan."

Tucked away in another drawer was a note from Susan dated November 27, 1991, commenting on this letter. Addressed to Jonathan, Nicholas, and Tom, and with "CONFIDENTIAL" scrawled on the envelope, the note read: "Jim forced me to sign and write a trumped up confession to something I did not do upon the threat of breaking my other arm. If that is found please don't believe it and please destroy it. You all know me better than that—he is a very deranged man. The 'confession' is dated Nov. 16 or 17, 1991. Love, Mom." I am not sure why Susan herself didn't destroy the copy of the letter she had; perhaps her thinking was that since Jim possessed the original and possibly planned to blackmail her with it, there was a good chance Jonathan and Nicholas would learn of it anyway, and she wanted to prepare them for that eventuality.

The episode these documents made reference to was not unfamiliar to me, although I had never been entirely clear about what had happened because Susan had given me two different stories concerning it. She had phoned me a day or two after she'd written the "confession," although she didn't mention anything at the time about that letter, and had tearfully told me how upset she was with herself because she had been picked up by a man at a bar and spent the night with him. She was also upset with herself for getting drunk, after having been sober for several weeks. When I pressed her for more details, she told me that she and Jim had gone out to dinner and she had become angry with him because he kept trying to talk her into having a glass of wine. She accused him of trying to undermine her efforts to stay sober, and that accusation led to a big argument, which ended with Jim's storming out of the restaurant and driving off in the car. Upset and feeling stranded, she went to the bar and began drinking, assuming Jim would eventually come back to get her. After she'd had a couple of drinks, an attractive black man came over and sat down and began to talk to her. Jim didn't return, and she remained talking and drinking with this man until around midnight, when he offered to drive her home. The rest of the evening, she cried to me, was a blank; the next thing she knew, she was awakening in the man's bed, whereupon she asked him to drive her home, and he did. She kept calling herself a sinner and saying she ought to go to confession. I tried to steer her away from her guilt and get her to think rationally about the riskiness of what she had done, and I repeated my warning that she needed to get out of the relationship with Jim since it triggered this kind of self-destructive behavior. But she countered that it was she herself, not Jim, who was the cause of all the problems between them.

However, a couple of weeks later, during a period when she and Jim had been fighting and he had gone off for a couple of days, she called me and this time put a different spin on the episode. She told me about Jim's forcing her to write the confession and trying to brainwash her into believing she had slept with the man. She said that while it was true that she had met the man at the bar and gone back to his apartment with him, she was sure nothing had happened. There were two other people at the apartment, they all had some more drinks, she fell asleep for a couple of hours, and then the man drove her home, whereupon Jim blew up at her and held her down while he forced her to write the confession under the threat of breaking her other arm (an allusion to his alleged breaking of her arm in 1986). Fuming about his treatment of her, she declared to me, "I may be a lot of other things, but I don't think I'm promiscuous." Her anger was targeted not only at Jim's manipulation of her but also at his apparent racism, for, she pointed out, it was the fact that the man was black that seemed to bother him as much as anything else.

However, after Susan reconciled with Jim some time later, she didn't mention the incident again. When I referred to Jim's forcing her to write the letter, she tried to dismiss the topic, saying she'd been so drunk she couldn't remember what had happened. So I relegated the incident to that gray area of reality where I stored all of Susan's allegations and retractions. But when I actually saw the confession letter, as well as the disclaimer to Tom and her sons and another note stating that Jim "twists everything I say and fabricates like mad," I was convinced that regardless of where the truth lay concerning Susan and the man she met at the bar, Jim had been in the habit of brainwashing and blackmailing her. Additional evidence of the way he tried to control her was a series of notes and cards we discovered in which he declared, in inflated romantic language, how much he loved Susan and how beautiful he found her. I suspected that these were written in the aftermath of a fight and were intended to blot out her memory of his abusive treatment.

The cumulative impression of all these documents found among Susan's possessions was that Susan and Jim's marriage fit the classic spousal-abuse pattern: fights that turned violent, followed by the abuser's lavish displays of affection to the victim and/or his attempts to brainwash her into blaming herself, followed in turn by the victim's convincing herself that all would be right from now on if she acted sweet enough—until the next episode when the pattern would begin all over again.[1]

Further signs of the confused thinking and shattered sense of self the relationship had effected in Susan were the many pathetic coping mechanisms we discovered: empty wine bottles, containers of anti-depressants and tranquilizers, self-help books. We found an empty wine bottle tucked among some cleaning supplies at the back of a utility closet, another one behind the refrigerator, another one under her bed. Susan had been trying to give the family the impression that she had her drinking completely under control since leaving Jim, and no doubt she feared that her sons, dropping in unexpectedly, might see the empty bottles if she threw them away in the wastebasket. She must therefore have stashed them out of sight until trash pickup days. The array of pills in the bathroom medicine cabinet, with purchase dates going back to the late 1980s, further opened my eyes to the extent of her emotional difficulties. I knew she had seen numerous psychologists and psychiatrists during her years with Jim, and I knew some of them had prescribed medications, but the spectacle of container after container of partially used-up Prozac, Xanax, Valium, and other pills suggested she had been feeling much more desperate than she had let on to the family. This search for a panacea had also apparently caused her to forage into pop psychology, for we found various self-help books and articles among her bedside reading materials. Tears came to my eyes when I picked up one of these, *Feeling Good,* and thought how that title must have hooked her, how the simple, ordinary mental state it describes, taken for granted by so many people, was what Susan yearned for but what eluded her.

By the end of the week, I was overwhelmed by revelations about the dangerousness of Susan and Jim's relationship and about the toll it had taken on Susan's mental health. The artifacts I had discovered in her cottage served, in my opinion, as compelling evidence that she had been caught in the battered-wife syndrome. There was one final artifact, although not discovered in the cottage, that clinched my conviction. It was a photo Jonathan showed me the last night of my Thanksgiving stay in Baltimore, a photo he had taken in July of 1993 for the purpose of documenting Susan's condition following an alleged battering by Jim. I remembered this particular fight well: Susan's description of it had so alarmed us that Jonathan and my three brothers rushed to Baltimore to help her take out a restraining order on Jim. But to their distress, Susan ended up changing her mind and getting back together with Jim. My brothers were shocked by the physical condition they had found her in; her appearance eliminated any doubt they'd had about her allegations of abuse over the years. Their description to me on the phone went a long way toward eliminating my own doubts as well, but not having viewed the injuries firsthand, I didn't have the visceral conviction my brothers had.

I hadn't been aware of the existence of the photograph until Jonathan mentioned it that night, and I asked to see it. Fetching it from his files, he handed it to me with the warning, "Brace yourself."

I took one glance at the 5-by-7-inch color photo of Susan's face and gasped. Then I doubled over in tears. As often as I'd had her appearance on that occasion described to me, I had not been prepared for the shock of the sight. My sister was barely recognizable, her face distorted by swelling, one eye partially swollen shut and the other almost wholly so and surrounded by a protruding purple welt. But what I found even more distressing than the bruises and blood and swelling was the expression I could make out in her eyes: a look of utter despair.

At that moment, any lingering doubts I'd had that my sister had been the victim of spousal abuse dissolved. The gray, fuzzy, obliquely viewed picture I'd had of her life with Jim was abruptly refocused. It made me sick at heart to think that only now, when it was too late, did I fully realize what had been going on.

Susan on Santa's lap at the Jordan Marsh
store, Boston, ca. 1944

Susan as a flower girl in a family babysitter's wedding, ca. 1947

Susan *(right)* with Molly and their mother
at Cape Cod, ca. 1948

Susan crowning a statue of the Blessed Virgin in the "May
Procession" at St. Joseph's Church, Taunton, Massachusetts,
ca. 1948

Susan *(extreme left)*, Molly *(center, standing)*, Bobby *(extreme right)*, and family friends, Cape Cod, 1949

Susan, age seven, 1949. Photo by Stu Frazier.

The Hurleys on Christmas Eve, 1950. *Left to right:* Dad, Bill, Bobby, Johnny, Molly, Susan holding doll, Mom. Photo by Stu Frazier, Reed and Barton photographer and family friend, who took photos of the Hurley family at Christmastime every year from ca. 1949 to 1970.

Susan and Molly on the side porch of the family's summer home, Cape Cod, ca. 1950

Molly, Susan, and Bobby, ca. 1950. Photo by Stu Frazier.

Susan, age twelve, in front of the barn at the family's Cape Cod summer home, 1954

Clockwise from top left: Johnny, Bobby, Susan, Molly, 1954. Photo by Stu Frazier.

Susan *(middle row, far left)* wearing flower crown at the Dana Hall School's traditional "Spread" celebration for juniors, spring 1959

Susan *(second from right)* with Bill *(extreme left),* June Gebelein, and Dave Larkin at a Pieta Club party at Harvard, 1959

Susan *(extreme left)* with her date, Paul McKenna, and friends Eileen Cotter (now Eileen Malouf, Susan's lifelong close friend) and Steve Brady (another old family friend from Cape Cod summers) at the annual summer Falmouth Regatta Dance, ca. 1960

Susan's engagement portrait for the newspapers, fall 1967

8 Growing Suspicions about Domestic Abuse, Mid-1980s–July 1993

𝒯here were a number of reasons it had taken my brothers and me so long to become convinced that our sister was being physically abused. The main one was Susan's denial: she had a strong need to pretend to the world, and to herself, that she was a happy, respectable upper-middle-class matron. But there were additional reasons for our delayed convictions. These included the infrequency with which we saw Susan and Jim; the diminished contact and communication we had with Susan's sons following their parents' divorce; and Susan's drinking problem, which tended to cloud the situation.

The pattern Susan had begun shortly after moving in with Jim of making periodic distressed phone calls to one or more of her siblings continued for the duration of their relationship. As I have already described, for the first year or so she gave the impression that the cause of her distress was the slow pace of their respective divorces, and her anger was focused on Tom or Molly. Then some time in 1985 or 1986, Jim himself began to figure in her complaints. She started mentioning arguments they had had, usually sparked by her impatience with the way he seemed to be dragging his feet in his divorce process (her divorce from Tom occurred in late 1987, almost a full year before Jim's from Molly). Every once in awhile, she would let drop a piece of information—such as that she had yelled at Jim, whereupon he had slammed out of the house and driven off and now she didn't know where he was—that made me realize these were more than arguments: they were ugly, chaotic, no doubt drunken fights. By now I'd figured out that Susan and Jim were drinking heavily. But it still didn't occur to me that there was any physical component to the arguments. It was bad enough to imagine how disturbed Susan must have felt at the realization that she was behaving like my mother and re-creating the very kind of home life she'd spent her childhood yearning to escape.

And then I began to pick up, at first almost imperceptibly, on hints that something darker might be going on. It's hard to put my finger on exactly when I first formulated my suspicion or what it was Susan said that caused me to do so. It may have been her third or fourth vague reference to Jim's shoving her, or it may have been her offhand mention of yet another recent injury or accident. Whatever it was, it caused a lightbulb to turn on suddenly in my head, and I blurted out over the phone, "Susan, has he ever struck you?" She was very quiet for a moment and then said in a small voice, "Yes." I inhaled audibly, and immediately she began to waffle, saying that, well, actually he'd only done it in defense a couple of times: when she'd pushed at him during arguments, he'd grabbed her arm to stop her. And then she proceeded to blame herself. I was bewildered, not sure at first what to believe; but as she continued defending Jim, I found myself buying her explanation. I knew she was drinking, and I figured maybe she had been thinking incoherently when she'd at first said yes in answer to my question. Besides, it was just too unreal to think my sister could be a battered wife, like the kind you read about in *Redbook* or see on sensational TV movies.

About two days after this conversation, which probably took place in late 1986 or early 1987, she phoned me back, in what I would eventually come to recognize as her post-crisis mood: cheery, reassuring, upbeat. She apologized for her recent incoherent phone call and reiterated emphatically that Jim had never hit her. He was a wonderful, loving partner, she said, and the problems all stemmed from the funks she would sometimes get into because the divorces were taking so long. She sounded so clearheaded and convincing that I believed her, and I began to counsel her about controlling her drinking, which I thought caused her to get into these low states of mind.

She latched onto this notion; and so for the next year or two, whenever she would call me upset about a fight with Jim, I would steer the conversation in the direction of the necessity of her getting help for her drinking and would try to dismiss my suspicions about violence. But I would also try to persuade Susan to leave Jim, reasoning that her drinking had become a problem only since she had gotten involved with him. In the heat of her initial fury at him she would often agree, but inevitably a day or two later she would call back and say that no, the problem was not Jim; it was herself and her drinking, which caused her to get upset too easily by things Jim said or did and to exaggerate her complaints. She would often go even further and describe how loving and good to her Jim was. During these phone calls, I could usually hear Jim in the background, and sometimes she would interrupt our conversation to say something sweet or solicitous to him. Her behavior at such times gave me the creeps: she seemed to have fallen under Jim's spell.

There would follow a period of about two or three months uninterrupted by hysterical phone calls. During this time, I would receive an occasional breezy note from Susan, usually containing no mention of the previous crisis. A stranger reading it would have the impression she was a happy, busy Junior League–type housewife, whose untroubled life was taken up with nothing more eventful than crafts projects, tennis games, and volunteer work at the art museum and her younger son's private school. Scrawled on an expensive monogrammed note card in her preppy handwriting would be lighthearted descriptions of a weekend trip she and Jim had taken to Middlebury to watch Jonathan play lacrosse, or of a festive dinner party she was planning for some of Jim's children and their spouses. Occasionally in one of these notes, she would break the facade for a moment and make a brief, embarrassed reference to our last communication, for the purpose of assuring me that she had her life under control and was doing much better.

Then in the late spring of 1988, she informed me that she and Jim had both stopped drinking and had joined Alcoholics Anonymous. I was encouraged by this news, for it suggested that Jim was giving her the supportiveness I had sensed had been lacking on his part prior to this. Maybe with this kind of commitment, the relationship could become a healthy one after all, I thought optimistically. I hadn't seen Susan and Jim together in almost two years—the one or two brief visits she had made to Massachusetts had been solo, and with their domestic life being so unpredictable and crisis-filled, I had been reluctant to visit them—but now I thought it would be a good idea to pay a visit, in order to show my support for the effort they were making. My husband and I were relocating from Rhode Island to Georgia—we had both accepted teaching positions at the University of Georgia—but Mike would have to move down there in the early summer, when his contract began, while I remained in Rhode Island a few more weeks to finish out my contract with the company for whom I'd been working as a technical writer. I decided Alison and I would stop for a two-day visit with Susan and Jim on our drive south in mid-July; with their having turned over a new leaf, I had no qualms about staying under their roof.

For the first day and a half of our visit, it seemed that my optimism had been well founded. Alison and I arrived late Thursday night, and were greeted by a sober, hospitable Susan and Jim. We sat up with them for about a half an hour, drinking soft drinks and making small talk, and then Alison and I retired, exhausted from our long drive. The next day Jim went to work, and Susan, Nick, Alison, and I spent a fun day walking around the newly created Harborplace mall, going out to lunch at the restaurant where Jonathan had a summer job as a waiter, having afternoon tea at McCormick's colonial-style tearoom, and then being taken on a tour of the spice mill—arranged for by Jim, who was still at that time an executive with the company. Susan was in good spirits, interacting affectionately with her sons and niece, delighting in having a little girl to buy feminine trinkets for (she'd always wanted a daughter), and laughing and chatting in a sisterly way with me. In front of the children—Nick was then thirteen and Alison seven—we avoided the topics of her drinking and her relationship with Jim; but a couple of times when we were alone for a minute or two, I broached these subjects and she would wax eloquent about how she'd turned her life around, thanks to AA. I was deeply encouraged; I really believed all Susan's problems and all of the problems with the relationship were a thing of the past. In the late afternoon, Susan wanted to take the children to the dog pound so that Alison could help Nick pick out the new puppy Susan had promised him for his recent birthday, and I opted to take a nap while they were out, in order to rest up for the long drive ahead of me the next day. I remember that as I lay my head down on the pillow in the guest room, hearing the happy voices of the three of them wafting up from the driveway as they piled into Susan's car, I was filled with a sense of relief.

For supper that evening, Susan, always one to make the most of traditions and special occasions, wanted to prepare her out-of-state guests a customary Maryland meal of hard-shelled crabs and corn on the cob, and in accordance with the traditional ritual, we sat outside cracking open our crabs over a picnic table spread with newspapers. It was intended to be a fun, festive occasion, but I couldn't quite relax into it. I sensed a strained manner on Susan's part when she was in Jim's presence—a contrast to the easy, confident manner she'd had during her day spent with Nicholas, Alison, and me. She seemed deferential and too eager to please Jim; he, though not obnoxious in the way I had remembered him being when he was drinking, was stilted in his manner. As I did the last time I'd visited with them, in June of 1986, I felt that he put up a wall with people and couldn't interact in a normal give-and-take way. At the end of the evening, when I said good-bye to Jim—he would be leaving for work before I got up the next morning—I concluded that I would probably never feel comfortable with or close to him and that I didn't like the way Susan behaved with him, but at least the relationship seemed to be stable now that they had stopped drinking.

The next morning, I awoke before Susan had gotten up, and I went downstairs to make some coffee. As I walked into the kitchen, the first thing I noticed was a note propped up in the middle of the table. Assuming it was a good-bye message from Jim to Alison and me, I went over to read it and immediately discovered it was a love note to Susan. In gushing language, he told her how deeply in love with her he was and how wonderful she was. The first thing that struck me was the inappropriateness of his leaving an intimate note prominently displayed for all to read, including children. I was suddenly less reassured about Jim's changed behavior: this kind of histrionic, attention-getting gesture seemed in keeping with the old Jim. And then I began to become suspicious: his protestations of love seemed extreme, as though he was either trying to coat over recent lapses or give other people (namely, me) the impression that he was a totally loving partner to Susan, one who would never abuse her. I left the note there, and when Susan came down a few minutes later accompanied by Alison, she glanced at it, then quickly and nervously tucked it away some place. I soon put my uneasiness about the matter out of my head, though, as I began to busy myself with packing for our journey and saying our good-byes.

The next day, after I'd arrived in Athens, I phoned my brother Bill to report my impression of Susan and Jim's relationship during my visit: how my initial optimism had been tempered by suspiciousness of Jim after I came upon that note he'd left for Susan. Then about five days after my conversation with Bill, he called me back to tell me my suspicions had been well founded: he'd just received a troubling phone call from Susan in which she described a violent argument she and Jim had had, in the midst of which Jim had thrown her out of the house and locked the doors. It was this incident that gave rise to the sequence of events described earlier, in which Bill convinced Susan to fly to Boston and arranged for the medical workup that resulted in the erroneous manic depressive diagnosis.

When Susan returned to Baltimore, under the illusion that her lithium treatment was going to be the answer to the problems in her relationship with Jim, I think she knew she had become like "the boy who cried wolf" with the rest of the family, and she was therefore determined to show us that she now had her life together and the relationship with Jim was fine. We didn't hear from her for about three months, and we tried to believe that maybe the lithium really was the answer. But, not to our surprise, in November there was another spate of distressed phone calls reporting another violent battle with Jim. In her conversation with me she sounded as if she'd been drinking, and so I asked what had happened to her commitment to AA; in a bitter voice she replied that Jim's involvement had been short-lived and that he always undermined her efforts by trying to get her to take a drink. This was a claim she would make again and again over the next few years; in fact, in one of the lists of scribbled complaints we found when we were cleaning out her cottage after her disappearance, she wrote, "I saw him through a window drinking beer at Woodies with his back against the bar. He appeared already be [*sic*] on his way and the fact that he had broken the sobriety pact that we had really disgusted me."

In this same November 1988 phone call, she also confessed that the lithium wasn't helping and she didn't believe she was manic depressive. I again emphasized the necessity of her leaving Jim, and I urged her to seek out a good psychologist and commit herself to a course of therapy, for she tended to flit from counselor to counselor, trying to find one that would help her to cure her problems without her having to leave Jim. By the end of our conversation, she was agreeing with me that she should leave Jim; but, as always, a few days later she entered her post-crisis, denial phase and claimed all was fine between the two of them. No doubt contributing to her optimistic mood this time was the fact that Jim's divorce from Molly had just come through and she and Jim were finally free to marry. Under the illusion that marriage would put their relationship on a stable, respectable footing and hence remove the condition that caused their arguments, Susan immediately wed Jim. The brief civil ceremony took place on December 2, 1988.[1]

My brothers and I were in a bind now. On the one hand, we didn't believe that the marriage was going to effect any improvement in Susan and Jim's relationship, but on the other hand, we felt that we had to give them the benefit of the doubt and treat Jim as a member of the family now that he was our brother-in-law. The next time we saw the two of them was in February 1989, when my mother passed away after a long illness. She died not knowing about either Susan's second marriage or her personal difficulties during the previous few years, because Susan had continued to be secretive about her life when communicating with or visiting my mother and because we had wanted to spare my mother heartache in her last years. Susan and Jim spent the week of the funeral with the rest of the family in Massachusetts, and they were on their good behavior on this occasion: she wasn't drinking, he drank moderately, and there were no arguments. But I had the same uneasy feeling about their relationship that I'd had the last night and morning of my visit in Baltimore the previous summer. As then, Susan was overly sweet and solicitous with Jim, as though she were walking on eggshells, and he was flamboyantly affectionate toward her. His behavior was doubly inappropriate when one considers the somber tenor of the occasion. Susan's birthday occurred during the week of the funeral, and Jim kept interrupting family discussions about funeral-related business by presenting her with lavishly wrapped gifts and insisting she open them then and there, in front of the whole group. My brothers and I repressed our annoyance and behaved civilly toward him, but we found it hard to interact with him in the easy, open way we did with our other in-laws. This was partly due to his odd behavior, but it was also due to our mistrust of him. We were all beginning to realize that there was a dark underside to his showy affection toward Susan and that the kind of honeymoon sweetness we were witnessing usually followed or was followed by a major fight. And sure enough, the night after I returned home from Massachusetts, I received a phone call from a sobbing, incoherent Susan.

The infrequent visits family members had with Susan and Jim during the next few years were equally awkward and uncomfortable, and always we sensed that their display of super-devotedness to each other was a sign of the calm before the storm. They seemed to be trying to prove to the world, and to themselves, that they were a loving, happy couple. For example, when I drove with them back to Bill's house in Hingham following the December 1990 dedication ceremony for the library in my parents' name in our Massachusetts hometown, I sat in the back seat of the car and was treated to the spectacle of Jim, who was driving, continually turning away from the wheel to lean over to kiss Susan. About a week later, I mailed Susan copies of the photographs taken at the ceremony; it was these photographs that I found torn to shreds when I cleaned out Susan's cottage in 1994, presumably the result of the alleged violent rage Jim had gone into following that period of sweetness.

The next time I saw Susan and Jim was a little over a year later, when they visited Mike and Alison and me in Georgia in January 1992. Jim treated Susan like a princess the whole weekend, squeezing fresh orange juice for her, constantly jumping up to refill her coffee cup, fetching a sweater for her whenever she mentioned feeling cold. And always he would present his offering to her with a flourish. When we went out to dinner on Saturday night, he ordered her meal for her in a cavalier manner, using the words "My lady will have the filet of sole." I couldn't help but think to myself cynically that this was the same "lady" he would allegedly call "whore" and "bitch" and "slut" during his rages. For her part, Susan seemed to love the treatment but also appeared to be guarded, as though aware of the fragile nature of Jim's mood.

The last morning of their visit, Susan and I were both getting washed in the upstairs bathroom, just off the guest room that she and Jim were staying in and where Jim was still in bed. This being the only time we'd been alone together all weekend, I took advantage of the moment to try to talk candidly with her. We hadn't had an extended conversation since her last crisis phone call, the previous November, and so I asked in a concerned voice, "Susan, how is everything going now with you and Jim?" A look of fear crossed her face, and she whispered in alarm, "Shhh, he'll hear you," and she pointed to the next room. Then she motioned with her finger to her lips for me to say no more. I had to leave for work, so we never got a chance to talk. Two days later, I received a charming, breezy thank-you note from her, with no mention of the subject I had tried to broach. And then, not at all to my surprise, about two weeks after this, another violent blowup erupted.

This cyclical pattern of crisis followed by denial followed by three or four months of my not hearing from Susan continued for the duration of their marriage. And Susan continued to go through periods of sobriety and periods of heavy drinking. My brothers and I were deeply confused about the situation and hence never able to hit upon a satisfactory, consistent line of action to take. When Susan was in a denial phase, she seemed so convinced that all was fine and so desirous of having us treat Jim and her like a normal couple that we tended to go along with her. In thinking now about this response of ours, I see that it was in keeping with our early childhood training, that is, our going along with our parents' pretense that everything was normal the day after a drunken middle-of-the-night episode of my mother's. In Susan's case, we would speculate that maybe she *did* exaggerate about their problems when her mind was muddled by alcohol, and maybe it *was* her drinking and her provocations that triggered the fights or escalated the violence. She had confided guiltily in me that on some occasions, she had become so angry at Jim's treatment of her that she had cut up and burned his clothes and destroyed some of his possessions, and she'd told us that she too sometimes became physical during their fights, hitting Jim or throwing something at him (of course, weighing eighty or ninety pounds less than he did, she wasn't much of a match).[2] Therefore, we rationalized when Susan was in a denial phase, maybe Jim was only responding to her provocations and trying to defend himself by physically restraining her, not abusing her. And so, during these periods, we would talk ourselves into thinking that perhaps our best approach would be to not get sucked in when she called us up in hysterics.

But then it would be impossible to maintain this attitude in a crisis phase, and the crises gradually grew worse—or perhaps she was just being more honest in her descriptions of them—especially after Jim was passed over for promotion to CEO at McCormick in the fall of 1991 and, stung (according to Susan), took early retirement. Now instead of veiled references to shoves and pokes, Susan was making outright mention of Jim's hitting her, pushing her down the stairs, pulling out her hair, bruising and fracturing her ribs. It was during this period that she finally admitted that the broken arm she'd supposedly suffered in a bicycle accident had really been caused by Jim. Although we knew she was going to retract each of these allegations a few days later, we would still react with alarm and would vociferously insist that she leave Jim and commit to getting intensive professional counseling, even that she consider entering an alcoholics' rehabilitation program. It was becoming clearer and clearer to us that what caused her both to use alcohol destructively and to remain in an abusive relationship was a serious lack of a sense of self-worth.

My emotions toward Susan during these volatile years were complex and shifting. In the midst of her crises, I would feel a deep, almost maternal pity for her; as a daughter who had grown up in the same family she had, I could relate on a gut level to the insecurities and fears that plagued her. Hand-in-hand with this pity would be a feeling of guilt at the knowledge that I, as similar to her as I was, had somehow escaped the weakness that made her unable to surmount her problems. But as she would come out of the crisis, these feelings on my part would gradually give way to contempt and anger: contempt that she refused to take action and *do* something about her situation, and anger that I'd wasted so much time counseling her during a crisis. These crises would usually last three or four days, and I would spend several hours of each day on the phone with her and often write her lengthy follow-up letters; but it would all be for naught, for she always made up with Jim and withdrew her allegations. Yet another strand in the tangle of feelings these crisis-denial cycles would create in me was total confusion about where the truth lay: hearing Susan's graphic allegations, I would be convinced Jim had abused her, but this conviction would dissolve in the face of her emphatic insistence a few days later that her drinking had caused her to fabricate or exaggerate Jim's role in their fights. My brothers, too, were subject to this confusion, right up until the incident that convinced them the allegations were true.

This incident, of course, was the one that occurred in July 1993. I first learned of it through a phone call from Susan. As soon as I put the receiver to my ear, I knew that this crisis was worse than usual. Normally the first sound that greeted me in these calls was a sob or a rush of furious complaints about Jim; this time, Susan's voice sounded dead and defeated. In almost a monotone, she began to describe the physical condition she was in: her right eye was so swollen she could barely see out of it, she couldn't rotate her right hand because of the wincing pain this caused to her wrist, her knees were sore and bruised. Horrified, I asked her how she had gotten this way. The account she launched into chilled me not so much by the content as by the contrast between that content—the sickening description of Jim's hitting her on the head, shoving her into walls, pouring *urine* on her!—and the flat voice in which she delivered it. It was as if the years of degradation she'd been subjected to had finally reduced her to a zombie. What a contrast, I thought, to the Susan of former years who had taken such pride in her refined behavior and impeccable appearance.

As I peppered her with questions and with exclamations of alarm and outrage, she began to warm to her usual initial-stage-of-the-crisis mood and became tearful and angry. I was relieved when she told me she'd already talked to Jonathan and that he was on his way up to Baltimore from D.C., where he was living and working that year. She was staying at a friend's house, and when he arrived, Jonathan was going to take her to the police station to file for a restraining order against Jim. "Susan," I said, "this has got to be the final straw. Surely this episode has proven to you that you've got to leave him for good." She said that yes, she knew that.

As distressed as I was, I felt optimistic after I hung up. I believed that this was the extreme situation she needed in order to make her see the light.[3] Later that day she phoned me back again, as I'd requested her to do, and told me she and Jonathan had just returned to her house from the police station and that Jim had been forced to evacuate the premises. She sounded 100 percent better than she had earlier that day, explaining to me in a clearheaded way the details of the restraining order: it was a temporary order, good for only six days, but at the end of that period she could petition in court for a permanent order, which she planned to do. A hearing was scheduled for the following Monday, and she was determined to go through with it. I congratulated her on her decision and told her I loved her and was proud of her.

Shortly after I got off the phone with her, my brother Bill called. He had been apprised of developments by both Susan and Jonathan, and he and my other two brothers had decided they would go down to Baltimore on the weekend to give Susan moral support prior to and through the court hearing. We decided that rather than my joining them, I, along with Mike and Alison, would stop and stay with her for a few days the following week, when we would be driving north for vacation. The idea was that the family would help get her through the initial, most difficult stage of separation, by offering both emotional and practical support. My brothers planned to spend Monday afternoon after the court hearing helping her look for an apartment; over the next few days, Jonathan and Nicholas would rent a truck to move her stuff; and when I arrived, I would help her find a battered women's support group and try to get her started on putting together a résumé and thinking about looking for a job.

To keep up Susan's morale in the days prior to the court appearance, I phoned her frequently. At first she continued to dwell on Jim's cruel treatment of her and on the rightness of her decision to take out the restraining order. But as the week wore on, I thought I was beginning to detect a relenting in her complaints. I brushed away these suspicions, though, for surely, I said to myself, she couldn't possibly soften toward Jim this time, not after he'd battered and bloodied and degraded her the way he had. When my brothers arrived in Baltimore, they too sensed that Susan was backpedaling in her decision. She kept telling them she didn't really need them to be there for the hearing, and they suspected she wanted to get out of it. She seemed very agitated; they could tell she was drinking on the sly. But they were determined to make her go through with the hearing and obtain the permanent restraining order, their determination redoubled by the sight of what Jim had allegedly done to her. Her appearance was shocking, they said; my brother Bob described her face as resembling that of a prizefighter. There was no longer any doubt in any of their minds that her allegations over the years had been true.

On Monday morning, my brothers, along with Jonathan and Nicholas, accompanied Susan to court. Thinking that the hearing would be a routine procedure and the judge would have no choice but to grant the restraining order after witnessing Susan's appearance and hearing the evidence, they were taken aback by what transpired in the courtroom. As soon as Jim's lawyer began to speak, it was clear the case was undone. To the shock of my brothers, nephews, and Susan's lawyer, Jim's lawyer informed the court that Susan had broken the terms of the temporary restraining order by agreeing to see Jim during the period it was in effect. Jim had phoned Susan the previous Thursday evening and apparently cajoled her into meeting him at the end of the driveway (this way, he must have figured, he could claim he hadn't violated the court order, because technically he did not enter the property covered by the restraining order). He had a bottle of wine in the car and talked her into getting in and drinking it with him. Then the two drove off to a motel and spent the night together! Susan was called to the stand and was asked whether this was true; she concurred. Her lawyer was astonished and mortified; my brothers and nephews were speechless. The judge, realizing Susan was not serious about wanting a restraining order, threw out the case.

In stunned silence, my brothers drove Susan back to Jim's and her house, followed by Nick and Jonathan in another car. Once there, they all began to plead with her to pack up a few belongings and go back to Boston with my brothers or to D.C. with Jonathan, or they could go out right then and find her an apartment in Baltimore. They could pack up the rest of her stuff later. Pathetic and disoriented, she refused. She needed some time, she mumbled. She needed to think things over. They warned her that she would be putting herself into real danger if she stayed with Jim. Again she lamely repeated that she needed some time.

Defeated and in despair, the five men walked out of the house, some of them struggling to hold back tears. As my brothers got into the car for the drive back to Massachusetts, Jonathan looked at them and, slowly shaking his head, said, "I feel like Mom is gone. Jim's killed her spirit and taken her over completely." My brother John told me a year later, after Susan disappeared, that that was the moment he felt Susan had really died.

Bill called me that night to report what had happened. I felt sick to my stomach at the mental picture of my sister in her bruised and bloodied condition being physically intimate with the man who had rendered her that way. I was also shocked by Bill's description of the zombie-like state Susan had been reduced to. And on top of all this, I was furious about the fact that I'd spent much of the previous week counseling Susan under false impressions: she hadn't even been honest with me about what was going on. My fury mounting, I picked up the phone and called her as soon as I was finished talking to Bill. The first words out of my mouth when she answered were, "Susan, how *could* you have?" Then I launched into a series of exclamations of incredulity and disgust at what Bill had reported to me.

If I hadn't been so worked up, I probably would have taken pity on Susan when I heard her response: in a lost, pathetic voice, she told me she was terrified of being alone, that anything was better than that, and besides, Jim could be so good to her when they weren't fighting. I retorted that living alone but having dignity and pride would be far better than being in a relationship with someone who degraded and abused her. She began to cry, protesting that she couldn't survive on her own, she would become a "bag lady." This is a fear she'd voiced before, and in the past I would always respond by pointing out what an irrational one it was, given all the resources she possessed: talent, intelligence, a supportive family, a comfortable inheritance from our parents. But this time I was in no mood to be patient; I lashed out at her that her real fear was of having to give up her luxurious lifestyle and that she needed to get out there and get a job like the rest of us. Then I hung up.

Later that night, I wrote her a long letter. Hoping that I could shock her into an awareness of the gravity of her situation, I pointed out that she was spiraling downward into mental illness as a result of remaining in the sick relationship with Jim and that the two of them were living like Bowery bums. I warned her that she was headed for tragedy if she didn't make a radical change in her life immediately. I have this letter in front of me right now (I retrieved it from Susan's desk when I was cleaning out her cottage), and two things in it jump out at me. One is my prediction, "I think you're on the road to disaster." The other is the date at the head of the letter: August 4, 1993. It would be exactly one year and one day later that my prediction would come true.

9 Susan Hits Bottom, Autumn 1993

The July 1993 episode marked a breakthrough in our understanding of the nature of Susan and Jim's relationship. My brothers had received what they considered proof, in the form of her physical appearance, that Susan had been abused by Jim. In addition, for the first time we began communicating openly with Jonathan and Nicholas about the situation, and their testimonies further supported this interpretation.

Following Susan and Tom's divorce and the granting of joint custody, the boys had split their time between their parents' respective homes; but as the relationship between Susan and Jim became increasingly tempestuous, Jonathan and Nicholas began spending less and less time under their roof. And so, like my brothers and me, the boys had only gradually become aware of the physical aspects of the conflicts; at first they had assumed Susan and Jim's fights were restricted to yelling and door slamming. Usually the boys would leave the house when the arguments started, and Jonathan would drive the two of them over to their dad's. The next day, Susan would be wearing dark glasses or would explain away a black eye or a bruise by saying she had clumsily injured herself falling or bumping into something. When they were younger and more gullible, they believed her; eventually they caught on.

Their eye-opening was assisted by some firsthand glimpses of Jim's potential for violence against their mother. Once, when Nicholas was twelve and was spending the night at Susan and Jim's, he awoke at 1:00 A.M. to a terrible fight and became so upset that he had to get away. His dad and brother were off in New England on a tour of prospective colleges for Jonathan, so Nick phoned Jonathan's girl-friend to ask her to come pick him up. Then he sneaked out of the house and waited at the end of the driveway for the girl. Suddenly, Nick saw his mom run out of the house carrying several of her lamp-shades (custom-designing lampshades was a craft she had become increasingly serious about), one of them badly torn. She was franti-cally trying to open the trunk of her car, apparently to stow the lamp-shades, when Jim lurched out of the house, ran over to her, and be-gan violently shaking her. Nicholas yelled, "Get off my mom!" Jim turned and smiled at Nick and then calmly walked back into the house, as though nothing untoward had occurred.[1]

Another time, Jonathan showed up at Susan and Jim's when the two were in the middle of a fight, and he discovered Jim holding Susan with one hand and brandishing a kitchen knife at her with the other. Jonathan rushed at him, threw him down on the sofa, and commanded, "Don't move until we're out of here." Jim complied, for by this time Jonathan was taller and stronger than he, and Jonathan ushered Susan out of the house. The next time Jonathan saw Jim, the latter acted as though nothing had happened.[2] My brother John has described witnessing similar behavior on Jim's part: when John stayed at Susan and Jim's to attend Nick's high school graduation, he was awakened in the middle of the night by a vicious argument, which caused Susan to seek temporary refuge in his room; the next morning, Jim pretended he didn't know what John was talking about when the latter confronted him with the question, "What was that all about last night?"

Although Nick and Jonathan's exposures were limited to inci-dents of incipient abuse rather than full-blown abuse, the boys saw enough to believe that Jim was capable of violence. And so, increas-ingly, they would not accept their mother's explanations for her bruises and injuries; they began urging Susan to leave Jim, just as my brothers and I were doing. As they grew older, Susan became more honest with them about her problems with Jim; sometimes she would even phone Jonathan at his dad's in the midst of a fight and ask him to rescue her from Jim, whereupon Jonathan would rush over to intervene. It was all he could do to keep himself from beating Jim up on such occasions, he later told us; wisely, he stuck to restraining

Jim. Two or three times, in a particularly bad crisis, Jonathan or Nick phoned my brother Bill, but for the most part the boys didn't report the fights to their mom's siblings.

In retrospect, after the tragic outcome, it seems astonishing that the extended family did not openly and continuously address Susan's situation and what could be done about it. But we did not possess the wisdom of hindsight, and as much as we warned Susan that she was flirting with disaster by staying in the relationship, I don't think any of us fully comprehended that her life was in danger. In addition, the boys felt a strong loyalty to their mother and knew how important it was to her to keep up the appearance of being refined and respectable, so they to a certain degree colluded with her pretense. Often she would beg them not to tell the rest of the family about an ugly fight that had recently occurred; similarly, sometimes she would phone only me, not my brothers, after a fight and later in embarrassment would ask me to please not tell the others. And so it wasn't until after things came to a head with the July 1993 incident that the six of us began to discuss Susan's situation openly. I think another reason for the new frankness was that both boys were now adults—Nick was starting college that fall, and Jonathan was twenty-three—and my brothers and I felt we could now talk to them as such, whereas when they were younger we felt awkward about discussing their mother's drinking and marital problems with them.

At our wits' end about how to get Susan to come to her senses and leave Jim, the six of us decided on a "tough love" approach: we would make clear to Susan that we didn't want her to call us up any more just to cry on our shoulders, that we resented the time, energy, and emotion we spent trying to help her, only to have her ultimately reject our advice, patch things up with Jim, and deny her previous allegations. She was to call us only if she was serious about finally leaving Jim and turning her life around. My brothers and I conveyed this message to her very bluntly, saying we would hang up the phone if all she did was describe Jim's treatment of her and not state her intention to leave him. She expressed anger and hurt when we announced this new approach to her, just after we learned in early August that she and Jim had gotten back together. But the message sank in, for she did not call my brothers or me for several months, even though she and Jim continued their pattern of fighting and making up during this period.

We learned secondhand about these fights, from Jonathan and Nicholas. They were not able to be as firm with Susan in their tough love approach as my brothers and I were, and consequently Susan continued to phone them when she was upset, and they continued to listen and counsel her. One might wonder why her sons were so loving and understanding with her, why they didn't become angry that despite their begging and pleading she continually returned to the man they abhorred. I think the answer lies partly in the fact that they were unusually mature, sensitive young men who realized it was their mother's lack of a sense of self-worth that kept her in an abusive marriage, not her lack of concern for her children's feelings. They also believed it was Jim's fault that Susan was unable to break out of the relationship: they felt he manipulated her by feeding her feelings of worthlessness when he abused her and then offering her relief from these feelings when he lavished her with praise and affection afterward.

But perhaps the main reason they did not give up on her was that they truly loved her and saw her as a good person, despite all her problems. When Susan was between crises, she was a remarkably warm, generous, and competent person, an attentive mom and a loyal friend. When the boys were in junior high and high school, she religiously attended their sports matches, helped them with homework, volunteered at their schools. When they got to college, she frequently sent them care packages and decor for their dorm rooms. Although they teased her about being a mother hen, they secretly loved it; they pretended to balk, for example, when she gave them dorm pillows she'd made from their old lacrosse jerseys, but they were pleased whenever friends would come into the room and be impressed.[3] Susan's attentiveness extended to their friends, whose names were also often on the care packages she sent. Once Susan had mail-order steaks shipped to Jonathan and his suite mates so they could enjoy a hearty dinner the night before final exams began. And when a lacrosse teammate of Jonathan's died suddenly and tragically, Susan urged Jonathan to make sure the boy's mother had a card for Mother's Day, which was only three days away, signed by the entire team so that she would know she was not alone.

Susan was always doing thoughtful, creative things for her own friends as well. A number of women she had been close to over the years contacted me following her disappearance to offer sympathy, and many of them reminisced about her gracious gestures. One talked about how after she'd given birth to a daughter, Susan had handed over to her all the beautiful "just-in-case-it's-a-girl" clothes she had sewn during her pregnancy with Nicholas. Another told me that once she had described to Susan a lamp she'd loved that was in her bedroom when she was a child, and Susan surprised her by making a replica of the lampshade that had been on it. Still another friend recalled how she had phoned Susan one time for advice when frantically trying to put together a fat-free luncheon for a visiting relative on a strict medical diet. Susan suggested a cold cucumber soup, but as she explained how to make it and realized she was not dealing with a gourmet chef, she insisted on making it for her friend to serve. When Susan dropped the soup off, she handed her friend a card with the recipe written on it, so that the latter could take credit if anyone asked how the soup was made.

It was such traits as these that Jonathan and Nicholas saw as constituting the "real" Susan. The way she behaved with Jim was an aberration, they thought, the result of the erosion of her self-esteem that the relationship and alcohol had effected. And so rather than being disgusted and angry with their mother for the mess she had let her life become, they saw her as a victim. It was only when she was upset by Jim that she drank too much, they claimed. And she had never yelled and carried on with them or anyone else the way she did with Jim. If she could just summon up the courage to leave him for good, she would return to her old responsible, gracious self, they felt.

But in the fall of 1993, they were beginning to despair that this was ever going to happen. If Jim's alleged battery of Susan the previous July had not motivated her to leave, they didn't know what would. Adding to their pessimism was the fact that Susan and Jim had gone on a vacation together when they reunited after the crisis. This was a trip that they had planned earlier in the summer. An artist friend of Susan's spent summers painting in Taos, and she had arranged to lead a bunch of her Baltimore friends on a sort of arts-and-culture tour of northern New Mexico in August. Susan had been looking forward to this trip all summer, but given the kind of physical and emotional shape she was in after the July episode, all of us assumed she would not go through with it, or if she did, would go on her own. When we learned that she and Jim had gone ahead with the vacation, we were more depressed than ever: Susan's ability to deny and to put up with self-degradation was even more extreme than we had realized. I was beginning to believe Susan was a lost cause.

A little over a year later, when my brother John and I were sifting through photographs we found while cleaning out her cottage, we came upon a batch of prints taken on this New Mexico vacation. They confirmed the feelings I'd had about what that trip must have been like for Susan. The prints were intended to be typical cheery vacation snapshots: almost every one features a group of smiling, well-dressed middle-aged people set against the backdrop of a gorgeous mountain or desert range. But in all the photos, Susan stands out, her appearance inviting uneasiness. Although she, like the others, is dressed beautifully, and although her spouse holds a "loving" arm around her, she seems out of place in the midst of this carefree group: her face is puffy, her knees appear swollen, and she wears dark glasses in every shot, even in those apparently taken late in the day, when no one else is wearing sunglasses.

From what I could infer, the autumn of 1993 marked a new psychological low for Susan. She was utterly chagrined by the fact that everyone in the family and virtually all of her friends, most of whom had gone through the same stages of eye-opening about Susan and Jim's relationship as we had, now knew of the degraded way she was living. My heart went out to her, but I forced myself to stick to my tough-love decision. When Susan broke down and phoned me in November with a sobbing account of how Jim, upset that his daughter Betsy had just failed the bar exam, had turned his rage on Susan, I repeated my position about not wanting to get involved unless she was serious about leaving Jim. She became angry at what she considered my heartless attitude and hung up. I felt awful: this happened right before Thanksgiving, and all I could think of was how bleak her holiday would be—she who loved holidays so.

Christmastime came, and I kept returning to these same kinds of thoughts. Then a few days after Christmas, I received a phone call that confirmed my fear that this holiday had been a nightmare for Susan, the polar opposite of the storybook Christmases she'd always striven for. This particular crisis, according to Susan, had once again been launched by a volcanic eruption on Jim's part. She claimed that the previous day, she had returned home from a meeting of the alcoholics' support group she had recently joined, in a good mood because she'd just completed a full month of sobriety. But when she walked through the door, Jim suddenly exploded at her for no reason. There ensued a fight that lasted through the night. She claimed that Jim threw her down under the Christmas tree and pinned her to the ground and that as she lay there, with smashed glass ornaments cutting into her back, he taunted her with threats of killing her and killing her dog. Then he locked her in a room for several hours, occasionally entering and throwing water or soda on her. Finally, in the early hours of the morning, she managed to escape. She ran barefoot to her car, jumped in, and drove to her friend Mary Jo Gordon's house. It was from Mary Jo's that she was phoning me.

I listened to all this without saying much. I was not going to get caught up in this crisis if it was all going to blow over as usual. Although upset by the description of what she'd been subjected to and by the physical injuries—bruises, cuts, fractured ribs—she described, I was determined to check my reactions and to keep the focus on what she was going to *do* about the situation. To my surprise, she had already given this question a lot of thought. She was going to stay at Mary Jo's until she found a place to live; Jonathan and Nicholas were going to rent a U-Haul and move her belongings out of Jim's house; she was going to file in court for separate maintenance and meet with a divorce lawyer. I was elated, and I began telling her how proud I was of her for finally taking action. It seemed to me that the strong, sensible person buried inside of Susan was finally emerging.

I allowed myself to hope.

10 Hopeful Beginning and Tragic Ending, January–August 1994

The first few days following Susan's decision to leave Jim were crucial, I knew, and so I called her frequently to give her support. She could easily slide backward, as the previous July's episode had demonstrated. But a sea change seemed to have occurred in her attitude this time; there was a resolve in her voice I'd never heard there before. It may have been that the Christmas episode was the proverbial last straw, or it may have been that numerous friends rallied behind her and wouldn't let her back down. Whatever it was, Susan seemed determined to stick to her decision this time. She stayed with Mary Jo for several days, and then with another friend, Gretel White. A bunch of her friends made it a project to find a house for her to rent, and they finally found just the thing they thought she'd like: the cottage in Ruxton. Jonathan and Nicholas moved all her furniture in and helped her get set up. I sent roses as a housewarming gift. We were all determined to keep up her morale.

It was a frigid winter in the Baltimore area that year, and Susan sometimes called me on nights when she was snowbound in her house, feeling scared and sad. She talked about how she used to love this kind of weather, when her little boys would play outside in the snow and then return rosy-cheeked to the house to warm up with the cocoa she would have waiting for them. Now the snow just made her feel isolated and lonely. She also talked about her fear of growing old alone. Despite these feelings, though, she did not seem to be having second thoughts about her decision. Other times, she was upbeat when we spoke on the phone. Her friends kept her busy socially, and Jonathan and Nicholas visited her on weekends whenever they could (Jonathan was still working in D.C., and Nick was a freshman at Middlebury). But what seemed to have been boosting her spirits the most was that she had finally taken a step toward developing a career.

For years, friends and family members, awed by Susan's artistic and domestic achievements, had exclaimed that she ought to market her talents. We siblings often used to point out to her how ironic it was that she was the only one of us without a job and yet the one who could probably make the most money if she set her mind to it. We would cite examples, telling her she could be another Holly Hobbie or Martha Stewart. But she had never had any real interest in a career outside the home, and the more time that passed, the scarier it was to her to re-enter the workforce. Now that she had finally found the confidence to live on her own, though, she was able to summon up the confidence to take that big step. Because in recent years friends had increasingly been offering to purchase her custom-made lampshades, she decided to start a lampshade business. She rented a studio in a reconverted mill next to the studio of a friend, Clara Arana, who designed jewelry, and she had business cards made up. The name of her new business was "The Shady Lady." (I still have the business card she proudly sent me; it sits in my desk drawer, sad testimony to what could have been.) It was thrilling to me to hear her describe how good she felt about getting up every morning and going to work. Once she said in a voice of delighted discovery, "Now I know what you've been talking about all these years!" I was certain she was on the road to achieving the self-confidence and self-esteem that would prevent her from returning to Jim.[1]

But as winter turned into spring, I began to detect a subtle change in Susan. Her phone calls to me became less frequent, and she gradually stopped talking about the rightness of having separated from Jim. So afraid was I of the answer I might hear that I didn't pose to her the question burning in my mind. Then, to my distress, she began to say things that confirmed my fear. With studied casualness, she would mention that she had recently seen Jim. She assured me they weren't getting back together; it was just that she was sometimes lonely on a Friday or Saturday night, and he was someone to go out to dinner with. Plus, he'd been very nice to her lately, helping her to get her studio set up and supporting her career efforts. I listened with a sinking heart and with increasing premonitions. At first, I raised challenging, confrontational questions whenever she referred to having seen him, but these would only cause her to become defensive or annoyed. Gradually, our communication began to taper off, as I became disgusted by her rationalizations and evasions. In hindsight, I wish I had never let up in my warnings about the dangers of getting back together with Jim.

In the sporadic phone conversations I had with Susan during the summer of 1994, Jim's name was not mentioned. I tried to tell myself that her silence meant she was no longer seeing him. I didn't really believe this, but I told myself that at least she wasn't calling up complaining about his treatment of her; maybe they really were just dating socially. Subsequent to Susan's disappearance and murder, I was gradually able to put together a picture, constructed on the basis of police reports, documents I found in her house, and conversations with her sons and friends, of what had really been going on between Susan and Jim that last spring and summer. From what I can gather, it seems that Susan had been serious about wanting a divorce but that Jim had persistently tried to get her to change her mind. His efforts ranged from wooing to threats: from blitzing her with romantic cards and notes to trying to convince her she couldn't survive without him. She complained to friends that he had threatened to leave her with nothing if she divorced him and that he had compiled a negative dossier on her that he threatened to show to people (this dossier must have included things like the "confession" he'd forced Susan to write about sleeping with the man she'd met at a bar and the letter from me to Susan in which I had referred to her so-called manic depression).[2] Her friend Mary Jo Gordon has said that "Jim was very cunning and would brainwash Susan into thinking she would have no life without him. He would say or do anything to that end, even coerce her into confessing things she'd never done IN WRITING."[3] Mary

Jo also told me, "Many times when I visited Susan she was in such a state brought on by his threats. [. . .] He had power over her and he knew it and he was not about to give it up."[4] After they separated, Jim insisted that Susan come in person to collect the monthly checks he was required by the court to give her in compliance with her suit for separate maintenance; by doing this, he ensured that she would see him regularly. The result of all Jim's pressuring and cajoling was that a few months into the separation, Susan began to succumb. She spent the night with him intermittently, and in July she accompanied him on a three-day vacation to Ocean City. There were sporadic flare-ups of physical violence, and Susan called the police a couple of times that spring and summer. The last recorded incident occurred on July 31. Police responding to a call from Susan arrived at her house to find her with a bruised, swollen hand. She told them that Jim had shown up wanting to take her out to dinner, and when she turned him down, he became angry and began twisting her fingers.

As the July 31 incident suggests, Susan made efforts to keep away from Jim, even though she occasionally slipped up and responded to his seductions. There is no indication that she had decided to get back together with him. Indeed, she continued to meet with her divorce lawyer, and she was allegedly putting pressure on Jim to sell the house they had shared, which she co-owned. In the summer, she consulted a realtor for advice on how to make the house more marketable—it had been deteriorating since she moved out—and the realtor urged her to return some of the drapes and other decor she had taken with her. It was for this reason that she went over to Jim's house a few times in late July, although Jim has claimed that she was moving her stuff back in because they were going to reconcile.[5]

We have good reason to believe that on Friday, August 5, Susan announced to Jim that she was definitely going through with the divorce. Nicholas had recently given her an ultimatum, telling her that if she didn't break with Jim completely, he would distance himself from her emotionally. This was the first time either of her sons had presented her with such a stark choice, and given her devotion to them, the ultimatum was effective: four nights before she disappeared, she telephoned Nick at his dad's to announce that she was going to break things off completely with Jim but that she needed to do so "in a delicate fashion."

In the days between her announcement to Nick and her disappearance, Susan was agitated and was drinking again. When Nick went to her house on Friday morning, thinking they were going to leave that day to drive up to Massachusetts for their visit, he found her depressed and hungover. She was too ill to drive, so they decided to fly the next morning. As Nick picked up the phone to call my brother John to inform him of their changed plan, Susan mouthed to him not to mention her being hungover. After Nick got off the phone, Susan explained that she was distressed about her drinking and wanted to get help but that she didn't want my brothers to know about her relapse. Nick proceeded to spend several hours talking with her about her drinking and discussing different kinds of treatment programs she might try. By the time they finished their conversation, she was in a more hopeful mood. Then Nick left to run errands.

In the early afternoon, Susan apparently drove over to Jim's; Jim's cleaning woman heard the two of them arguing loudly in the driveway. By the time Nick returned from taking the dog to the kennel around 4:30, Susan had returned home and the two of them talked for awhile. Then she said she was going to rest while he went over to his dad's to finish his packing. Some time after Nick left, she made the phone call to my brother John that he had to cut short because of his imminent softball game. And after this, we can only surmise what happened. What provoked her to dash out the door, not even bothering to shut it behind her, and drive over to Jim's? Did she inform Jim that evening that she was divorcing him? And if she did, did this announcement have anything to do with her disappearance? These are questions we will probably never have the answers to.

I have thought often about my own final conversations with Susan that summer. At the time, they seemed unremarkable, but they have taken on a special poignancy now, in light of my knowledge of what was about to befall her. She called me in late June to ask about my husband's experience several years earlier riding a bicycle across the country because she was trying to talk Jonathan into taking a cross-country bike rather than motorcycle trip; he wanted to do something adventurous in his final summer of freedom before start-ing law school (he ended up going to Europe). Susan was terrified of the dangers of motorcycle riding. She said to me, "If anything ever happened to him [she couldn't bring herself to use the word *die*], I couldn't go on living." I shuddered with her, the two of us united in our acknowledgment that this is the worst fate a mother can imag-ine. Now her sentiment carries a sad irony, for while she was preoc-cupied with averting a tragic fate for her child, her own tragic fate was awaiting her. And although her primary concern was the wel-fare of her children, she was living her life in a way that would result in that welfare's being shattered—by their loss of her. In a further irony, I learned from Jonathan after Susan's disappearance that just a few days after she'd made this phone call to me expressing her fears for *his* safety, Jonathan had tried to warn her to watch out for her own. The two of them, like most of the rest of the nation that night, had been riveted to the television screen watching O. J. Simpson inch along the L.A. freeway in his Bronco trying to forestall his arrest for the murder of his wife, when Jonathan suddenly turned to Susan and said, "Mom, do you realize how dangerously close you are to that?" But, said Jonathan, "Like anyone close to that situation, she couldn't see it. She brushed off my warning, saying 'Oh, no, no, no.'"[6]

The very last phone conversation I had with Susan was on July 21. She called me for two reasons. One was to ask whether tropical storm Alberto, which was ravaging parts of Georgia, was affecting my area. As we discussed this topic, we both commented on a ghoulish phe-nomenon that had been aired on the national news that night: flood-ing caused by the storm had dislodged coffins from their graves, re-sulting in the gruesome sight of coffins and corpses bobbing along on the flood waters. Susan and I had always been drawn to macabre stories like this. Now I think how ironic our discussion was: less than a month later, I would be frightening myself with equally ghoulish images of Susan's own corpse.

Her other reason for calling was to give me the phone number of her friend in New Mexico, Helen Lamberton, whom she wanted me to look up when Mike and Alison and I were out there on vaca-tion in a couple of weeks. This part of the conversation would also return to haunt me, but for different reasons. After giving me the phone number, Susan went on to tell me a bit about Helen, whom she'd become acquainted with through her volunteer work at the Baltimore Museum of Art. She said that Helen was a talented painter, had attended Sarah Lawrence, summered in Taos and wintered in Baltimore, and possessed a number of other attributes that all added up, in my mind, to a picture of the kind of cultured society woman Susan admired and emulated. Then just before we were about to say good-bye, Susan's tone shifted from breezy to almost pleading. She said to me, "If you do get together with Helen, *please* don't mention anything about my past drinking problems because she doesn't know anything about all that, okay?"

Later I would recall this last, anxious request of Susan's and be filled with sadness at the thought that right up until the end of her life, she was conflicted about her identity: she wanted to appear to the world a refined "lady," but she feared that in reality she was an alcoholic like my mother, and she was desperate about keeping this reality a secret. I would also later be struck by the tragic irony of Susan's request: while she was worrying about her reputation, she should have been worrying about her life, for just a little more than two weeks later she would be dead.

In the early months following Susan's disappearance, I would often find myself bemused by the question of why her life ended up the way it did. When I arrived home from Baltimore in late November, following the eye-opening I'd received about Susan's final years while cleaning out her cottage, I began to think more deeply about this question. I delved into family photo albums and scrapbooks, as well as into my own memories, to explore the roots of my sister's psychology and to figure out why she had made the choices she did. Certain emblematic scenes from Susan's life flooded my memory.

Part Two

Susan's Beginnings

11 Irish Roots

"The baby!"

My parents, temporarily preoccupied by some need of four-year-old Billy, turn in alarm at the sound of the woman's shriek and see one-year-old Susan toddling toward the edge of the precipice at the top of Mount Washington. My mother lets go of Billy's hand and, crying "Jesus, Mary, and Joseph!" rushes over to scoop up the child, thereby averting the disaster that would have prematurely ended my sister's life.

This is a tale I heard recounted innumerable times in my childhood, so many times that I felt as though I had witnessed the event, although it occurred four years before my own entry into the world. The vivid mental picture of the baby being rescued just before she toppled off the mountainside took on almost mythic dimensions for me, with its suggestion of the precariousness of human existence and of the role luck plays in an individual's destiny. Reflecting on the incident in late 1994 in the wake of Susan's disappearance, though, I couldn't help but note the irony: Susan had been spared one disastrous fate only to be saved for another, fifty-one years later.

The scene above serves as a fitting introduction to Susan's biography because it contains ingredients that capture symbolically the nature of our family life and dynamics: the excursion to New Hampshire's Mount Washington arranged by my father, a family man intent upon educating his children about the history and geography of their native New England; the frequently harried but intensely protective attitude of my mother toward her growing brood; and the

threat of impending disaster lurking amidst our otherwise wholesome, Norman Rockwell–like family life.

My sister was born Susan Mary Hurley on March 2, 1942, the
second child of my parents, Mary Lynch Hurley and William Tho-
mas Hurley Jr. In trying to discover the deepest currents of Susan's
psychology, I found myself dwelling on the prominent role our family's Irish identity played in my parents' consciousness. Both my
mother and my father grew up in Dorchester, Massachusetts, at the
time an Irish-Catholic enclave of Boston whose residents' ethnic
pride was rivaled only by their sharp sense of inferiority. These were
the days when "INNA" ("Irish need not apply") was a commonplace
inclusion in job advertisements and when Boston Brahmins would
disown a Harvard-educated son who brought home a girl with a
brogue—the situation underpinning the plot of the well-known
social satire *The Late George Apley* by John P. Marquand, whose son,
ironically, Susan would one day become engaged to. The paradoxi-
cal attitude Boston's Irish Americans held toward their ethnicity was
embodied in the person of my paternal grandmother: an immigrant,
she changed her name from the obviously Irish "Bridget" to "Ber-
tha" in order to increase her job prospects; but her loyalty to her ethnic heritage was so well known in the family that in later years when
her grandson, my cousin Dave Rafferty, was dating the non-Irish girl
who would become his wife, he so much wanted his grandmother
to accept her that he initially lied about the girl's last name, claiming it was "Kelly."

My parents grew up in the same neighborhood, and their two
families had many things in common. My father's mother and paternal grandparents had emigrated from Ireland, as had my mother's
father and maternal grandparents. My father's three sisters were
"chums" with my mother and her two sisters; and my mother's
brother was best friends with my father (both were named Bill and,
as was traditional for the eldest sons in Irish families, were called
"Brother" by their siblings and parents). A further coincidence was
that my mother's father had dated my father's mother years before
their respective marriages.

As a shy young girl, my mother was flattered by the interest her
big brother's friend, four years her senior, showed in her whenever

he was at the house; a diary she kept when she was thirteen mentions, in code, how thrilled she was when he talked with her on the front porch swing one summer evening. My father was a self-confident, ambitious young man with the kind of drive that characterized the children and grandchildren of immigrants. His family had no money for college, so he worked his way through Boston University, graduating in three years at age nineteen (his mother, skeptical of the "Protestant" character of the school, would blame any unfamiliar notion he brought home on "that BU."). Like many young men of his generation who had pulled themselves up by their bootstraps, my father wanted to achieve the American Dream, so he studied business. But his ambitions were loftier: he read widely—the classics, English literature, history—and gained the reputation among his friends and, later, business associates of being something of a scholar and Renaissance man. These traits—his ambition, his business acumen, and his culture—combined with an Irish gift for humor and storytelling proved to be an excellent foundation for success in his career.

My parents courted for several years. In Irish tradition, my father as the eldest son was not free to marry until he could afford to support a wife as well as his widowed mother's household. During these years, he lived at home and worked as a salesman for the Gorham Silver Company; his job involved frequent traveling, and while on these trips he wrote my mother letters, some still extant, that reveal his romantic nature and suggest the deep attachment that would hold my parents' relationship together despite its eventual problems. My mother, also living at home and expected to contribute to her widowed mother's household, worked from the time she graduated from high school until her marriage, first as a secretary at Sharpe and Dome, a pharmaceutical company in Boston, and then as assistant director of the press bureau at Northeastern University. A product of her era and her socioeconomic class, she never considered college and assumed she would stop working and begin having babies as soon as she married.

The marriage took place in 1936, when my mother was twenty-six and my father thirty. They moved into a small apartment in West Roxbury, the first place either had lived besides the house each grew up in. These early years were apparently happy ones. My father advanced in his career and was proud of his pretty, domestic wife, a frugal housekeeper who could impress his business colleagues with dinners she prepared out of her old high school home economics cookbook. My mother was content to cook and keep house and meet her sisters and old school friends for occasional lunches or ice cream sodas at Schrafts. Soon, with the arrival of my brother Bill in 1939, this happy routine expanded to include frequent outings to the Boston Public Gardens and the swan boats with her sister Arline, also a new mother, and the two babies. My mother adored little Billy, and Bill's own early childhood memories are of a loving and fun-loving mother.

In 1941, my father, intent on moving up the career ladder, accepted the position offered to him of sales manager at Reed and Barton, a well-respected silver manufacturing firm in southeastern Massachusetts. The job meant that my parents had to move from the Dorchester/West Roxbury area of Boston to Taunton, forty miles away. By today's standards, such a distance seems like nothing; indeed, Taunton is now considered a bedroom community for Boston. But in the 1940s, especially for a couple like my parents who had lived always among people of their same background, a move like this was major. Not only would they no longer be living a few minutes from their families and the old neighborhood but they would also be moving into a different social and ethnic world. The latter change actually had more to do with my father's new position than with the demographics of Taunton. As a manager and eventually an executive at Reed and Barton, my father would have as his colleagues scions of Massachusetts blueblood families; furthermore, his position meant that my parents would socialize with the upper echelon of Taunton society, many of whose members were non-Irish and Protestant. However, my parents proved to have no problem being accepted into this new world: my father's raconteurism and wit made him the center of attention at parties, and people were charmed by my mother's shy, smiling manner.

As time went on, the Hurleys became one of the most prominent families in Taunton. My father was not only a business success but a civic leader, active in the Red Cross, the Rotary Club, and numerous other organizations and philanthropies; my mother involved herself in charities as well as full-time homemaking and motherhood; and both my parents acquired the reputation of being devoted to their five children. They were always taking us on family trips, most of which had a cultural or educational purpose; they provided us with music, dance, and skiing lessons; they bought a summer home on Cape Cod and a boat so that we could all learn to sail; and they sacrificed so as to save for our educations. Although well-to-do by most standards, we lived comparatively frugally, wearing hand-me-downs and mended clothes, rarely dining out, putting off purchasing a television set until several years after most families had one, and forgoing many of the material luxuries that other families in our economic bracket possessed. We children struck people as a wholesome, happy lot: Bill was a protective big brother, intensely devoted to his younger siblings and always coming up with wonderful projects for the five of us, such as building an elaborate snow fort or making a raft and floating it on the brook at the bottom of our backyard; Susan was a traditional, pretty little girl, with blond pigtails and smocking-style dresses, who loved playing dolls and baking cookies and performing in ballet recitals; and then there were the "three little kids"— as I, Bobby, and Johnny, all born within three years of one another, were dubbed—who with our curly hair, freckled faces, and grass-stained overalls seemed to come right off the cover of the *Saturday Evening Post.*

In many ways, our childhood was idyllic. There were wonderful rituals, such as my father's bedtime telling of the ongoing saga of "Fussy and Crabby," a cautionary but hilarious tale he concocted about two sisters who were never satisfied with anything they were given; the nightly summer "car walks," in which my father would take the three little kids on a walk and then when we reached a particular spot about a quarter of a mile from our house would say, "Oops, I forgot the car," and we children would sit down on the grass and wait while he walked back to the house, got the car, picked us up, and drove us to Silver Beach, about ten minutes away, to buy ice cream cones; the silly dance my mother would do to cheer one of us up when we were sick—she would make her body go completely limp and flop around like a rag doll, a sight so funny that the sick child would go into uncontrollable spasms of laughter; the magical Christmas Eves when all five of us children would sleep in Bill's big bed and stay up half the night in excited anticipation, we three little kids listening for Santa on the roof and Susan and Bill, too old to be believers, indulgently going along with our fantasy. Mostly I remember the laughter. We had all to one degree or another inherited my father's wit, and family gatherings were always characterized by intense humor. As we grew older, the Hurley kids' reputation for being funny became so well known that our friends were always wanting to congregate at our house—especially if Bill or Bob were there—because they were sure to be entertained.

But the laughter had a dark side. I recall a college course in modern Irish drama in which the professor started to talk about Irish "graveyard humor"—the Irishman's survival strategy for laughing in the face of the bleak conditions of his existence. A click of recognition went off in my mind: *that,* I thought to myself, describes my family to a tee. For increasingly while we were growing up, we children had come to use humor as a coping mechanism, a way to stave off the depression and fear that threatened us as a result of the presence of a skeleton in our family closet. This skeleton—this shameful, scary secret—was that our mother could suddenly change from being the sweet, devoted parent she was much of the time to a disturbed, coarse, witch-like stranger, and that alcohol played a large role in this transfiguration. We will never know what the cause of my mother's problem was—whether it was a congenital personality disorder, or the changed social circumstances in which she found herself as a result of my father's growing success, or purely and simply alcohol—because the problem was never diagnosed. These were the days before people talked freely about family problems—before the phrase "dysfunctional family" had become fashionable—and when there was a real stigma attached to seeking psychiatric help; so my parents' way of dealing with the situation was to go into denial, and we children never mentioned the situation to anyone outside the family, nor, when we were very young, even discussed it among ourselves. In today's parlance, this would be described as "enabling behavior."

According to my father, whom we finally confronted about the situation when we were all grown up, my mother never manifested her personality problems in the early years of their marriage. It wasn't until after they had moved to Taunton and entered the world of cocktail parties and social drinking—my parents had rarely drunk alcohol prior to this—that she began to do so. Because the problem worsened as she got older, my eldest brother's memories of early childhood are quite different from those of us youngest children. During my childhood, weeks or months would go by when everything would be fine; then suddenly my world would change from a normal, secure place to a chaotic, nightmarish one: I would awaken in the middle of the night—usually after my parents had been at a party—to the terrifying sound of my mother's slurred, snarling speech. From what I am able to put together, often when she was at such a party she would feel socially inadequate or threatened by people she thought were looking down at her, and to cope with these feelings she would drink; the more she drank, the more paranoid she would become. Then, as soon as she and my father were in the car driving home, she would begin to abuse him verbally—sometimes accusing him of considering himself superior to her, other times accusing him of being attracted to a woman at the party. Her ranting and raving would continue after they arrived home, often going on for hours. She would wander the house, turning lights on and off and continuing her verbal rampage. My father would try to hush her or would go to sleep; sometimes he would leave the house for awhile and then come back, whereupon her ranting would begin again. Meanwhile, Susan and Bobby and Johnny and I (Bill was away at boarding school by the time these episodes became frequent) would be lying terrified in our beds. To make matters worse, the next day my parents would not talk about what happened; my father would act as though everything was normal, and my mother would go about her household tasks, although in a subdued mood.

As the years went by, my mother's scenes became more sustained, more public, and more frightening. My brothers and sister and I would be afraid to have friends spend the night; we braced ourselves for family trips, knowing my mother might cause a scene in a hotel; we became experts at reading "danger signs" and developing coping strategies. For example, on a summer day at our house at Cape Cod, if my parents left us a note telling us they had gone out on a friend's boat for the afternoon, we would know that they would be drinking cocktails on board and that my mother would most likely be drunk when they arrived home and dinner would be forgotten; so we would decide to go out for the evening to avoid the trauma the scene would cause us, or we'd try to combat the craziness by having dinner all cooked when they arrived home and pretending things were normal. A major coping strategy we used was humor. We hated the confusion and scariness of these episodes, and joking was our defense. One time, for example, following a disastrous family trip to Montreal in which, first, the hotel management had to ask my raving mother to keep it down (guests in the room adjacent to my parents' complained) and, second, my mother scowled and wouldn't speak for the rest of the trip, my siblings and I took to referring to this vacation as "the Canada caper." Another such humorous epithet we developed was "Taunton tea," a reference to the tea spiked with vodka we discovered my mother sneaking one time.

We children became experts at keeping this family skeleton in the closet. Not until we were grown up and it had become socially acceptable to admit to having a family member with a psychological problem did any of us discuss the situation with our friends. Eventually we confronted my mother about her alcoholism, but we were never able to get her to seek help. This fact brought us real sadness, for despite the trauma her behavior caused for us, we all loved her. When she wasn't drunk or paranoid, she was a loving, cheerful mother. Since her death, we have often talked about how different our lives would have been had she sought help. Susan's life in particular would have probably taken a different course, for Susan suffered the most from my mother's behavior.

12 Childhood

"Susan, now come on, get up and stop pretending."

My mother is leaning out an upstairs window overlooking the backyard. Susan and Bill and a bunch of neighborhood children have been playing a game in which they jump, one by one, off the low branch of a tree into the sandbox. Susan has just had her turn and is now lying in the sand claiming she can't get up because her leg hurts. My mother, with a one-year-old baby (me) needing attention and with another baby (Bobby) about to be born, doesn't have the energy to put up with Susan's antics.

This anecdote, told and retold through the years, became our family's version of "The Boy Who Cried Wolf": it turned out that Susan really *had* broken her leg, but at the age of six she had already become saddled with the "wuss" reputation that would characterize her role in the family. Of the five children, she was the only one with a frail constitution, and the rest of us often became impatient with her physical fearfulness and athletic ineptitude. We tended to turn a deaf ear to her physical complaints, only to discover sometimes with chagrin that they had been legitimate, as was the broken leg complaint. Thinking about this incident again the winter after Susan's disappearance, I suddenly saw that our lifelong habit of doubting her physical complaints must have played a role in our delayed realization that Susan was the victim of domestic abuse.

The recollection of this backyard scenario caused me to reflect not only on the way we siblings habitually regarded Susan but also on the way my mother did. From the time Susan was a small child, the relationship between the two was problematic. Being the elder daughter in a family like ours put Susan in an unfortunate position in certain ways. In Irish families, the eldest son is placed on a pedestal; this had especially been the case in my mother's family. My grandfather had died prematurely, when my mother and her sisters were quite small, and so their big brother had had to take on many aspects of the father role in the family. He was thus doubly looked up to and adored. I can recall my mother talking nostalgically about how she and her sisters used to love to iron their brother's shirts and handkerchiefs for him when they were growing up. This paradigm of sibling relationships influenced how my mother brought up her own children: Bill was to be unquestioningly admired, and the boys in general were given a much wider scope for behavior and behavioral infractions than were the girls. Susan's sex and her place in the sibling lineup combined to put her in a second-class position of sorts. As a daughter, she was expected to do many more household chores than her brothers did, and this expectation was multiplied by the fact that she was the elder daughter, with a considerable age gap between herself and the three youngest children, who were five, six, and eight years her junior. Susan's childhood was therefore in some ways a dreary affair: while her girlfriends played dolls or jumped rope after school, Susan would often be required to return home to fold laundry or mind her little brothers and sister. My mother, having had three babies in a row relatively late in life, tended to feel overwhelmed, and her elder daughter received the brunt of her crankiness.

Susan was also the occasional target of my mother's irrational jealousy. With her blond hair and delicate physique, Susan fit the stereotype of the pretty little girl of that era, an image that was enhanced by her interest in traditional female concerns. My parents often repeated the story about how when Susan was two and they were shopping in the girls' department at Jordan Marsh, she saw a dress she wanted that was actually for an older girl; when they pointed out that the dress was much too long for her, she protested, "But I could wear it as an e'ning gown." They were amazed, they would exclaim, that she knew about evening gowns at that age! Susan loved pretty clothes, and after learning how to sew at about age ten, began making many of her own skirts and dresses. She also early on showed a flair for cooking and domestic crafts and would bake fancy cakes for family birthdays and make elaborate decorations for Christmas and other holidays.

On the one hand, my mother was proud of this accomplished, feminine daughter, but on the other hand, she felt threatened by her. My mother seems to have felt that implicit in Susan's domestic activities was a criticism of herself: that Susan was baking the cakes and decorating the house because she could do these things better than my mother could. This feeling of my mother's was partly based on paranoia but also partly based on Susan's attitude. Susan did not hide her desire to have a fancier home, a fancier life, and a fancier mother; often she would try to persuade my mother, who was so busy running a large household that she didn't pay much attention to her appearance, to dress more stylishly or change her hairdo. There was an oil-and-water quality to their relationship, and I can remember tempestuous arguments triggered by Susan's criticism of my mother's ways or by my mother's accusation that Susan was being *flaithiuil.* This was a Gaelic term (pronounced "flah-hool"), passed on to us by my maternal grandmother, that evidently originally meant "generous" but over time took on the additional meaning of "acting above one's station" or "putting on the airs of aristocracy."[1] At least this is the way my family used the word. My mother's tirades at Susan would often end with the warning that Susan would never be happy because she always wanted something better than she had.

Had my mother been of a more reflective, analytical nature, and not beset by her own personal problems, she would probably have arrived at the same insight that I did as I pondered Susan's psychology, and that is that Susan's desire for a higher-class life was the result of her picking up on my mother's deep sense of social inferiority and my father's status seeking. My father's job with a company that manufactured sterling silver products entailed his establishing contacts with representatives of other businesses involved with the accoutrements of fine living, such as crystal, china, and jewelry. He was always traveling to New York to meet with an editor at *Vogue* or with an advertising tycoon, such as David Ogilvie, or flying off to Europe to meet with Italian designers or heads of international companies. I do not mean to paint a picture of him as a wide-eyed rube or as a crude social climber—he was too smart and too discriminating to be either of these things—but he *was* perceptibly taken with the sophisticated way of life to which his career increasingly exposed him. And he found a willing listener in Susan when he returned from his trips and described the people he'd met, the products he'd viewed, the gracious homes in which he'd been entertained. Often he would seek out Susan's opinion on a new flatware line Reed and Barton was developing, and as part of the promotional portfolio for one such pattern, he had the company photograph a place setting featuring Susan's graceful hand resting on a fork handle. And so, while my mother was threatened by Susan's "uppity" ways, my father encouraged them. As a result of his influence, as well as of her innate artistic inclinations, Susan at a young age developed precocious, sophisticated tastes.

She could also not help but pick up on my father's never-entirely-dispelled sense of being a fish out of water in the aristocratic world to which his career introduced him. All of us children noticed the way his style of speaking would subtly change when he was on the phone with his colleagues Roger Hallowell or Sinclair Weeks, members of the Yankee patrician family whose ancestors had founded Reed and Barton. My father's ordinary-man's Boston accent, with its broad *a*'s and dropped *r*'s, would be replaced by the dignified, slightly haughty tone of the Harvard-educated WASP. We kids used to joke about this, but I think it contributed to the developing notion that we all had that there was a very basic gap between us—the Hurleys—and the kind of people we must move among in order to be successful in life.

When I recall my sense of identity as a child, it seems to have been almost schizophrenic, to use that term in its casual sense. On the one hand, we were immersed in an Irish-Catholic world: most of us spent several years in parochial school; confession, abstinence from meat on Fridays, Mass attendance on Sundays and Holy Days, and all the other rules and regulations of the Church were conscientiously enforced by our parents; my father often lectured us on the history of Ireland, and my mother talked fiercely about the inhuman way "our people" had been treated by the English. On the other hand, much of our social life took place in the predominantly Protestant, non-Irish world of the country club, of (for my parents) cocktail parties, and of (for us children) ballroom dancing lessons and friendships with the upper-middle-class children we met through these lessons. I can remember the uncomfortable sensation of my two worlds colliding when I would spend a Saturday overnight at a Protestant friend's house and the next morning, while the friend slept in, would have to arise early and be picked up by my family for Mass. It wasn't the "hardship" of the situation—the early rising and the fasting from food prior to receiving communion—that bothered me so much as the sense of being marked, of being an underdog in comparison to my friend and her family. Life was in a sense more coherent in the summers because our summer home was in a section of Cape Cod where almost everyone was Irish Catholic and upwardly mobile like us. But then there would be occasions, such as a sailing regatta at a yacht club in a WASP resort, when the sense of being second-class would suddenly overtake me: I would look at the tanned, preppy youngsters milling about the yacht club and would feel that an unbridgeable social chasm existed between them and the pale-skinned, freckled, Irish-looking tribe to which I belonged.

I think Susan and I experienced this sense of inferiority more sharply than our brothers did. Being boys, they were not preoccupied by appearance and impressions. Also, they had as a role model our father, whose self-confidence and ability to hold his own in social situations were evident. We girls, on the other hand, had as a role model our mother, who clearly felt threatened by those she considered her social superiors. Susan's reaction was to try to be as different from my mother as she could be. Accordingly, from an early age she strove to create an elegant life that she felt was far removed from what she'd been born into.

These attempts on Susan's part invited frequent scorn from not only my mother but also my brothers and me, particularly later, when I was in my hippie and feminist phases. But in my musings on my sister's psychology the winter following her disappearance, I revised my view of Susan's efforts to live more elegantly. Whereas before I'd seen them solely as a reflection of her social climbing, now I saw them also as a reflection of her creative drive and her generosity. She had a true zeal for creating a beautiful environment, and from a young age she channeled this enthusiasm into a wide range of areas: sewing, knitting, designing her own patterns and recipes, cooking, baking, doll making, interior decorating, drawing and painting, designing murals and sets for school plays, and numerous other handicrafts. Although a major force behind her creativity was the desire to enhance her own life, another force was simply generosity. From childhood forward, she used her gifts to benefit others as well as herself. She would knit sweaters and scarves and caps for my brothers and father for Christmas and would sew outfits for my mother and me. When I was starting third grade, I had in mind a particular kind of "back-to-school" dress I wanted but my mother couldn't find in any of the stores: I had been reading *Little House on the Prairie* books and wanted an old-fashioned calico dress with lots of buttons down the front, a style not readily available in the mid-1950s. So Susan, only thirteen, found a Simplicity pattern that roughly approximated what I wanted, modified it, and sewed me a dress that matched my vision almost perfectly.

Another example of her generosity toward me was the birthday parties she would give me. Susan had such a flair for planning parties that my mother let her take over the running of the younger children's birthdays beginning when she was around ten. My birthday is May Day, and Susan would make the most of this theme, creating little May baskets and filling them with "flowers" made of gumdrops stuck on toothpicks. I loved dolls, and so she would usually make me a doll cake: she stacked up three or four round layer cakes of decreasing circumferences to form the skirt, cut a hole down the middle and placed a Barbie-type doll in it (this must have been a precursor, though, because these were the days before Barbies), and covered the "skirt" with glossy boiled-sugar icing, which she had tinted with food coloring. The effect, to my five- or six- or seven-year-old eyes, was that of a lovely lady in a pastel gown.

There were also, I now believe, compelling emotional forces behind Susan's desire to enhance and beautify her life and her environment. I think she was trying to cocoon herself in a storybook-perfect reality that would protect her from the ugliness and chaos lurking in our family closet and that would give her the security she lacked as a result of my mother's non-nurturing treatment of her. It was thus a combination of factors—insecurity, a sense of inferiority, a longing for increased social status, and a strong creative drive—that caused Susan to try to re-create herself and her world. As she moved into adolescence, these goals expanded from artistic achievements to include social ones. Like the famous Becky Sharpe of Thackeray's *Vanity Fair,* Susan possessed a genius for being able to size up a social situation and conquer it. Although in later years she would apply her powers to more sophisticated worlds, as an adolescent she set her sights on the world of public junior high school. She acquired the look—blond pageboy hairdo, full skirts, sweater sets, scarf tied jauntily around the neck—and the talkative, flirtatious manner that characterized popular girls of the time, and she was immensely successful. The phone was constantly ringing with calls from girlfriends, her current boyfriend, boys who had crushes on her, and—the most telling indication of female adolescent popularity in that era—girls who were jealous of her and wanted to menace her. Susan's life was a whirl of dates, dances, football games, and after-school Cokes at Durand's, Taunton's teenage hangout in the 1950s. By the time she got to high school, she had perfected her skills and was soon going steady with John Cullen, a handsome athlete who was one of the most popular boys in her class.

Looking back, I think that these years—junior high and the first two years of high school—were among the happiest of Susan's life. While she continued to have a difficult relationship with my mother, she had gained confidence and a sense of belonging as a result of her social success. But this period of relative security was to come to an end when she went away to prep school, an experience that left an indelible mark on Susan's psyche.

13 Prep School, College, and Early Adult Years

$\mathcal{I}$ am standing at the top of the back stairs, feeling shy and nervous about going down to greet my big sister, who has just arrived home from boarding school for the first time. She has brought some friends with her, girls with names like "Margot" and "Muffy," and I can hear them all talking in the kitchen. What has made me shy is that Susan suddenly seems like a stranger: her accent has changed—I hear her pronouncing *r*'s in words—and she has affected the preppy manner of her friends. I don't know how to relate to her, and so I put off going downstairs to say hello.

Susan's transformation at Dana Hall, the boarding school in Wellesley to which she was sent for her last two years of secondary school, was dramatic. When she first arrived there in September, she felt scared and out of her league, whispering in alarm to my father as they carried suitcases into her dorm room, "Daddy, these girls are all so *sophisticated*." But by mid-October, she had mastered the idiom, the accent, and the manner of a prep school girl. She was no longer "Susan" or "Sue"; she was "Susie." Her big brother no longer went to "Haavid" but to "Ha*hrvahr*d." And she sprinkled her conversation about boys with references to Exeter and Andover and other prestigious schools. To a certain extent, this transformation was just typical teenage-girl herd behavior; but I think it also reflected her desire to eliminate all vestiges of her background, a desire that in turn stemmed from the underlying sense of inferiority she had picked up from my parents.

My father's growing acquaintance with the world of Massachusetts Brahmins had made him aware of the social cachet that a prep-school education provided. In addition, as a lover of books and learning, he wanted his children to have the kind of schooling he wished he himself could have had. With a mix of meretricious and noble motives, then, he decided that all of his children would have the advantage of attending prep school—and not just any prep schools but the *best*. Exeter was the choice for the boys (Bill, however, ended up going to Tabor Academy instead because the local Catholic boys' high school where he attended his first two years missed the deadline for sending in certain application documents) and Dana Hall, founded originally as the preparatory school for Wellesley College, the choice for the girls. There was never any discussion about this decision, never any weighing of the pros and cons or any explanation to us children about the different social world we would be encountering. Perhaps if the first of us to go off to boarding school had had a difficult time, my parents would have reconsidered their decision, but Bill's experience at Tabor was almost idyllic. Tabor was a smaller institution than Exeter, with a fatherly headmaster who ran the school like one big family, and Bill proved to be something of a star there: a top student and top athlete whose wit and sociable nature made him extremely well liked. Bill's experience must therefore have confirmed my parents' belief that they had made the right decision about sending us all away to school.

However, for the rest of us, prep school was more problematic. Exeter, where teachers were to be addressed as "Master" and where students had formidable pedigrees (David Eisenhower, for example, was a classmate of my brother Bob's), lacked the family-like atmosphere that made Bill feel so at home at Tabor. And Dana Hall was socially daunting to both Susan and me. Not only were most of the girls extremely wealthy—hailing from upscale areas like Greenwich, Connecticut, and Winnetka, Illinois—but they came from "old money." Susan and I were among the handful of Dana Hall students each year whose educations were being funded by our fathers' earnings, as opposed to trust funds or inheritances or rich grandparents. Girls talked casually about summering in Europe, skiing in Aspen, and preparing for their debutante parties. It was very easy for someone like Susan or me to feel socially inadequate. I developed some of the same kinds of strategies Susan had done: I unofficially changed my name, no longer going by "Mary Ellen," which seemed to me to be a dead giveaway of my background (my Catholic grammar school had been filled with "Mary Margaret"s and "Mary Catherine"s, and my cousins had such names as "Mary Louise" and "Mary Jane"), but instead by the nickname "Molly"—not realizing, ironically, that this was a stereotypical Irish nickname![1] And I too developed the habit of pointedly not mentioning certain facts about my family, such as that my grandmothers lived in Dorchester and that my mother had not gone to college.

But I was never quite as dazzled as Susan was by the upper-class society to which Dana Hall introduced us. Part of the reason for this was that I had early on, when I was in elementary school and Susan in junior high, realized I could never be the kind of social success my sister was, and so I had striven to develop other strengths, purposely trying to achieve in areas where she had not. One of these was academics. I do not mean to imply, however, that Susan was unintelligent—on the contrary, she had a very high IQ and was quick and witty; it's just that, being more interested in socializing and working on artistic projects, she put only enough time into her schoolwork to get by with B's and C's. I also became more involved in sports and physical activities—skiing, ice-skating, and modern dance—because this was an area Susan was notoriously unaccomplished in. At Dana Hall, then, although I had my moments of wishing I were a debutante, I focused more on academics and athletics than on the social scene and consequently staved off the feelings of inferiority that gnawed at Susan. In addition, my years in prep school coincided with the early stage of the 1960s counterculture movement, and like most people my age I grew increasingly skeptical of class distinctions and of such manifestations of social elitism as debutante parties. My sister, however, whose prep school experience took place in the late 1950s, had already gone through her formative years before these influences began to be felt.

Susan's drive to escape her background and fashion a new identity caused her to pour her energy into becoming a social success at

Dana Hall. She acquired the image of the typical prep school girl of the time, she had a wide circle of friends, and she was often invited to dances at boys' schools. But, as she confided to me in later years, she always felt she was wearing a mask. I think she feared that if she let down her guard, she would slip into talking in her natural accent and reveal her true background. She steered away from inviting classmates home for weekends or vacations because they would see that her mother was not the well-heeled, self-confident society matron that their mothers were, and, worse, they might witness one of my mother's degrading, drunken scenes. When she would visit friends at their homes over vacations, her sense of difference and her longing for both the pedigree and the emotional security her friends possessed became even sharper.

Susan's choice of college ensured that she would continue both to climb the social ladder and to feel socially inferior. She attended Manhattanville College of the Sacred Heart, near White Plains, New York, a school that she liked to point out was considered by many to be "the Catholic Wellesley" (she would have loved to have gone to Wellesley, but her grades were not strong enough). Many Manhattanville students came from prominent Catholic families—several of the Kennedy sisters and wives went there—and Susan, of course, gravitated to the crème de la crème. She cultivated a close friendship with two sisters from a wealthy Puerto Rican family, Grace and Encarnita Valdez, and visited them at their family's villa in San Juan during one vacation. She befriended a princess, from some defunct royal line, named Catherine Hohenloe, and during the summer would frequently drive over to visit her at her family's summer home in Hyannis Port, near the Kennedy compound. The young men Susan dated, such as Eli Lilly Jr., usually attended Princeton or Harvard or belonged to families in the Social Register.

As Susan became increasingly sophisticated in her tastes and friendships, her relationship with my mother became increasingly difficult. The latter felt threatened by Susan's friends and sometimes, to Susan's deep humiliation, made scenes in front of them (something she did much less frequently in front of her other children's friends). Numerous occasions that should have been celebratory ones for

Susan were ruined by my mother. For example, at a luncheon following Susan's graduation from Manhattanville, my mother launched into an alcohol-induced verbal attack on one of Susan's close friends, a girl from a wealthy, cultured family who my mother thought "put on airs." My father got my mother to stop, but a pall was cast over the occasion, and Susan once again had her superstition confirmed that she was doomed never fully to escape her shameful background. (Perhaps the most upsetting incident of this sort was my mother's drunken, attacking phone call to Tom's stepfather, a doctor in Alabama, about a week before Susan and Tom's wedding. The two had not yet met, and Dr. Owsley was unaware of my mother's psychological problems. Alarmed and thinking she was sick, he got off the phone and immediately called Tom, who enlightened him about my mother. An understanding man, Dr. Owsley behaved graciously toward my mother at the wedding, acting as though the phone call incident had never happened. When Susan was informed by Tom about my mother's behavior, she was mortified, and the day that should have been the happiest of her life, was, like her college graduation, ruined by the family's skeleton in the closet.)

Following Susan's graduation, she moved to Boston and took a job at the Museum of Fine Arts. It was through the social circle she joined there that she met Lonnie Marquand.

It is a weekday afternoon in January 1966, and I am home from Brown to study for my final exams in the quiet of the Taunton house. My parents are on a trip, Bob and John are away at school, and Bill and Susan are both living and working in Boston. Unexpectedly, Susan and her soon-to-be fiancé, Lonnie Marquand, drop in. The scene becomes like something out of *The Great Gatsby.* Lonnie and Susan are lounging around idly, trying to think of something to do, when Susan, in the whimsical manner of Daisy Buchanan, suddenly decides we should all drink champagne. She sends Lonnie out to purchase some, and he returns with a bottle of Dom Perignon and a motley array of expensive liquor. Susan laughs gleefully at his extravagance, and the two of them talk me into joining their party. We proceed to drink the champagne and sample some of the other stuff, and as the lost afternoon dwindles away, I notice Susan's high-jinks mood being replaced by anxiety. She doesn't have to tell me how she's feeling, for I know we are experiencing the same insight: this drunken scene is reminiscent of the occasions when my mother's drinking would cause her to become sloppy and irresponsible and our household to become chaotic. Susan is deeply disturbed by the realization that she has re-created this situation.

Susan's engagement to Lonnie, described in chapter 6, represented the culmination of her lifelong effort to enter the upper class. I remember being struck by this insight as I watched Mrs. John D. Rockefeller III, Lonnie's aunt, walk through the front door of our house in Taunton for the occasion of Susan and Lonnie's engagement party. But the engagement also represented the dangers that Susan's social climbing could lead to, for the relationship with Lonnie came at the cost of her psychological well-being. To her credit, she realized this and broke off the engagement. But, as I have explained, she was unable to stick to her decision and resumed dating him, a situation that filled her with self-doubt. It was of course the fortuitous introduction to Tom Owsley that ended this unhealthy chapter of her life.

In retrospect, it is eerie to note how similar the Lonnie Marquand chapter was to the Jim Harrison chapter (except for one crucial difference: Susan never complained that Lonnie abused her). Susan's involvement with both men grew out of her deluded notion that wealth or social status would bring her the elusive security and happiness she yearned for and would banish the feelings of inferiority that had dogged her all her life. But in entering each relationship, she found that she had entered a world of alcohol and psychological chaos, the very features of her childhood family life that had most frightened her. Like a character in a Greek tragedy or a cautionary fable, then, my sister discovered that in trying to escape her past, she had unwittingly re-created it.

Part Three

The Search for Susan and the Pursuit of Justice

14 The Search Continues, January–May 1995: Appeals to Jim and His Family

My extensive reflections about my sister's past a few months after she disappeared resulted in my having a much better understanding of her and a much deeper sympathy for her than I'd had when she was alive. Whereas then I had been contemptuous of her social climbing and her involvement with men like Lonnie and Jim, now I understood that her actions had grown out of deep feelings of inferiority and insecurity. These forces had caused Susan to make wrongheaded and disastrous choices, but she had ultimately recognized her mistakes and tried to rectify them. She had succeeded the first time, when she finally extricated herself from Lonnie; but she hadn't been allowed to succeed the second time, because her attempt to extricate herself from Jim was cut short by her murder.

With this enlarged understanding of my sister, I felt more keenly than ever the tragedy and injustice of her end. She had not been a saint, and she had no doubt provoked and escalated some of the fights with Jim; but she did not deserve to be murdered, her body discarded and denied the dignity of a funeral and the crime gone unpunished. No, I was determined that justice would be served for my sister. As the new year, 1995, began, I felt a renewed conviction to make this happen.

The rest of the family felt the same way, increasingly so as the six-month anniversary of Susan's disappearance approached. It was time, we decided, for another powwow in Baltimore. The weekend before Valentine's Day 1995 was the date we settled upon.

On Friday night and Saturday morning, the six of us arrived at Tom's house at staggered times, my three brothers coming in from Massachusetts, Jonathan from New York, Nick from Vermont, and I from Georgia. Then on Saturday afternoon, a cold, gray one, we gathered in Tom's living room, a fire blazing in the fireplace and the seven of us, including Tom, armed with strong cups of coffee, legal pads, and pens. Bill, who was the family's primary contact with the police, began by summing up details of the official investigation thus far, and then he opened up the floor for suggestions about new avenues we might urge the police to pursue and efforts we ourselves might undertake. Over the course of the next several hours, our discussion yielded a lengthening list of possible angles and strategies, ranging from the feasible to the far-fetched.

Observing this exercise, I found myself noting the way it caused the individual personalities and talents of family members to be thrown into sharp relief. John, for example, with his cerebral, intellectual bent, would suggest an elaborate scheme for using psychological theory to trick the killer into divulging the whereabouts of Susan's body. He would propound his proposal at length, until, say, Jonathan, with his incisive legal mind, would point out a possible obstacle, or Bob, blunt and no-nonsense, would object to the plan's impracticality. Bill, ever the wise big brother and consensus maker, would step in and suggest some kind of compromise. My observations also caused me to reflect on how we Hurley siblings were, in a way, in our natural element in a situation like this: since childhood, we'd had extensive experience in banding together to deal with the emotional upheavals of family crises. And as we so often did as children and adolescents, we turned to humor to relieve us in the present crisis.

The Susan case, indeed, provided much fodder for humor, given the strange, hitherto alien worlds it introduced us to, including the worlds of psychics, private eyes, and soft-news journalists. In particular, the new experience of media interviews was the occasion for many jokes. Bill, Bob, and John, quick to note the way many of the female television reporters who interviewed us had clearly been chosen for their looks rather than their journalistic credentials, got into the habit of referring to them behind their backs as "info-babes." Once when we were asked to pose for a newspaper photograph following an interview, Bill, whose struggle with his weight has long been a family joke, deadpanned to the disconcerted reporter, "Well, gee, if I'd known I was going to have my picture taken, I'd have worn something slimming: I photograph heavy."

Like many of the reporters who interviewed us, the police were sometimes taken aback by our family's humor. During our February visit to Baltimore, we met with Detective Ramsey, and in the course of our discussion he mentioned something about a psychic who had called in expressing her hunch that Susan's mind and spirit were in one place and her body in another—a pronouncement that caused Bob to quip, "Yep, that sounds like Susan." Ramsey stared at him, not sure how to take his remark. At another point that weekend, when we were meeting with Frank Napfel, the private investigator who was trailing Jim, Napfel reported that Jim never left the house except to go to the liquor store or a bar; after hearing this description, Bob let out a wistful sigh and said, "Aaaah, the simple life," causing Napfel at first to look startled and then to crack up.

Because we were losing faith in the police investigation, we focused in our brainstorming on ways we ourselves could help either to find Susan's body or to implicate her killer. Many of the ideas we entertained were wild-eyed and were never followed through on, but they reveal how desperate we felt. These suggestions included persuading the local media to declare a "Susan Hurley Harrison Day" on which Baltimore County residents would voluntarily go out and search for Susan's body; asking Boy Scout troops in the area to take on the search as a scouting project; having me telephone Jim pretending I was Susan (everyone had always confused our voices on the phone) and taping his response, which might betray his knowledge that it couldn't be Susan because she was dead; getting hold of a Colombian truth serum that Bill had read about in the *Wall Street Journal* and hiring a prostitute or some kind of operative to slip it into Jim's drink, in the hopes that Jim might divulge the location of Susan's body.

One rash suggestion we did decide to act on, though, was to confront Jim ourselves. The police had advised us to keep our distance and to avoid voicing our suspicions publicly; they were afraid that any hostile or confrontational gesture on our part might cause Jim to stop cooperating with the investigation, and they felt that the only way the case was going to be solved was through keeping him talking to the police. We, however, had become increasingly skeptical about the chances of a confession. We decided to take matters into our own hands and to work on Jim ourselves. Our reasoning was that if he witnessed our grief firsthand, his conscience might be pricked; or if he really was going crazy due to guilt, in the manner of *Crime and Punishment*'s Raskolnikov, we could either work on his conscience or keep him talking until he let drop some clue as to Susan's whereabouts.

Accordingly, the following day Bill, Bob, John, and I got into Bill's rental car and set out for Lutherville, about a ten-minute drive from Tom's house. As we rode along the quiet Sunday-afternoon streets, I gazed out the backseat window at the snow-covered lawns and the houses with smoke coming from their chimneys. Suddenly I felt like a child again, packed into the family car with my siblings on a winter Sunday afternoon, being taken by our parents on an outing to our grandmother's in Boston. How had the Hurley kids traveled from that Norman Rockwell–like scenario to the present nightmare? As we got closer to our destination, my feelings of nostalgia were replaced by those of dread. How would Jim react when he saw us? How would I feel being in the house where my sister had probably been murdered? Would I be overwhelmed with fear at the thought that I was in the same room as my sister's probable killer?

We slowed to a cruise as we approached Jim's house. Yes, he was home: there was his Lincoln Town Car in the driveway. We pulled in behind it, parked, and, taking a collective deep breath, got out and walked silently to Jim's front door. My heart was pounding. Bill knocked once, then again. After about a minute the door was opened, and we were face to face with the man whom we suspected to be our sister's murderer.

Holding a lit cigarette and wearing a disheveled layering of shirt, sweaters, and rumpled jacket, his face a florid red, Jim greeted us in a befuddled way, seeming confused about which brother was which

and what my name was. Then he suddenly shifted into his master-
of-ceremonies mode and waved us into the family room, offering us
a drink, which we declined. We could tell by his breath that he himself had been drinking, and there was a glass of some kind of dark-
colored liquor on the coffee table. We had been somewhat prepared,
from descriptions by police and reporters who had interviewed Jim
at home, for the mess we encountered, but still it was shocking. The
last time I had been in that family room, when Susan was mistress
of the house, it had looked like a page out of *House Beautiful* or *Martha
Stewart Living,* elegantly furnished and impeccably maintained; now
what greeted my eyes were a soiled rug and shabby sofa, a cracked
framed picture on the wall, and old newspapers and mail spilling off
tables and chairs and stacked a foot deep along the walls. The scene
was not only messy but bizarre: country-western music blared from
a radio in the kitchen, competing with the sound of a golf tourna-
ment turned up to normal volume on the TV; Christmas cards were
strewn about; and a knee-high plastic Santa Claus grinned inanely
from the hearth. Jim made no motion to turn off the TV, behaving
as though we were casual pals who had just dropped by to watch golf
with him. Bob asked if he could turn the set off so we could talk;
Jim said no, he wanted to see the score, but Bob could turn the volume down. Then Bob asked if he could also turn down the volume
of the radio; Jim consented but acted as though he thought this was
a strange request, adding the non sequitur that he and Susan had
become fans of country-western music.

Bill then opened the conversation by explaining that we wanted
to talk to Jim about Susan's disappearance, to which the latter replied,
"Have you seen her?" When Bill said no and that we were sure she
was dead, Jim launched into a tale about how some "black man" had
told a friend of Jim's that Susan was hiding out in Boston with a
boyfriend named "Dave," planning a lawsuit against Jim, and that
her family knew she was there. In accordance with our agreed-upon
plan to try to get Jim to talk as much as possible, we bit our tongues
and let him continue. Over the course of the next couple of hours,
he rambled on incoherently, regaling us with absurd hypotheses about
Susan's disappearance. He continually returned to the theme that Su-

san had had a number of mysterious "boyfriends" and that he'd heard rumors about her being involved with a black man. (In retrospect, I am struck by the similarity between this seemingly racist red herring and the stories fabricated by Boston murderer Chuck Stuart and North Carolina murderer Susan Smith, both of whom claimed that a black stranger was responsible for, respectively, the shooting death of Stuart's pregnant wife in 1991 and the kidnapping and drowning of Smith's two young sons in 1995.) Jim claimed to have received much of his information from a new friend whom he'd met in a bar, a man named Christopher Kennedy Hughes who, Jim proceeded to tell us with a straight face, had been adopted sequentially by President Kennedy, Marilyn Monroe, Aristotle Onassis, and Howard Hughes and who was formerly an agent with the CIA and possibly the FBI. We held in check our laughter and expressions of incredulity as Jim went on to inform us that Chris Kennedy Hughes was going to run for president in 2000 and that the previous week he, Jim, had driven Hughes to the airport to catch a flight to England for a two-month stay with Queen Elizabeth in Buckingham Palace!

Another striking aspect of Jim's behavior during our visit was his speech habits. Not only did he frequently refer to himself in the third person, but he employed a limited, childlike vocabulary and limited, childlike reasoning. For example, when we asked him to recount for us what happened the last night he saw Susan, he said that when she first came to the house she was "good" and then she had a glass of wine and fell asleep, and when she woke up she was "bad." Similarly, in response to our question about his taking the lie detector test, he said that Detective Ramsey and the FBI agent who administered the test were "good guys" who were being "nice" to him for the first half hour but then started saying "these bad things" about him and accusing him of murdering Susan. This type of strange childlike behavior and speech of Jim's would in fact be noted and quoted by many of the reporters who interviewed him in the next few months. To Loni Ingraham of the *Towson Times,* for example, he remarked, "Normally the police are very nice and very helpful. . . . But every once in a while, they come and accuse me. Then they go back to being nice again."[1] Margaret Guroff, in her *Baltimore Magazine* article, quotes Jim as describing his relationship with Susan in these words: "It's really neat. Life is full of so many different people. But then you meet somebody who is the person above all. We couldn't stop it, so I had to leave my wife and six children. She left her husband and two children."[2] And *Baltimore Sun* reporter Laura Lippman describes how during her interview with Jim, he plugged in the plastic Santa—still on display in June!—and began merrily singing along with the snatches of Christmas songs that issued from it; then, after leaving the room for a minute to answer the phone, he shouted "Merry Christmas!" upon his return.[3]

Jim's odd performance on the day we visited him fueled our puzzlement as to whether he was losing his mind due to guilt, denial, and alcohol, or whether he was putting on a supreme act. What led us to suspect that the latter might be the case was the way he would often stare at us after he'd said something outlandish, almost as though he were watching to see the effect it was having. Perhaps he was playing a mind game with us and enjoying the feeling of power. In some ways, he did seem to be controlling the whole event, for although we got him to ramble on, we were not successful at getting him to let drop any clue that would help us figure out where Susan was.

We were also not successful in achieving our other goal: to move him with the spectacle of our anguish. In advance of our visit, we had decided that if one of us felt like crying, we should give in to this urge. I had occasion to do this: at one point when we were talking to Jim about our strong need to give Susan a proper funeral, I began to describe how unbearable it was to me to think of Susan lying dead and uncared for somewhere, and I broke down and wept. Jim's reaction was chilling: he merely looked at me, as though I were a curiosity, and then he changed the subject. He did the same thing when my brother John broke down. And when John subsequently looked him in the eye intently and said, "Jim, we *have* to find Susan's body," Jim averted his eyes, looked up at the ceiling, and said he loved Susan and hoped she'd return to him soon.

Arriving at the tacit mutual conclusion that we were not going to get Jim to confess or to betray the location of Susan's body, my brothers and I decided, after about two hours, that it was time to wrap up the visit. But we had one more piece of business to accomplish before we departed: our invitation to Jim, on the off chance that he was innocent, to work *with* us in our attempts to find Susan. As we stood up to leave, Bill said something to the effect of, "Jim, you know we've suspected you, but we want to give you the benefit of the doubt. If you didn't kill Susan, we want to work with you. We have to pull together to find out what happened to her." Jim broke into a big grin and started nodding his head, only too happy to go along with this pretense of camaraderie. We each wrote down our phone number to give him and asked him to call us if he thought of any leads or came across any possibly helpful information. Then, suppressing our repulsion, we each shook his hand and departed, politely declining his last-minute invitation to stay for dinner!

Not to our surprise, Jim's show of wanting to work with us in our efforts to find Susan was hollow: we never heard from him again. Bill made another attempt at pricking Jim's conscience about a month later. In my constant lookout for articles about cases like ours, I had come upon and been following the case of a missing Emory University student, Shannon Melendi, who had disappeared a year earlier. I sent Bill a copy of the article that appeared in the *Atlanta Constitution* in March on the one-year anniversary of her disappearance, describing her family's anguish. Bill decided to send a copy to Jim. He attached a note saying, "Molly sent me this news clipping from the *Atlanta Constitution*. We sympathize with the Melendi family. We must do *more* to find Susan's body!," and in the article he underlined the following quote from Mrs. Melendi: "This animal removed something very precious from our lives. I call whoever it is an animal because he's had a year to reflect on what he's done. A human would not leave this family in limbo."[4] Jim, needless to say, did not respond.

Another one of the ideas that had come up in our brainstorming session was to try to work on some of Jim's family members. Perhaps one of them could be moved by our plight to pressure Jim to confess, or perhaps one of them was holding back information and would be moved to go to the police. Over the years of Susan and Jim's marriage, we had had little contact with Jim's relatives— in fact, most of us had not met any of them—because matters were always so awkward between our family and Jim. But we thought that some of his family members might be approachable under the present circumstances.

Jim's older daughter, Wendy, seemed the most likely one to appeal to, for she had been at Jim's house when Susan arrived that final night, and according to Susan, at one point the two of them had been close, although in later years Wendy turned against Susan and sided with her father. Susan had told me that on a couple of occasions when she had been upset after a fight with Jim, Wendy sympathized with her and confided that Jim had sometimes had temper outbursts and been physically abusive to her and her siblings when they were children. My brother John and I each tried several times to reach Wendy by phone, but our attempts were in vain. When I finally realized she did not intend to return my calls, I tried to squeeze all that I wanted to say into two or three lengthy recorded messages. I made one of these calls right after I'd started crying while looking through old photographs of Susan, and I tearfully described to Wendy how much I missed Susan and how I needed to talk to Wendy because she had been one of the last to see Susan alive. I tried to appeal to her on the basis of our common situation of each having just one sister and on the basis of the special closeness she and Susan had at one point shared. Another time, I left an extended message after I'd learned from Detective Ramsey that Wendy had contacted him to say she had information about people who hated Susan but that Ramsey couldn't get Wendy to come down to headquarters to give him this information. In my recording, I begged her to go see Ramsey, pointing out that it was her moral obligation to divulge any information that could help solve this case and thereby alleviate a whole family's pain. But all my appeals seemed to fall on deaf ears: she never responded. Nor did Ann Offutt, Jim's sister, to whom I wrote an imploring letter.

We often speculated about whether Jim had confided in any of his family members or whether any of them had suspicions about his role in Susan's disappearance. This question suddenly became a burning one about three months after our visit to Jim. On Tuesday morning, May 9, I was glancing at the Southeastern section of the *Atlanta Constitution* when the word "Harrison" jumped out at me.

In those days, I had antennae out for any word or phrase ("murder," "missing woman," and so on) even remotely relating to the Susan case. Scrolling my eyes back up to the beginning of this story, I read the headline "MAN SHOOTS BUS RIDER, SELF," and, my curiosity aroused, I proceeded to read the article in full: "Without saying a word, a man shot another passenger on a bus in Fort Lauderdale, Florida, then killed himself. William Harrison, 35, walked to the end of the bus, pulled out a sawed-off shotgun and shot Byron Dean Flowers, 38, who was traveling with his common-law wife and 2-year-old son, police said. Then Harrison shot himself. There was apparently no connection between the two men, police spokeswoman Sonya Friedman said."[5] Could it possibly be? I asked myself. I knew Jim had a son named Bill who was in his mid-thirties, lived in Florida, and was troubled; but on the other hand, I told myself, "Harrison" is a pretty common name and Florida is a pretty big state. So, after mentioning the coincidence to my husband, who agreed that the chances that the murderer was Jim's son were slim, I put the thought out of my mind.

Two days later, however, I received a call from our attorney, Carey Deeley, informing me that this *had* been Jim's son! Over the next week, Carey faxed me the various articles about the crime that had appeared in Fort Lauderdale area newspapers. These told the tale of a disturbed young man, an out-of-work loner who harbored an inexplicable anger and whose apartment the police had occasionally been called to when neighbors complained that he was firing off guns. I experienced a barrage of thoughts and emotions as I read these stories: pity, of an almost maternal nature, for Bill Harrison (his landlady spoke poignantly about how unhappy and lost he always seemed, despite his good looks and wealthy background);[6] anger and disgust at him for pointlessly taking the life of an innocent bystander—and the father of a young child, to boot; the thought that perhaps Bill Harrison had inherited from his father the selfish tendency to disregard the suffering they inflicted on others (Jim on our family, his son on the wife and child of the man he murdered); speculation as to whether the son's violent behavior was the result of his having grown up with a violent father; and the teasing question as to whether this desperate act could have been prompted in part by guilty knowledge

Bill was harboring about his father's role in his stepmother's disappearance. I knew that Jim had gone to visit Bill and another son living in Florida the month after Susan disappeared, and one of the newspaper articles described how Bill had spent five days in mid-April at his father's home recuperating from surgery following a frostbite injury.[7]

As shocked and saddened as I was by this news of the murder-suicide, I felt excited about the fact that it opened up a new avenue of investigation for us, and hence new hope of finding Susan. My family put pressure on the Baltimore County police to alert the Fort Lauderdale police about a possible connection between our case and Bill Harrison's. However, neither set of investigators explored the connection with the sense of urgency and commitment we felt the situation warranted. Fort Lauderdale police looked through Bill Harrison's apartment and, finding no revealing diaries or letters, let the matter rest. We would have liked a more thorough investigation: a questioning of anyone the younger Harrison had had a meaningful conversation with over the past several months. Surely there was someone—a counselor, perhaps, or a minister (his landlady was quoted in the newspaper as saying he had joined a church for a spell in an attempt to make friends)[8]—to whom he might have confided what was troubling him. There was a flurry of newspaper articles, in both Fort Lauderdale and Baltimore, mentioning the parallels between the elder and younger Harrisons' troubles, and then interest in the connection fizzled. The hope we'd had that this crisis might break Jim down emotionally and make him more vulnerable to the police's efforts to work on his conscience also amounted to nothing. Indeed, his response to his son's death was characteristically bizarre, ranging from his denial of the facts (which were never in dispute)— "There were six people on the bus," he told reporter Margaret Guroff. "I wonder if something else happened. Like, they killed him and the other guy"[9]—to odd, detached musings about his son's problems, among them: "Every once in a while we'd see him, and every once in a while he'd act unusual. But then again, he'd act beautiful too."[10]

My one final attempt to move Jim was to send him a letter of condolence a few weeks after his son's death. The motive was partly sincere sympathy—my heart goes out to *any* parent who suffers the loss of a child, the most unbearable pain I can imagine—and partly strategy: maybe my magnanimous gesture would prick his conscience about the way he was making my family suffer. But, of course, nothing came of my attempt. By this time, it was obvious that the police had been wrong in their premise that the way to solve this case was to get Jim to crack. I suspected that either he was a sociopath, totally lacking in conscience, or he was in deep denial. Our family was beginning to lose hope that the case would ever be resolved.

15 The Memorial Service, June 1995

By the spring of 1995, after living for almost a year in the peculiar limbo of mourning a loved one who is not officially dead, the family felt the need for some sort of formal service memorializing Susan. We had come to realize that her body might never be found and therefore that we might never be able to have a real funeral. While we knew that such a service wouldn't "provide closure" (a psychobabble phrase we had grown to hate, for as anyone who has lost a loved one to murder or presumed murder knows, there is no such thing as emotional closure in such cases), we thought a formal ritual would be a cathartic outlet for our grief and a way of dignifying Susan's memory. In addition, planning such a service would fill our need to keep active; it would give us something purposeful to do at a time when we were beginning to feel helpless in our efforts to solve the case.

A mini-memorial service of sorts had been held on Susan's birthday in March: Bill had had a Mass dedicated to her that day at his church in Hingham, Massachusetts, and friends and relatives in the area had attended the service and an informal reception following it at Bill's house. The larger memorial service that we planned for late spring would be held in Baltimore, we decided, so that the many friends Susan had had in that area could attend. Jonathan and Nicholas wanted it to be a ceremonious affair, and they wanted to hold it at the Gilman School, which they were both graduates of and where Susan had been an active parent volunteer. The headmaster, Arch Montgomery, graciously gave them permission to do so, and the service was scheduled for Saturday, June 17, at 2:00, with a reception following at Tom's house, close by the campus.

It would be an understatement to say that planning this event was a challenge. Emily Post does not cover memorial services for missing-and-presumed-murdered loved ones in her etiquette book, and we were moving in uncharted territory. Plus, the one person in the family who would have had the social and artistic know-how to create the kind of affair we were envisioning was, ironically, Susan. Never did I feel her absence more keenly than I did during this time. With every decision that had to be made—about invitations, flowers, music, reception arrangements—I found myself instinctively thinking, for a brief second, "I'll ask Susan." However, we managed, with the help of some of Susan's friends who shared her tastes, to fashion a ceremony that we felt she would have approved of.

The service was a remarkable occasion, combining elegance, poignancy, and humor—a true celebration of Susan's spirit. Printed invitations had been sent to approximately two hundred guests, virtually all of whom showed up. They were greeted at the entrance to the alumni building by an attractive group of young people, Gilman and Middlebury friends of Jonathan's and Nicholas's, and ushered into the auditorium, a dignified, old-fashioned room with ornate sconces spaced along the paneled walls. Seated with the family at the front of the auditorium waiting for the service to begin, I kept thinking how fitting the setting was. Susan had loved Gilman, which she'd been involved with since first moving to Baltimore when Jonathan had enrolled in its middle school. She was, of course, drawn to the school because of its patrician atmosphere, but also because her boys had been so happy there, excelling in both athletics and academics and respected by peers, teachers, and administrators. It suddenly occurred to me that just two years earlier, Susan had been seated in this very same auditorium, at the baccalaureate service for Nicholas's graduation. I swallowed hard, telling myself I wouldn't be able to make it through my speech if I started crying now.

The service began. Bill, having inherited my father's skill as a raconteur, was our natural choice for master of ceremonies. After welcoming the large crowd and on behalf of Jonathan and Nicholas and the rest of the family thanking them for joining us to remember Susan, he launched into his own personal reminiscences, beginning with his earliest memories of his little sister. He recalled how he would come into the house after playing in the backyard and Susan, three years younger than he and not yet walking, would catch sight of him, drop the toy she was playing with, crawl eagerly across the floor, and, her face lighting up with a great big smile, pull herself up on him. Bill's voice cracked as he finished this recollection. He said, "Excuse me," took a deep breath, and continued. I heard several sniffles behind me and knew that the tears had already begun to flow in the audience.

Bill then proceeded to recount a number of anecdotes, many of them humorous, about Susan's and his childhood escapades, all of which pointed to the strong sibling bond they shared, a bond that eventually expanded to include "the three little kids." He talked of "all the great times" the five of us had had together in our childhood and on into adulthood. Then, in a more solemn vein, he described how after the deaths of our parents, we'd had a headstone placed over their grave with five shamrocks engraved on it: two on one side, standing for Bill and Susan, and three on the other side, for "the three little kids." Bill didn't put it into words, but I could tell that for him, as for me, one of the most disorienting things about Susan's disappearance was this changed paradigm: we had *always* been "the five Hurley kids," and now where there had been five there were only four. As I dwelled on this subtext of his speech, I found myself thinking of Wordsworth's poem "We Are Seven," about a small child who cannot accept the fact that the number of her siblings is reduced, to five, now that two have died. That poem, which ironically my father used to read to us when we were little, had always brought tears to my eyes, and now it held added poignancy for me.

Bill's talk captivated the audience because of its wit and emotional power and because of its big brother's perspective on Susan. This was followed by several of Susan's friends' speeches. Each was captivating in its own way, and each opened a window onto a particular stage of Susan's life, beginning with her teenage years. Terry MacMillan, who couldn't be at the service but who wrote a speech that was read by my brother John, recalled antics from their Dana Hall days, including the time the two of them and some other girls skipped vespers one Sunday night. Those who were caught didn't tell on Susan so that she could go to the Spring Formal weekend she'd been invited to at Lawrenceville, a boys' school in New Jersey. Terry's postscript to this anecdote triggered affectionate laughter from those in the audience who knew that Susan's fun-loving streak often conflicted with her Catholic sense of guilt: "Susan went on the weekend, albeit not without a pang of conscience, for she apologized up until 1994 for not sharing in our punishment way back then." Terry went on to describe how she and Susan had shared their lives since then, staying close by spending "hours, or should I say years, on the phone," and concluded her talk on a bittersweet note: "I will miss the phone ringing, her being there for me, and me for her. But in a way it will be like time standing still, because I can still hear the ringing, and her lilting voice with all its charm . . . and these sounds will live forever in my memory as I join you in saying good-bye, for now, to your dear friend and mine."

Connie Weeks, whom Susan roomed with in Boston after college, mentioned a similar lingering impression of Susan, that of her radiant smile: "Each time I reunited with Susan, there it was! A reassurance that beauty of spirit and love of life was an unwavering constant with her." She described how that love of life was expressed through Susan's many artistic interests and talents and recalled how in awe she had been of Susan's sophistication when they were young working girls living in an apartment together. She cited a humorous episode in which Susan introduced her to gourmet cooking, tactfully trying to teach her that meatloaf isn't appropriate for a dinner party. "To this day," smiled Connie, "moussaka will always evoke memories of Susan."

Carol Even, whom Susan had become friends with in Reston, Virginia, when they were neighbors and young mothers, echoed this sentiment: "Susan once made a lemon soufflé that I can still taste as I remember it. She was a memorable cook." Carol and Connie and other friends who spoke were all quick to point out that Susan used these talents not to impress her friends but to express her love for them. Carol described Susan's dinners as being "works of art that you felt had been created just for you."

The same themes sounded through all the speeches by Susan's friends: Susan as talented and generous, Susan as a true-blue friend,

Susan as beautiful and sophisticated but also fun and down-to-earth. Lister Bradley, one of the women in a close-knit group of tennis-playing friends Susan had been part of since moving to Baltimore, mentioned how the group had gone to see the movie *Steel Magnolias* together and went on to say, "Susan was the 'magnolia,' who represented the epitome of culture and refinement—not in a remote way but in terms of living everyday life with a style Martha Stewart would envy." But the most prominent theme was Susan's maternal devotion, which every speaker dwelled on. Carol described the sleepless cribside vigil Susan maintained when Jonathan as an infant developed a serious staph infection and had to be hospitalized for a week. Both Terry and Connie characterized Susan's phone conversations with them as being filled with talk about her sons. "She was their greatest fan," said Terry. "They were her best friends," said Connie, "and she always stressed the fun she had with them. Her greatest joy and priority was motherhood. She would catch up with me in terms of Jonathan's and Nicholas's accomplishments and interests well before she would share her own interests, such as her lampshade business." Lister recalled with a smile the way Susan would entertain their tennis group with stories about "her two perfect sons. We enjoyed following Nicholas and Jonathan through Gilman and into college—and if we were skeptical at all in the beginning, we soon realized that she was not bragging; she was just being truthful. She showed us with pride and obvious love her display of Mother's Day cards they had made for her over the years. Her gifts to them, in turn, were creative expressions of her love. . . . Nothing was too much trouble to do for her boys. Any of the rest of us would have been overwhelmed to have the whole lacrosse team drop in for two or three days, but not Susan. She delighted in that sort of thing."

As eulogistic speech after speech brought Susan vividly back to me, I found myself experiencing the old inadequacy compared to her that I had so often felt as a child. I was therefore in an appropriate state of mind when it came time to give my own speech, which was intended to present a younger sister's perspective on Susan. As Bill had done, I began with my earliest distinct memory of Susan, from when I was around four or five and she was around nine or ten. I had been playing with my little brothers all morning in the back-yard when my mother called us in to lunch. We scrambled into the house, little ruffians full of high spirits. At that same moment, Susan walked into the kitchen—these were the days when mothers didn't work and schoolchildren came home for lunch—and my exuberance was suddenly checked when I registered the difference between my big sister and me. Susan, with her neat blond pigtails, her feminine blue dress, her clean fingernails, and the enviable drawing of a duck—with all the crayon coloring *inside* the lines—she had done that morning in school, formed a sharp contrast to me, with my unkempt reddish hair, dirty fingernails, and mud-stained overalls and with no morning's artistic achievement to show off. I felt ashamed and inferior; I wanted to be like Susan, and I made this my goal. But with the shortsightedness of a child, I had forgotten this plan by the next morning and that day at lunch was once again chagrined by the contrast between my appearance and Susan's. It was this incident, or so my memory tells me, that launched my lifelong awe of my big sister's beauty and talent.

I moved on to describe how, although I was sometimes jealous of Susan as a child, I was also grateful to her because I was often the beneficiary of her artistic talents: the clothes she sewed me, sweaters she knit me, haircuts she gave me, parties she planned for me, birth-day cakes she baked me, song-and-dance routines she taught me. I concluded my talk with a list of the things I would miss about Susan: "Not a day goes by that I don't come across something Susan made for me or that I don't think of something funny I would like to share with her, in the way only sisters can do. Not an Easter will pass that I won't hear her laughingly recounting to me the time when I was about three and I begged her to dress me up so that I could 'go Easter.' Not a Thanksgiving will pass that I won't watch my daughter making stuffed dates—a Hurley family tradition—and see Susan and me performing this same ritual when we were girls. Not a Christmas will pass that I won't watch the film *White Christmas* and picture Susan and me as kids imitating the famous 'Sisters, Sisters' song-and-dance routine from that movie. No, not a day, not a season, not a holiday will pass that I won't continue to miss my sister,

Susan." It took me three attempts before I could complete that last sentence without breaking down.

When the talks by Susan's friends and siblings were finished, it was time for her sons' perspectives. Everyone knew that these testimonies would be the emotional high point of the service. A hush fell over the audience as Jonathan, lanky and handsome and looking every bit the product of this refined setting, walked to the podium, swallowed hard, and launched into a lengthy "letter" to his mother, a brilliant piece in which he recalled, in graceful prose, the fiercely devoted mother Susan had been. His recollections, of which the following is an example, were both moving and humorous: "I remember other things, like telling you, no matter what, never, ever run down onto the field if you think that I'm hurt, I don't care how bad it looks. I told you that it's not cool for a guy to have his mother run down on the field in front of everybody and be treated like a little boy. I never told you how wonderful it felt to know that you would run down onto that field, in front of fans, teammates, and coaches, you didn't care who objected, yell at whoever had hit me, and then push past them all to see if I was all right." By the end of Jonathan's speech, the audience was emotionally drained, having been catapulted from laughter to tears and back several times. But more emotional intensity was to come. What Jonathan had done with words, his brother was to do with images, in the form of "A Video Memory by Nick."

Splicing together still photographs from Susan's childhood, excerpts from grainy family movies Tom had made when the children were small, and videotapes of extended family gatherings of more recent years, Nick had created a moving mosaic of his mother's life. Shortly after Jonathan concluded his talk, a movie screen was unscrolled at the front of the auditorium and the lights were dimmed. After several seconds, the silence was broken by the intoning of the plaintive lyric "Long ago it must be, I have a photograph / Preserve your memories, they're all that's left you," from Simon and Garfunkel's early album *Bookends*. Against this musical background there emerged on the screen the smiling face of seven- or eight-year-old Susan, a front tooth missing and her eyes shining in anticipation—

I think it was a clip from one of the family portraits we used to have taken every Christmas Eve by a photographer friend of my parents. Immediately the sobs and sniffles started up again.

They did not let up for the duration of the video, as we watched Susan being transformed from wide-eyed child to self-conscious teenager to stylish young woman to blissful new mother, and so on. Nick, as skilled with his medium as his brother was with words, accompanied the various visuals with related audios, excerpts from popular music his mother had loved. For example, in a home-movie clip of Susan building sandcastles on the beach with toddler Jonathan, the Crosby, Stills, and Nash song "Teach Your Children Well" played in the background. For me, some of the most wrenching clips were of family gatherings at my parents' home in the early 1980s, particularly the video of Thanksgiving 1983, the last time all of us had been together. As the camcorder's eye roamed about the living room, capturing shifting configurations of family members and generations in the midst of various activities—a toast being raised, a joke being shared, a child being tossed in the air by an uncle, my mother waving us all into the dining room for dinner—I experienced a sharp sense of loss. The scene brought to mind James Joyce's story "The Dead," in which the protagonist, attending his spinster aunts' annual Christmastime gala in Dublin, finds himself dwelling on the ephemeral nature of the occasion and on the mortality of all those laughing, drinking, flush-with-life revelers who are "[o]ne by one . . . all becoming shades":[1] less than two years later my father would be dead, followed by my mother in another four years, and then Susan in another five. I longed to step into the time frame of the video clip and re-experience that moment, this time fully alive to its preciousness.

The last segment of the video, portraying Susan's final years, had no doubt been the hardest for Nick to put together, for many of the photos and clips of that period hint at the dark, troubled turn Susan's life had taken, especially those in which her face appears swollen and she seems to be hiding behind sunglasses. But Nick wanted an honest portrait and so included some of these, along with pictures of Susan in the rare happy moments of her last few years—working in her garden, laughing with her sons, playing with her dog. The cumulative effect was a portrait of his mother in all her complexity: a troubled soul but one in whom there still burned a love of life and a gracious spirit, one who could have given so much to the world and could have enjoyed the world so much more if only she had believed in herself. The final image that filled the screen was a color photo of Susan's head and shoulders, taken by Jonathan in her garden a year or so before she disappeared. In it she is smiling, and her green-brown eyes are squinting in the sunlight. Except for a trace of sadness, they are the same shining eyes seen in the video's opening childhood photo. As this concluding image lingered on the screen in the dark, hushed room, Ted Jackson, the soloist who had performed a number of hymns and songs during the service, sang a haunting rendition of "When Irish Eyes Are Smiling." By the time he was finished, there was not a dry eye in the house.

The lights came on, and there was a moment or two of silence while everyone tried to regain their emotional composure. Then the audience began to rouse themselves, and the stricken looks on faces were gradually replaced by sociable smiles as acquaintances spotted and greeted one another. Someone—it must have been Jonathan or Bill—went to the front of the auditorium and reminded the guests that they were all invited back to the Owsleys' home for food and drink, and immediately the atmosphere of the room lightened—a phenomenon I've often observed following funerals and memorial services. It's as though the reminder of our mortality has the effect of making us want to immerse ourselves in the pleasures of living; hence, the intense need for a party.

And what a party it was! It was just what Susan would have loved: a garden party on an idyllic June afternoon, with a canopy set up in Tom's backyard, waiters circulating with trays of fancy hors d'oeuvres, and a bartender dispensing drinks from a well-stocked bar. I kept having moments of déjà vu as friends from various stages of Susan's life swirled about me. I felt like I was back at Susan's wedding to Tom or at one of the many dinner parties I'd attended at her home over the years. The only thing missing in this hubbub of talk and laughter was . . . Susan. Her absence felt palpable, and I'm sure I was not the only one to experience this sensation. I kept expecting her to waltz around the corner, wearing a wide-brimmed garden hat and a floaty dress, making me feel suddenly conscious of the shortcomings or inappropriateness of my own outfit. How I longed to experience that sibling envy again! As much as I used to resent her social superiority, how strange and sad it was not to have her in charge at an occasion like this.

To a passerby, the gathering in the Owsleys' backyard that afternoon probably appeared to be some kind of typical celebration of the season, a wedding reception, perhaps, or a graduation party. But a closer look would have revealed unusual goings-on at it: the presence of reporters, mingling with guests and gathering material for articles that would appear in the *Baltimore Sun* and *Baltimore Magazine;* a police detective hovering near the front door, dressed in plain clothes, with his gun artfully concealed (in case Jim Harrison showed up drunk and insisted on coming in); and, toward the close of the reception, a conference in the master bedroom between family members and investigators. But despite these reminders of the dark underside to the occasion, the memorial service and reception had accomplished what we had hoped they would: people who loved Susan had come together to remember her and to celebrate her spirit.

Tom and Susan at the Hurley family home in
Taunton, Massachusetts, Christmas 1970.
Photo by Stu Frazier.

Susan holding Jonathan in his christening
dress, with Susan's maternal grandmother and
mother, Christmas 1970. Photo by Stu Frazier.

Celebrating the Hurley parents' fortieth wedding anniversary, December 31, 1976. *Back row, left to right:* Mom, Dad, Jessica (Bill's older daughter), Bill. *Front row, left to right:* John, Bob, Susan, Molly.

Susan with Jonathan *(left)* and Nicholas *(right),* ca. 1980

Left to right: Tom, Nicholas, Jonathan, Susan, April 1983

Susan, with a broken arm, and Jim, Washington, D.C., spring 1986

The five Hurley children at the dedication of the Mary L. and William T. Hurley Jr. Library at the Taunton Historical Society, December 1990. *Left to right:* Bob, Susan, Bill, Molly, John (the portrait on the wall behind Molly is of their mother; a portrait of their father hangs on the opposite wall). Photo by family friend and photographer Herb Borden. It was a copy of this photo, along with others taken on this occasion, that Jim allegedly destroyed in a rage.

Susan at the house she shared with Jim in Lutherville, Maryland, early 1990s. Photo possibly taken by Jim.

Also accused me of drinking Sat. Feb 23, 1991
alcohol in my Piña Colada which
he knew was not true

Cheeca Lodge
Islamorada, Florida Keys

He also twists every thing I say and fabricates
like mad.

1) forces me to perform a sex
act which I clearly did not want to
— I begged twice - no, no - no, no.
C a form of spousal rape

2) Insisted we watch female bimbos
(Miss USA) afterword — something
that would insult anyones intelligence
He also called me a slimey ugly whore

3) a) would not let me have trunk
key to get my clubs — said I would
steal the car

b) told me he had plans for entire
3 days - race track, fishing etc — abvious
lies

c) told me to get out — go to Miami
- wait for a plane until I could get on
but that he would not help me — I had
$50 and had to beg for money — finally throw
$100 at me for whole trip home —

→ all meant to render his power
over me and the situation — very sick
and very crude and ungentlemanly.

P.O. BOX 527 • Islamorada, FL 33036 • TEL: 305 • 664 • 4651

Early Sun. Morn, Feb 24, 1991
Came home very drunk — driven
home by a security guard who
found him passed out under a tree.
I saw him drinking beer at Woodes
thru a window
with his back against the bar.
He appeared already be on his way
s and the fact that he had broken
the sobriety pact that we had really
disgusted me so I took the beer
and poured it on him.

When he came home he called
a "fucking whore", "fucking whore"
"common whore", "sleezy slut"
unnumerable times — over and over
and over. Also he kept saying
"go Fuck yourself"

I really should remove myself
from this intolerable situation once
and for all

Notes written by Susan that we found in the fall of 1994 when we cleaned out her
cottage after she disappeared

Nov 16, 1991

Dear Jim
First of all, I love you very, very much
I am sorry at my drunken behavior on Sunday
Nov 10, 1991.
Even though I was so angry with you,
I do not, in any way, think it was an excuse
for what I did consuming so much alcohol
and crazily escalating the problem.
Here is what I did:
I started talking to a black fellow in a bar
where you and I had an argument during dinn
about 10 pm. You left me there

and he drove me home — it was 3 am.
I am writing this of my own free will — I am mort
bied and sorry.
Love, Susan

Parts of a "confession" letter Jim allegedly forced Susan to
write in 1991 that we found among her possessions when
cleaning out her cottage after she disappeared

Nov 27, 1991

Dear Tom, Nichols and
              Jonathan.

Jim forced me to sign
and write a trumped up confession to something I did not
do. upon the threat of breaking
my other arm. If that is found
please don't believe it and
please destroy it. You all
know me better that that –
he is a very deranged man.
The "confession" is dated
Nov 16 or 17, 1991.

           Love
           Mom

Susan's disclaimer note to Tom, Jonathan, and Nicholas concerning the "confession" Jim allegedly forced her to write. This note was also found in her cottage when we cleaned it out.

Susan, ca. 1992. This is the photo that was
widely circulated on missing person flyers
and in newspaper and television coverage.

Susan with Jonathan *(left)* and Nicholas *(right)* at Middlebury
College, Vermont, ca. 1993

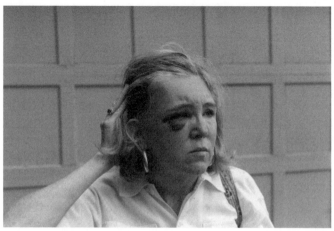

Susan after alleged battering by Jim, July 1993. Photo by
Jonathan Owsley.

> I Susan H. Harrison
> being of sound mind & battered
> body leave my entire estate
> and all personal possessions
> to my two sons Jonathan
> Hawkes Owsley & Nicholas
> Barrett Owsley. I appoint
> William Thomas Hurley II, &
> Jonathan Hawkes Owsley as
> my executors.
>   July 27, 1993
>   Susan H. Harrison
>
> witness
> _____
> Hazel K. White 7/27/93

Susan's impromptu will written after the alleged battery,
July 1993

> 8/6
> 12:00 am
>
> Mom—
>
> I waited and waited
> for you. I couldn't
> sleep so I went to
> Dad's. Call me
> when you get in —
> anytime!
>
> love
> Nick

The note Nicholas left for Susan the night she disappeared

P.O. Box 23713
Baltimore,
Maryland 21203

Phone 727-4144
24-HOUR HOTLINE:
276-8888

REWARD: MISSING PERSON

SUSAN HURLEY HARRISON

Susan is a white female, 52 years old. She is 5'6" tall and weighs approximately 115 lbs. She was last seen August 5th in the Towson/Timonium area. She is driving the following car, which we are also seeking to find:

1992 SAAB, 2 door sedan, GREEN in color, CONVERTIBLE
MD Tags: 043 AVF

If you have <u>any</u> information regarding this case, call **METRO CRIME STOPPERS 24 HOUR HOTLINE AT 276-8888.** The tip you provide could make you eligible to receive a
CASH REWARD of up to $6,000
YOU DO NOT NEED TO GIVE YOUR NAME. We are also willing to pay for information leading to the recovery of the missing car, as it may provide clues to help find Susan. Outside the Baltimore area, call our toll-free number 1-800-281-6666.

A copy of one of the missing person flyers that were posted throughout Baltimore County shortly after Susan's disappearance, August 1994

The billboard the Hurley and Owsley families had put up at the Timonium Road exit off Interstate 83 in Baltimore County following Susan's
disappearance, 1994

Susan's brother Bill walking away from the site where Susan's remains
were found in Frederick County, Maryland, December 1996. Photo by
John Hurley.

St. Paul's Rectory
147 NORTH STREET
HINGHAM. MASSACHUSETTS 02043

January 13th, 1997

Dear Mr. Hurley:

This "strange" postcard was received here this morning. I'm forwarding it to you because I don't know what to make of it.

Evelyn
(Fr. R's secretary)

UNITED NATIONS
INTERNATIONAL YEAR OF THE CHILD
31c

TO: The Susan Harrison Family & Friends
C/o ST. Paul's Church
Hingham, MASSACHUSETTS
02043

From: WASHington D.C. Bill Clinton, Newt Gingerich etc;
Well Susan guess GOD couldn't WAIT, needed ya
Help now!! Ya Ya always bragged about N.Y. N.Y!!
but Loved Boston also The Same Jonathan, Nicholas
+ Robert, Wild Bill, + OF Course Mary Moran From GA!!
Ya was always a "SHady Lady!!" with "Fine ArTs!!"
Every Time we GoTo The MeSeum (Boston) we See Ya
Works & How ya Cured Every Thing!! Luv Ya From US+A
Funded By: Paul Revere Brady VIII

The strange postcard sent to the Hurley family ten days after
Susan's funeral, January 1997. A handwriting analyst concluded
that the handwriting was Jim Harrison's.

16 Unsolved Mysteries and Other Desperate Measures, Summer 1995–Autumn 1996

The purpose of the meeting in the master bedroom toward the end of the memorial service reception was for the family to be updated on the investigation. Although there was nothing concrete to report, certain developments in Jim's behavior had given the police an idea for a new strategy to pursue.

Detective Ramsey informed us that Jim's habit of showing up drunk at social or business events and making a spectacle of himself had in recent months taken a more outrageous turn, resulting in run-ins with the law. In March, he had appeared at a cocktail and dinner reception to open the golf season at the Green Spring Valley Hunt Club and, red-faced and unsteady, had begun picking an argument with one of the guests. His combativeness escalating, he was ejected by the club's manager. He left the club and began walking home, stumbling along the road and causing cars to have to swerve to avoid hitting him. A policeman came to his aid, but Jim took offense and got into a physical altercation with him, culminating in Jim's arrest for disorderly intoxication and for assault and battery on an officer. At the Garrison precinct, where he was taken and handcuffed, he yelled "Fuck you" over forty-five times in succession (the rest of the prisoners and other officers started to count). A similar incident occurred in June, when Jim showed up at a Maryland Bar Association meeting in Ocean City. Maneuvering his car out of the hotel parking lot afterward, he bumped into a parked truck and was arrested for driving while intoxicated. The arresting officer claimed Jim had slapped him and offered him a bribe. Jim denied these acts. Trials were scheduled for both of these indictments—the March one and the June one—for the following autumn.[1]

It was these run-ins of Jim's, Detective Ramsey said, that had given the investigative team their idea for the new strategy. Their thinking was that if Jim was eventually convicted of one of these charges and given a jail sentence, he would be forced to dry out while incarcerated; without the crutch of alcohol, he might well be more vulnerable to their attempts to work on his conscience and get him to confess. Even if he were not charged in either of these two recent cases, there was a good chance—given his reckless, drunken tendencies—that sooner or later he would land himself in jail and the police would be able to carry out their plan.

This meeting left us encouraged, with renewed confidence in the police. We were also re-inspired to press on with our efforts to keep the case before the public, for Ramsey had stressed once again his conviction that media exposure is often the key to solving cases like ours. Two in-depth feature articles were, in fact, currently in the works at local publications, and we thought these might be the means of attracting the attention of the national media. Baltimore journalists Laura Lippman and Margaret Guroff had been working for months on articles for the *Baltimore Sun* and the *Baltimore Magazine,* respectively. They had researched the case extensively and conducted lengthy interviews with family members, the police, Jim, and others. With both women possessing excellent reputations as journalists, their articles were sure to have a big impact.

Laura Lippman's "The Mystery of Susan Harrison," which took up almost the entire "Today" section of the Sunday, August 20, edition of the *Baltimore Sun* (published two weeks after the one-year anniversary of Susan's disappearance), was an eloquent, sympathetic treatment of Susan's sad tale. Margaret Guroff's twelve-page "Susan's Choice" (a triple pun, with references to Susan and Jim's horse of this name, to the tragic novel *Sophie's Choice,* and to Susan's own tragic choice), published in the October edition of the *Baltimore Magazine,* was a provocative, warts-and-all portrait of Susan's life, of Susan and

Jim's marriage, and of "former golden boy" Jim Harrison's professional and psychological decline.

The ramifications of these articles were what we had hoped they would be: a stirring of national interest in the case. Well-known true-crime writer Ann Rule picked up on the *Baltimore Sun* article and e-mailed Laura Lippman with questions about the case; we were hopeful this meant she might decide to write a book about it. She didn't, but her interest was still encouraging, for it demonstrated that word about the case was spreading beyond the Baltimore region (Rule lives in Seattle). A producer with the television soft-news magazine *American Journal* also noticed the article and telephoned me to ask if the family would agree to be interviewed for a segment on that show. I consulted with my brothers and nephews, and we decided that the national exposure the show would give to Susan's disappearance would be worth the sensationalism the producers would probably clothe the story in. We agreed to the interview, and I flew to Massachusetts in early September for the taping, which was done at Bill's house. The segment was scheduled to be aired toward the end of the month, but it kept getting bumped to make room for late-breaking developments in—ironically—the O. J. Simpson trial. It was finally aired in mid-October. Much to our disappointment, though, many of the facts and pleas we tried to include, which we hoped might trigger someone's memory or prick someone's conscience, were edited out. The *American Journal* segment thus did not result in any call-ins to the Baltimore County police, as we'd hoped would be the case; however, we consoled ourselves with the thought that this show might be the stepping-stone to others that were more focused on solving crimes.

For the previous year, I had been making sporadic attempts to interest producers and reporters of such programs, but they had continually put me off. *Prime Time Live*'s Jay Schadler thought that if I could come up with a unique angle or slant on the situation, he might be able to convince the show's executives to do a story on it. I was never able to think of a satisfactory hook, though. *America's Most Wanted* strung me along for months, telling me they ordinarily didn't air missing person cases or feature crimes that lacked a fugitive but that sometimes they did, and so they would keep my proposal on file. Every time I'd watch the show and see a case covered that was similar to ours, especially if it contained less evidence or was less compelling, I'd phone them and ask why they had chosen that story instead of ours. Some of their explanations were maddening. For example, the reason they gave for airing one particular missing person case rather than Susan's was that the victim was a child—the implication being, I thought, that because Susan was an adult, her disappearance and her family's grief were less significant. Eventually, I wrote a personal plea to John Walsh, the show's founder, appealing to him as a fellow sufferer (as is well known, his child was kidnapped and murdered about twenty years ago), but I never received a response.

Unsolved Mysteries, though, did finally respond after I sent them a tape of the *American Journal* segment in the late fall. They told me they would assign the case to a team of researchers who would determine whether there was enough evidence to do a story on it. Shortly after the new year began, I was informed that they had made a positive determination. I was ecstatic: having the case featured on this well-known show, which has a high success rate for solving crimes, vastly improved the chances that someone somewhere who knew or had seen something critical would step forward. This would especially be true if Susan's body had been disposed of in another part of the country. Now I had a new project to preoccupy me and give me hope.

Throughout the winter and spring of 1996, I was involved with the development of the *Unsolved Mysteries* piece. It was fascinating to observe the elaborate behind-the-scenes work that goes into creating such a show. First, lengthy phone interviews were conducted with most of the family members and other principals involved in the case; this took a couple of months. Then in early spring, my brothers and nephews and I all had to fly to Baltimore for the group interview with the East Coast producer, who would be coming in from New York. As we sat in Tom's living room awaiting this man's arrival, I was half-expecting someone like Robert Stack, clad in a trench coat and emitting an ominous aura, to appear; I was taken aback when Eric Taylor, an affable aging-hippie type, bounded up the front steps, wearing sneakers and jeans—the first of the many times I would find myself revising the stereotype I'd had of this show. Eric interviewed us for several hours, asking detailed questions about every aspect of Susan's life, including her childhood, her marriages to Tom and to Jim, our family background, and the ages of all of Susan's siblings and children. Out of all this material, he explained, the writers would fashion the story line.

The next step was the on-camera interviews and the filming of the dramatized reenactment scenes. This stage of the production took place during the first couple of weeks of May and was a complicated, multi-pronged affair. The show's producers rented a posh country estate in Baltimore County to serve as the crew's on-site headquarters and as the setting for some of the taped interviews. During the first week, the crew held auditions with local actors for the roles of the main characters in the reenactments: Susan, Jim, Jonathan, Nicholas at age twelve (for a flashback scene), and Nicholas at age nineteen (the age he was when Susan disappeared). They also scouted out and then rented houses to serve as Susan's and Jim's in the dramatization scenes, paying the owners handsome fees for the inconvenience of vacating their homes for a week.

The taping sessions were staggered throughout the second week. I flew in just for the day of my interview, renting a car at the airport and driving out to the sumptuous estate where the taping would be done. Seated in an elegant wingback chair in a parlor that looked like something out of a Merchant Ivory set, I was once again struck by the foreign worlds the Susan case had caused me to enter. To think that a few years earlier I had scoffed at *Unsolved Mysteries,* assuming that the kind of people who appeared on it were kooks or those who liked to sensationalize their lives. Not only was I now intimately involved with *Unsolved Mysteries,* but I had a new-found appreciation of the show and an empathy with the people who turned to it for help. As I looked intently into the camera during my interview, I willed that I was making contact with a viewer who held the key to the mystery of my sister's whereabouts.

Although an actor had been hired to play Jim in most of the reenactment scenes, the director had asked Jim if he himself would participate in the reenactment of his alleged boarding of the Light

Rail the day after Susan disappeared (this portion of the script was cut from the final version, however). He agreed to do so. The day after this scene was filmed, Eric Taylor called me to describe something strange that Jim had done. While the camera crew were setting up the equipment for the shooting, Jim suddenly walked onto the train tracks and sat down. Eric hollered, "Jim, what are you doing? Get up." But Jim remained where he was. A train was suddenly heard approaching, and people began shouting at him to get off the tracks. Finally, as crew members hastened toward him, he stood up and walked off. Hearing Eric's description of this incident, I felt a fluttering of hope that maybe Jim's guilt was making him suicidal, and if this were the case, perhaps he would be more amenable to the efforts of the police to get him to confess. More likely, though, I thought, was that it was another instance of his play-acting, trying to manipulate people into believing either he was a grief-stricken, suicidal husband or he was insane and hence could not be charged with murder if Susan's body was ever found.

With the East Coast part of the show's taping completed, the family had no further active role in the production. It was now just a matter of waiting for the airing, which was initially scheduled for September. We were impatient for this to happen: more and more we were pinning our hopes on *Unsolved Mysteries,* because the police investigation seemed to be stalled. The police often tried to assure us that they were working on leads and strategies they couldn't tell us about; we wanted to believe they were doing all sorts of smart, savvy things behind our backs and were harboring important secret information, but whenever they finally would tell us what they had been working on, it would be because that lead had turned out to be a dead end, and so we had grown skeptical of their claims. Perhaps the prototype of the kinds of false pursuits the police team engaged in was their first one, which occurred early in the investigation. They thought they had discovered dried blood on the floor of the family room when they had done the search of Jim's house, and they therefore took scrapings and sent them to a lab for DNA analysis. In order to determine if this was Susan's blood, they would need to know her DNA; they did not have that information, but they found out that her DNA could be inferred from that of several of her blood relatives. The police therefore had Jonathan, Nicholas, my brother John, and I all have blood drawn while we were in Baltimore during Thanksgiving weekend 1994. Squeamish though some of us were about this procedure, we gladly went through with it, thinking it might lead to the cracking of the case. But, we learned a few weeks later, the procedure had been in vain: it turned out that the "dried blood" the police had scraped from Jim's floor was dried red paint that had been spilled there.

The one current strategy the police had seen fit to share with us—the plan to work on Jim's conscience if he was incarcerated and deprived of alcohol—seemed to be doomed to failure since it didn't look as if Jim was ever going to be sentenced to jail. The trials for his two drunken assaults on officers had been delayed and delayed and ultimately resulted in a mere slap on the wrist: probation and required participation in an outpatient alcohol treatment program at Shepherd Pratt Hospital, a requirement that was only loosely enforced, as it turned out. Jim had hired an aggressive defense lawyer named Steve Allen who argued that the incidents were "an aberration" in "a distinguished career" and cited Jim's "former position as a top executive of McCormick and his service on many volunteer boards." Jim himself pleaded "to be allowed to continue helping people and to continue searching for his wife."[2] When I read this account in the newspaper, I couldn't help but mutter sarcastically to myself, "Yeah, right, you *really* care about other people and you've been making a *real* effort to find your wife." I also couldn't help but be reminded of O. J. Simpson's claim during his defense trial that he wanted to be acquitted and freed so that he could devote his time to finding his wife's killer. And a further parallel with O. J. occurred to me: I was certain that if Jim were just an ordinary Joe rather than a bigwig with wealth and influence, he would have had to pay the consequences for his unlawful behavior. But Jim appeared to be immune to the law: although he continued to drink, thus breaking the terms of his probation, and to become intoxicated and combative, he was never incarcerated for these infractions.

So discouraged had we become about the possibility that the case would be solved by the police that we had begun to revisit an idea that had come up in one of our early brainstorming sessions: the possibility of hiring an undercover agent to befriend Jim and elicit confidences from him. Over the summer of 1996, we discussed and honed this plan. At first we thought we would hire an attractive woman for the role, but then we decided that the sexual elements of the situation might complicate things, so we turned instead to the idea of hiring a man, a male confidante, reasoning that Jim had few friends and was always trying to get reporters and cops who interviewed him to go drinking with him. Further refining the plan, we decided the agent would pose as an author writing a book about Susan's disappearance and wanting to hear Jim's side of the story; in this capacity, the "author" would become sympathetic to Jim and gain Jim's trust, thereby eventually eliciting the truth about Susan's disappearance. As we explored this plan in greater depth, we realized it would make sense to hire an actual author, who really would be writing a book about the case. That way, if Jim or his family members became suspicious and looked into the man's credentials, there would be no problem. Also, the author would have a double incentive in taking the job: he would not only be paid by us for the operative work but would also make money eventually off the book if it were published. With the plan finalized, we began the process of researching potential author-operatives.

By the fall of 1996, then, having pretty much given up on the police, we were pinning our hopes on a positive outcome either to our operative plan or to the airing of the case on *Unsolved Mysteries*. The original date scheduled for the latter had been moved back a couple of times, but we were finally given a firm date of November 8. As that day grew closer, I braced myself for the weird sensation I knew I would experience watching my family's private tragedy being played out before a national audience. This happened sooner than I'd expected, though. I hadn't realized that *Unsolved Mysteries* does promos, and so I was taken aback the night of November 7 when, turning on the television just before the start of *Seinfeld* at 9:00, I was suddenly confronted with my sister's familiar face on the screen, incongruously accompanied by the otherworldly voice of Robert Stack intoning, "Two young men are desperately searching for their mother and need your help. . . ." The promo was run throughout the day on Friday, and every time I saw it, particularly when I was in a public place—

picking up clothes at the cleaners, running on the treadmill at the gym—I was jolted anew.

When the show finally aired that night, I watched it with riveted attention, bringing to bear all my training in literary and rhetorical analysis to try to determine whether the presentation would be likely to have the effect on viewers that we wanted. I cringed at some of the show's distortions of the facts, such as the statement that Susan had grown up in a "wealthy" family and the selection of a platinum-blond to play her, but I also realized that ingredients like these probably attracted viewers' attention and thus hooked them into watching the segment, which of course is what we wanted: the wider the audience, the greater the chance that there was someone in it who could help us. The reenactments were very faithful to the truth, and I was pleased with the scenes they chose to dramatize, such as Nick's childhood witnessing of Jim's shaking Susan when she tried to escape with her lampshades, and Susan and Jim's drinking and arguing in Jim's family room on the night of her disappearance. All told, the show did an effective job of presenting Susan as an abused woman, which would make audiences sympathetic to her and hence more willing to help us find her, I thought. It also clearly spelled out the facts about Susan's disappearance and presented ingredients that might jog viewers' memories, such as photos of her car, a description of the clothes Susan was wearing the day she disappeared, and several pictures of Jim as well as the interview with him. The segment ended with Robert Stack's delineating what we wanted viewers to ransack their memories for and what number they should call if they had any information.

The show over, I immediately got on the phone with various family members to compare our reactions. But none of us wanted to stay on the phone for too long: we wanted to keep our lines open in case the police tried to reach us with news of a promising call-in. Alas, we waited in vain all weekend. On Monday, I called Judy Storch, a producer at *Unsolved Mysteries* with whom I had developed a telephone friendship during the lengthy period that our segment was in production. She explained that, as usually happens with the segments they air, there were numerous call-ins concerning our case for the first twenty-four hours following the show, but only a couple of these had seemed worthy of passing on to the police (the staff at *Unsolved Mysteries* does the initial screening; they can tell from experience which calls are probably hoaxes or otherwise not worth pursuing). If the police considered them promising leads, they would notify the family. But, she assured me, although the call-ins slow to a trickle after the first few days, many times there is a delayed reaction and a crucial call comes in a week or more later. Plus, she reminded me, the show would be rerun on their network in about six months—maybe sooner if a new development occurred—and then would continue to be rerun on the network that had bought the rights to the old shows.

I tried to take her reassurances to heart, but I was terribly let down, increasingly so as the first week with no leads bled into the second and then into the third. In the fourth week, though, something happened. But it was not the result of *Unsolved Mysteries*.

17 The Search Ends, November 1996–January 1997

*T*hanksgiving 1996, like the previous two Thanksgivings and all the other family holidays since my sister's disappearance, was for me a sad day. This one was particularly depressing, because a major hope— that the *Unsolved Mysteries* feature would yield a break in the case— had been dashed: three weeks had passed since the airing of the segment, and not one solid lead had been phoned in.

The other major hope, concerning the use of an operative, had also dimmed in my estimation. Our research had yielded the names of a few retired journalists who might possibly be interested in doing a book about the case and who seemed as though they might possibly be the kind of men Jim would be inclined to "buddy up" to, but the obstacles to hiring any of them struck me as being overwhelming. First, feelers would need to be put out to try to determine what each man's reaction might be; obviously, we didn't want to propose the scheme to someone who would react with alarm or indignation and maybe blow the whistle on us. Then we would need to figure out how to approach those we thought might be amenable to the proposal. The more I thought about the whole idea, the more discouraged I became: I couldn't imagine that a reputable writer, with no prior spy experience, would want to take on such a job.

In this pessimistic state of mind, I made my usual beginning-of-the-week phone calls the Monday after the holiday to check with various family members as to whether there had been any new developments—a vain gesture, I always knew, since they of course would have notified me if anything important had occurred. As I'd expected, there was nothing to report. There had been one false hope, though, that Tom told me about in my call to him. In perusing the Sunday *Baltimore Sun,* he had come across an item in the state news section that caught his eye, a brief article about the discovery of an unidentified woman's skeleton in Frederick County. He'd immediately telephoned Carey Deeley to ask him to look into it, but when Carey did so, he learned from Frederick County police that the skeleton appeared to be that of a woman about five-foot-two-inches tall and in her thirties—considerably shorter and younger than Susan. By now we had become used to such false leads: on three or four previous occasions, we'd had our hopes raised by news of unidentified female skeletons' being discovered within a day's drive of Baltimore—the most recent discovery occurring the previous summer in southern Pennsylvania—but the autopsies always yielded negative results. So, said Tom, there were no new developments to report.

The week proceeded uneventfully. I finished up my semester's teaching on Wednesday, December 4, and planned to treat myself to a restful day on Thursday, the university's reading day before the start of final exams. I awoke early that morning, looking forward to my free day, when suddenly the phone rang. Within seconds, my world had turned upside down.

The call was from my brother Bill. Almost before the words were out of his mouth, I knew, by his tone, why he was calling. He spoke the grim sentence I had been both dreading and wanting to hear for twenty-eight months: "They found Susan." Immediately my heart began pounding and my lips began trembling, so much so that I could not speak. My husband, sensing what the message was, sat up in bed and took my hand. In a broken voice, Bill went on to explain how she had been discovered, but I could make no sense of what he was saying. Random words flew out at me—"hikers," "hunters," "skeletal remains," "wild animals"—each one like the lash of a whip. The early graphic images associated with Susan's disappearance that I had gradually replaced with abstractions over the past twenty-eight months bombarded me anew. My beautiful, vibrant sister was now nothing but a scattering of bones and some shreds of clothing! "Nooooo!" I moaned and began sobbing uncontrollably.

Bill waited until my crying had subsided and then asked me if I'd rather not hear the whole story right now. I said that no, I wanted the facts. So he began his account again. Late in the afternoon on the previous Friday, the day after Thanksgiving, two young men who were amateur paleontologists were hiking in a densely wooded area near Wolfsville, a small Catoctin Mountain town in Frederick County, about ten miles from Camp David and about fifty miles northwest of Baltimore. The men were looking for animal bones because they knew that this was an area where hunters often tossed the carcasses of deer, the flesh of which would be picked clean by wild animals and the bones left to decay. Suddenly the men stumbled upon a skeleton partially hidden beneath some brush. At first they thought it was an animal's skeleton, but when they looked more closely, they thought it might be a human's. They rushed to a nearby general store to phone police, who came out to the spot and immediately identified the remains as human.

It was the same discovery that Tom had read about in the paper. Although at first the police had thought the skeleton to be that of a short woman in her thirties, closer examination suggested an older, taller woman. They therefore contacted Baltimore County police to request a copy of Susan's dental records. Late yesterday afternoon, Bill said, a positive identification had been made. He received word around midnight; he had called me but I didn't answer, so he'd left a message for me to call him first thing this morning. (I hadn't heard the bedroom phone ring—it was turned to low—and the answering machine is on the first floor, so I wasn't aware that a message had been left on it.) The police told Bill that they had already gone out to Jim's house to inform him, but they planned to question him at length the next day, as well as to drive him out to the spot where Susan had been found. They were hoping that the shock of seeing the place where, they suspected, Jim had disposed of her body would cause him to break down and confess. News that the remains had been identified as Susan's had not yet been divulged to the press, Bill said, and the police wanted to hold off on publicity until they'd had a chance to work on Jim. I was therefore not to respond if any reporters contacted me that day to ask about a rumor they'd heard that Susan had been found.

I spent the day in grief-stricken shock, reeling at the thought of the utter finality of the situation. Although for more than two years

I had been certain Susan was dead, the lack of confirmation had kept that knowledge abstract; now I was having to deal with the reality that she was gone for good. But I also began to experience a feeling of excitement about the promising development in the investigation that this discovery had wrought: there was now a much greater chance that Jim would be charged. If he was indeed her killer, his conviction would mean that Susan's murder would be avenged and justice served; it would also mean we would learn, finally, what her last hours had been like. I waited eagerly to hear the outcome of the police officers' questioning of Jim and of his visit to the Wolfsville gravesite.

Bill called me the next morning to report that the hope that Jim might confess had not panned out. Jim had seemed stunned and sad when the police first informed him about the discovery of Susan's remains, saying things like "It's so horrible, it's so sad," but then he lapsed into his mantra about hoping and praying that she was still alive. When the police escorted him to Frederick County, he said that he and Susan used to drive up Route 70, toward that county, in the fall to view the foliage, but they had never been to Wolfsville. He said he couldn't imagine how she had gotten there; maybe she'd become "manic depressive" and driven there with a man who killed her. Then he added that the fact that her car had been driven to Washington National Airport made him think she planned to leave the country by herself or with another man.[1] It looked like he wasn't going to crack, said Bill, but at least the police now had physical evidence—Susan's remains—to work with and a whole new source for leads: people in the Wolfsville area who may have seen Jim there around the time Susan disappeared. Furthermore, the fact that Susan's body had apparently been dragged along the dirt for about seventy-five feet (this was the distance from the road to the spot where she was found) and then buried in a shallow grave strengthened the hypothesis that the excessive dirt Jim's cleaning woman had found in his bathroom may have been the result of these activities on Jim's part. If Jim was the murderer, Bill said, then after disposing of Susan's body, he probably jumped back into her car and drove to Frederick, about twenty minutes from Wolfsville, where he knew he could pick up Interstate 270. From there it was a clean sweep down to Washington National Airport, where he could abandon the car and travel anonymously via public transportation back to Baltimore and from there to Lutherville. The pieces seemed to be coming together nicely, and if the state medical examiner ruled the cause of death to be homicide, the case would no doubt be clinched.

Over the course of the next three days, Tom faxed me the various front-page articles that were appearing in the *Baltimore Sun* about the discovery. Halfway through the second paragraph of the first article, I had to stop reading, overcome suddenly by nausea and hysteria. The clinical description, in black and white print, was too much for me. "She's NOT some 'remains'!" I screamed. "She's my SISTER!" I eventually made my way through all of the articles, weeping copiously as I did so. They confirmed my worst fears: Susan had been abandoned in a forest, cruelly left exposed to the elements and to wild animals. While the rest of the family had been inside cozy houses eating and drinking during the subsequent Thanksgivings and Christmases—the holidays she had loved so much—she had been lying in the cold, rain, and snow, wearing nothing but a sleeveless shirt and shorts, being preyed on by wild animals. The recurring urge I'd had in the early days to place a warm blanket over her came back to me full force.

In graphic detail, one of the articles described the location of her skull, the arrangement of the bones, which suggested she had been left with her ankles crossed and her arms above her head, and the few remaining shreds of her clothing. These last details were especially poignant for me—a "piece of a nylon or silk blouse," "a tag with the size 'petite,'" and a "section of black underwear . . . found on a hip bone" the only testimony to the fashionable, elegant woman my sister had once been. Another wrenching detail included in the article was mention of the fact that there was now a covering of snow on the ground where Susan had lain: a heavy snow had fallen in western Maryland the day before, and it was causing a delay in the police examination of the gravesite. The article was accompanied by a photograph showing the wooded spot, covered with snowdrifts and cordoned off with yellow crime scene tape.[2] I couldn't help but be struck by the symbolism and irony of this setting, recalling the role snow played in so many emblematic scenes of Susan's life that I held in my memory: the howling snowstorm glimpsed through the window of her snug Connecticut cottage, suggesting to me at the time the safe haven she finally seemed to have found in life; the snowy evening I'd watched her ominously walk off into with Jim Harrison fifteen years later; the snowed-in nights she had braved out alone during her final winter, when she'd at last managed to take the courageous step of leaving Jim. And there also came to mind another symbolic snow scene, one from Susan's early childhood that she had dwelled on several times when she phoned me in her last, troubled years.

In these calls, she would often try to analyze the roots of the insecurity that caused her to be unable to leave Jim, and she always came back to what she saw as my mother's non-nurturing treatment of her when she was a child. One example she frequently cited was a memory of being cast out into the snow by my mother; specifically, she recalled that she had done something bad and her punishment was to stand out in the snow until my mother called her back inside. Tearfully, Susan would keen, "I was only a little girl, only about four years old, and she made me stay out in the cold. She made me feel like I had done something horrible. But how can a four-year-old have done something that bad?" Listening to this tale for what seemed to me the umpteenth time, I would grow impatient. I was certain that Susan's memory was exaggerating the situation; but even if it weren't, I thought it was counterproductive to dwell on such memories. A couple of times I lashed out at her, "Okay, Susan, so you had a terrible childhood. So did a lot of people, but they don't use it as an excuse. Get over it!" Now, gazing at the photograph of her final, forlorn resting place, I found the question of whether she had exaggerated the childhood incident and used it as an excuse to be beside the point. The real significance of this memory, it seemed to me, was that it revealed Susan's deep-seated emotional insecurity, her sense of herself as being metaphorically cast out into the cold and barred from the warmth that others inhabited.

When the snow had melted enough for the probe of the grave to continue, Tom and my brothers Bill and John, who flew down to Baltimore at the beginning of the following week, went out to the site with the police. They described the spot to me over the phone. (Thus far, I have not been able to summon up the emotional strength to visit it myself.) They said that near where Susan's skeleton had been found, there was a fallen tree that had apparently been blown over in a storm some time subsequent to the body's being left there. Tom pointed out that if the tree had gone down in the opposite direction, it would have covered Susan, and she would probably never have been discovered. I caught my breath at the thought of how near we had come to never finding her. Another observation their visit to the site yielded was how closely the area resembled the Bermuda psychic's prediction. The distance between the road and the gravesite, the way the hill sloped down from the road, the dense woods, the proximity of a stream—all these fit with the psychic's description of where she pictured Susan. Although I didn't really give any credence to the psychic's visions, this coincidence couldn't help but give me pause. Perhaps, I thought unrealistically, if we had taken the psychic more seriously and insisted the police search through every area matching her vision within a day's drive of Baltimore, Susan would have been found two years earlier, before her body was completely decomposed.

Given the current condition of Susan's remains, however, we knew there was a good chance the autopsy would not be able to determine the cause of death. The deputy chief medical examiner stated in a newspaper article about the autopsy that remains like Susan's, containing no soft tissue, are "the ultimate challenge" for forensic scientists.[3] And if the death was not ruled a homicide, we knew, there would be much less of a chance that Jim would be charged. We were therefore in a state of agitation while awaiting the ruling.

There being a backlog of autopsies for the state medical examiner's office to perform, it wasn't until December 20 that they issued their finding. Chief Medical Examiner John E. Smialek ruled the death a homicide, stating that Susan had died as the result of fractures caused by severe blows to the bone above one eye and to the back of her skull. She may have gone in and out of consciousness for some time before she died, he said. This fit the scenario we had imagined; the blows were of the kind—but greater in degree—that Jim had allegedly inflicted on Susan in the past, and the fading in and out of consciousness fit with reporter Frank Mann's theory that for awhile after Susan died, Jim probably thought she was merely sleeping. The possibility that Susan had been alive for some time after being knocked out increased Jim's culpability in our minds: it would mean that he had had time to call 911 and probably save her life. But saving his own reputation—if he called 911, he would be opening himself up for a battery charge—was, we suspected, more important to him than saving Susan's life. What a heartless, immoral coward, was all I could think.

As gruesome as the facts about Susan's manner of death were, we were thrilled by the news of the homicide ruling, for now Jim would be arrested, we assumed. At our family's first comprehensive meeting with authorities involved in the investigation, in the fall of 1994, we'd been told by Ann Brobst, assistant state's attorney for the Baltimore County judicial circuit, that if Susan's body were found and her death ruled a homicide, an arrest would in all probability occur. Detective Ramsey had frequently assured us this would be the case. And Lieutenant Bowerman, the criminal profiler, had conveyed this same message to Margaret Guroff in 1995 when she interviewed him for her *Baltimore Magazine* article. Guroff writes, "Police say that Susan's killer is better off revealing her whereabouts now. 'When that person is able to admit that they've done something, there's a huge sense of relief,' says Lieutenant Sam Bowerman. Besides, he reminds any guilty party who's reading, a cooperative killer might face a lighter sentence: 'Once we find the body, we won't be interested in your side of the story.'"[4] Not only had her body now been found and the death ruled a homicide, but the placement of her body in a remote spot further supported Bowerman's long-held theory that Susan's killer was someone close to her. This theory is explained in the 1995 *Towson Times* article:

> "We think we know what happened and why," says Baltimore County police Lt. Sam Bowerman. . . . "But we don't have Susan to prove it.
>
> "A thorough search of wooded areas, routes she may have traveled and places in which a body could have been concealed has revealed nothing," says Bowerman. He

is an FBI-trained criminal profiler who tries to identify the link between the victim and the attacker in unsolved cases.

"We don't believe it was a stranger type of thing," he says. "This was somebody who knew her and was associated with her. It was a thinking individual—you see some post-planning, after the crime was committed.

"A stranger doesn't need to cover his tracks. This was very, very, very personal. I don't believe somebody was hired.

"And I don't think this started out as something planned. I believe she became involved in a spontaneous type of incident with somebody she was very close to. Words were exchanged, words led to a physical altercation and, unfortunately, what started out as a dispute had fatal consequences for her.

"Then it became a matter of self-survival [for the killer]."[5]

Given the impression we had received that Jim would be arrested immediately if Susan's body were found in a hidden area and her death ruled a homicide, we were surprised and disappointed when this did not happen. But then we learned that the police investigation was being temporarily stalled while the question of jurisdiction was decided. Normally the county in which a crime is committed has jurisdiction, but in this case it was not known whether the murder occurred in Baltimore County or Frederick County, although we of course believed it was the former. Until the state could decide on this, the investigation would be handled by the state police. They had a lot of catching up to do on the investigation and so naturally could not immediately arrest Jim. This news was a disappointment, but we assumed it would be just a matter of time before Jim was arrested, by either the state police or the police of whichever county was given jurisdiction. Meanwhile, we had other matters to preoccupy us—namely, Susan's impending funeral.

Planning the funeral presented at least as many challenges as planning the memorial service had done. We decided to hold the funeral Mass at my brother Bill's church in Hingham and to have

Susan interred in the plot in Dorchester where our parents and several relatives are buried. But since the tale of Susan's disappearance and murder had not been publicized in the Boston area, we were not sure how to word her obituary. How could we convey the routine facts usually included in obituaries—the time and cause of death—without creating a sensational stir? We wanted a dignified funeral; we didn't want it to be marred by the intrusion of morbid gawkers or members of the local press eager for a hot story. Bill finally devised an obituary that presented the facts about Susan's death in spare, neutral language—stating that a funeral Mass would be held at St. Paul's Church, Hingham, on January 3, 1997, for Susan Hurley Harrison, who had disappeared August 5, 1994, and whose remains had been found in Wolfsville, Maryland, on November 29, 1996—and then went on to give a brief bio and a list of the names of her survivors. Despite our attempt to downplay the gory details, though, local television stations picked up on the obituary and contacted my brothers to try to line up interviews, which they turned down. Although we formerly would have welcomed such publicity about the case, we did not want to enshroud Susan's funeral in sensationalism; plus, we no longer felt the need for publicity now that Susan had been found and Jim's eventual arrest, we assumed, was certain.

Another challenge was how to prevent Jim from showing up at the funeral and making some sort of scene. We had, naturally, sent an obituary to Baltimore newspapers, but in this version we were vague about the date of the funeral, and we asked Susan's friends in the Baltimore area to remain close-lipped about it, lest this information leak out and make its way to Jim. Nonetheless, we experienced trepidations about this issue right up until the beginning of the service. Adding to our anxieties in the days prior to the funeral was the news that Jim had suddenly decided to hire his own forensic medical examiner because he wanted to challenge the official ruling that the skeleton was Susan's. Jim had his man, along with Jim's lawyer, flown to Boston, where Susan's remains had been shipped, to conduct an additional autopsy. Essentially this doctor was a hired gun, looking for anything that could be helpful to Jim and his lawyer. Apparently finding nothing useful on his initial examination, he claimed he needed more time and wanted to take the skull to a dentist's office. Carey Deeley, with John Smialek also in attendance, told Jim's hired medical examiner he would have to have his examination wrapped up by the evening before the funeral, when visiting hours began. The man's response was to request that either the skull be kept out of the coffin during visiting hours and the funeral service or that he be allowed to excavate the coffin after the burial and remove the skull. Carey said absolutely not, that our family had been put through enough already, and the examiner backed down and finished up his autopsy on time—apparently finding nothing of use to Jim. Awareness of these gruesome behind-the-scenes doings only added to an already extremely painful occasion for our family.

The funeral was a sadder, more solemn affair than the memorial service had been. The latter had been primarily a tribute to Susan's blithe spirit, with only a nod toward her troubled last years and her tragic end. The funeral, in contrast, although containing some of the elements of the memorial service (the eulogy I read, for example, was a pastiche of the speeches friends and family members had given at the memorial service), was frankly focused on her death. The Mass began with the ceremonial laying of the cloth shroud over the casket at the entrance to the church, performed by my brothers and me, followed by the slow, stately carrying of the casket down the aisle by the pallbearers. The casket was placed at the front of the church, just before the altar, where it remained for the entire service. This, of course, is the traditional procedure at Catholic funerals, but usually the casket has been open prior to the Mass, and friends and relatives have viewed the body at the funeral home during the previous few days. In Susan's case, however, because of the condition of her remains, the casket had remained closed at the funeral home, with a large framed photograph of her, smiling, placed on the lid—a sight so heartbreaking that virtually everyone walking into the funeral parlor burst into tears when their eye first alighted on it. The closed casket, both at the funeral home and sitting there center stage throughout the Mass, seemed to me to be a mute reminder of the way Susan had died.

Still, it was comforting to be able finally to give Susan a proper funeral and to know that her physical remains were present in the church. The feeling that we had her back with us was strengthened by the fact that the service was a Catholic one. Although not all of my siblings are still practicing Catholics, Catholicism is an integral part of our family identity, and it was important to us to say good-bye to Susan via the ritual of a funeral Mass. Numerous family members participated in the liturgy, presenting eulogies, doing the Bible readings, and carrying the Eucharist and wine up to the altar. Jonathan and Nicholas, however, were emotionally unable to participate. Just before we had left the funeral home for the church that morning, the two had requested a brief time alone with their mother's casket. Passing by the open door to the funeral parlor on my way to get my coat a few minutes later, I witnessed perhaps the most heartrending sight I've ever seen: the two young men standing in front of their mother's coffin gripping each other in a sustained embrace. At the Mass, they sat straight-backed and rigid throughout the service, too stricken to cry.

Following the funeral, the family made the slow, sad drive in limousines behind the hearse out to New Calvary Cemetery in Dorchester. As we wended our way quietly through the lanes of the cemetery, headed toward the Lynch family plot, purchased decades earlier by my mother's mother, Mary Lynch, I thought of all the interments I'd been to at this cemetery during my life. The last one had been my mother's, in March 1989. I remembered how Susan had reached for my hand and held it tightly as we watched my mother's coffin being lowered into the ground. As then, snow covered the ground now, but this time it was Nicholas's hand I held during the interment and Susan's coffin I watched being lowered into the snowy grave.

After this, we all drove back to Bill's house for food and drink and much-needed emotional relief. Like all Hurley gatherings, this one was rife with talk and wit and laughter. But of course, not far from anyone's consciousness was the same unspoken thought: Susan should be here, Susan would have loved this. This was her kind of scene: the Christmas tree and decorations were still up, fires were blazing in the fireplaces, through the windows could be seen nieces and nephews sledding down the backyard hill in the waning afternoon light, and inside the warm, firelit rooms the adults—Hurley siblings and relations and old family friends—milled about drinking and laughing. As had been the case at the memorial service reception, Susan's absence felt palpable at this lively family gathering. Suddenly, in the midst of the activity, I felt a surge of outrage at the thought that Susan had been robbed of all this. That monster who had snuffed out the life of my life-loving sister, I vowed, was not going to get away with what he had done.

18 Justice Pursued and Justice Denied, January 1997– August 1999

*N*ow that Susan had finally been found and the family had given her a proper funeral and burial, we could turn our attention fully to the remaining business that needed to be accomplished: the achieving of justice. We assumed it would only be a matter of weeks before Susan's killer was arrested and charged.

Our confidence began to wane, however, as we watched the debate over jurisdiction being drawn out longer and longer. For some reason, the Baltimore County State's Attorney's Office had lost their early enthusiasm about the case and seemed to have forgotten their assurance to us in 1994 that an arrest would occur if Susan's body were found and her death ruled a homicide; they appeared to be getting cold feet and argued that the investigation should be turned over to the county where Susan's body had been abandoned. But Frederick County also seemed to want to avoid involvement and argued that the murder had to have taken place in Baltimore County and that therefore that county should have jurisdiction. This prolonged waffling meant that for several months the state police, who were now handling the case, did not have a prosecutor to direct them. We hoped that once the jurisdictional issue was resolved, an aggressive prosecutor would be appointed and Jim's arrest would immediately be ordered. But on the chance that we were assigned a weak prosecutor who felt there still wasn't enough evidence, we wanted to do everything we could to help the police make a strong case for arrest.

One thing we could do, we realized, was search for possible witnesses who had seen Jim in the Wolfsville area, ideally in the early hours of August 6, 1994. To try to reach such individuals, I wrote a letter to the *Frederick News-Post,* the local newspaper, asking readers to rack their memories of that time frame for anything that might help us solve the case, and my brother John spoke with a reporter at that paper about the possibility of running a series of articles on the case highlighting certain memory-joggers and including photos of Jim and of Susan's car. I also informed *Unsolved Mysteries* of the new development and asked them to emphasize these same features when they did their update. And I contacted *America's Most Wanted,* thinking they might agree to air the case now that it had been upgraded to a homicide and the specific geographic area where the killer had driven Susan's body was known. None of these efforts, however, proved fruitful: *America's Most Wanted* still wouldn't commit, and although *Unsolved Mysteries* did do the kind of update I'd requested and the *Frederick News-Post* did publish a detailed piece, neither the rerun nor the article resulted in any new leads.

We also wanted to find witnesses who had seen Jim, or Jim and Susan together, in the Wolfsville area some time before Susan's disappearance. Such testimony would put the lie to Jim's claim that he had never been there before and would suggest that he knew the area and perhaps that he knew it would be a good place to dispose of a body. We therefore urged the state police to question people in local stores, gas stations, and inns.

Having heard that Jim was making noises about wanting to visit Susan's grave, we came up with another possible way to implicate him: we could bug the family plot in New Calvary Cemetery. That way if Jim, thinking he was alone, made some kind of graveside confession or apology to Susan, we would have it on tape. Certainly such testimony would constitute hard evidence. However, when we explored this possibility further, we discovered that it is illegal in Massachusetts to tape-record someone without that person's knowledge.

There was one very strange development that occurred during the period while the jurisdiction was in limbo that we thought could be used as helpful evidence in the case. Ten days after Susan's funeral, my brother Bill was notified by the secretary at his church, where the funeral had been held, that a bizarre postcard with a Washington, D.C., postmark had been received at their office addressed to "The Susan Harrison Family & Friends," in care of St. Paul's Church. She enclosed the postcard in an envelope and sent it on to Bill, who made photocopies for the rest of us. The message on the card read:

> From: Washington D.C. Bill Clinton, Newt Gingerich [*sic*] etc.
>
> Well Susan guess God couldn't wait! needed ya help now!! Ya ya always bragged about N.Y., N.Y.!! but loved Boston also the same Jonathan, Nicholas & Robert, Wild Bill, & of course Mary Moran from GA!! Ya was always a "Shady Lady!!" with "Fine Arts!!" Every time we go to the Museum (Boston) we see ya works & how ya cured everything!! Luv ya from US & A
> Funded by: Paul Revere Brady VIII.

Bill forwarded the postcard to Carey Deeley, who sent a copy to the police. Although conceivably some nut in the D.C. area could have read Susan's obituary in the *Baltimore Sun* and gleaned from it the biographical details alluded to in the card, more likely it was someone who knew her well, who felt hostile toward her, and who wanted to give the appearance of being mentally unbalanced. Moreover, the clever punning—the references to Susan's being a shady lady (the name of her business) and to her curing everything (a play on the term "curator")—suggested the author was someone who fancied himself very clever and who enjoyed the game he was playing. Finally, the references to historical and political figures (Paul Revere, Bill Clinton, Newt Gingrich) smacked of self-importance, of the author's seeing himself as being on a par with people of power. In short, the postcard seemed to have "Jim Harrison" written all over it, and, sure enough, a handwriting analyst who worked with the police concluded after examining the card that the handwriting was Jim's. Although the card of course didn't prove that Jim killed Susan, it at the very least suggested that he was not the grieving husband he claimed to be. And the cruel nature it betrayed—only a terribly heartless person would send such a card to a grieving family—would no doubt make a jury unsympathetic to him.

Finally, in April, a decision was made about jurisdiction: the state attorney general's office announced that it would take over the investigation in order to resolve jurisdictional issues between Baltimore County and Frederick County. Carolyn Henneman, assistant attorney general and chief of the criminal division, was assigned to serve as prosecutor. Now, we thought, things were going to happen.

But they didn't. Ms. Henneman appeared to want to move very cautiously. However, we were assured by Sergeant Roger Cassell, the lead officer in the investigation, that the state police were building a solid case. Ms. Henneman explained that it would be risky to prosecute before her team had enough evidence; if they did so and lost, that would be the end of it, for even if compelling evidence was later discovered, they could of course not prosecute because this would constitute double jeopardy. So we tried to be patient.

But as the summer got under way and there still had been no arrest, our faith began to weaken. Those in the family with legal know-how—namely, Jonathan and Tom—suggested that we begin to consider the possibility of bringing a civil suit against Jim in the eventuality that the criminal case was never prosecuted (a gambit similar to the one used by the Browns and the Goldmans, who sued O. J. Simpson in civil court after he was acquitted in criminal court). We asked Carey Deeley to look into the feasibility of doing this. Carey came up with a plan: Susan's sons could file a civil suit against Jim charging him with the wrongful death of their mother, as well as with spousal abuse. Although the statute of limitations may have been exceeded for many of the incidents of abuse (under Maryland law, the statute is three years for battery, intentional infliction of emotional distress, negligence, and false imprisonment, and one year for assault), Carey planned to ask the court to consider the pattern of abuse rather than the individual incidents. This approach had been used in a New Jersey case in which a spouse sued her husband for a continuous pattern of abuse, which extended beyond the statute of limitations. The plaintiff's attorney combined into one legal theory the series of abuses inflicted on the spouse, seeking a single damage award for the whole. Carey hoped the court would accept this novel theory. If they wouldn't, he would try an alternative plan: he would argue that Susan's disappearance extended the traditional statute of limitations, specifically that the statute was tolled between the date she disappeared, August 5, 1994, and the date Jonathan was appointed Personal Representative (following the discovery of her remains and hence the declaration of her death), January 22, 1997, because neither she nor her eventual representative could have filed claims during that period. This tolling argument would extend the applicable statute of limitations period by roughly two and a half years. Finally, if the court would not accept either the pattern-of-abuse argument or the tolling argument, Jonathan and Nicholas would still be able to file claims for two of the episodes of abuse if they filed immediately, before July 31, 1997. These two episodes were Jim's injuring of Susan's hand on July 31, 1994, and what Carey would argue was his negligence that resulted in her death on August 5 or 6, 1994.

Persuaded by Carey's reasoning, in late July Jonathan and Nicholas filed a $17 million civil suit against Jim, accusing him of the wrongful death of their mother and of a pattern of spousal abuse, and barring him from inheriting her share of the Lutherville house, which she was co-owner of, as well as her china, silver, jewelry, furniture, and other assets. With the filing of Jonathan and Nicholas's civil suit, we now felt we had a fallback in case the criminal case was never prosecuted, or was prosecuted and lost. There would be satisfaction in having Jim declared liable in a civil trial, even though it would not be the same satisfaction as a guilty verdict in a criminal trial. And although we would have preferred that his punishment be jail time— ideally life in prison—we knew that being forced to part with his money would constitute only a slightly lesser punishment for Jim, since his identity was so tied up with his wealth.

Shortly after the civil suit was filed in July 1997, however, a development occurred that made us more optimistic about the chances of the criminal case's being prosecuted. This development provided further evidence that Jim was prone to physical violence and that he habitually denied his wrongful behavior when accused. On August 12, he was charged with second-degree assault on a police officer, disorderly conduct, and resisting arrest. The incident was sparked when authorities for US Airways at Baltimore-Washington International Airport refused to let him board a plane to Florida because he appeared intoxicated: he had alcohol on his breath and was swaying and stumbling as he walked. Jim became belligerent, yelling that he was going to Fort Lauderdale to see his grandson. He was told he could board a later flight after sobering up, but he insisted that he wasn't drunk, claiming to have consumed only a small glass of red wine. When airport police officers tried to lead him away, he punched one of them. He swung again, and the officers wrestled him to the ground, handcuffed him, and took him to the Airport Police Office, where they booked him and held him for a few hours. Shortly after midnight, he was released on his own recognizance.[1] We were disappointed by the fact that he had been released—recalling bitterly how, two years earlier, the Baltimore County police had assured us that one of these assaults of Jim's would land him in jail—but encouraged by the thought that this incident could only push Carolyn Henneman further down the road toward prosecution.

Then in September, we ran into a roadblock in our contingency plan, when Jim's lawyers attempted to put a halt to the civil suit. They filed a motion requesting the Baltimore County Circuit Court to postpone the suit until the criminal investigation was complete, accusing Jonathan and Nicholas of using the civil suit to help prosecutors implicate Jim. They argued that the taking of depositions or any other discovery in the civil suit would violate their client's rights while the criminal investigation was active.[2] This motion caused us concern, for a delay would mean potential witnesses' memories would fade and potential evidence might be lost—testimony and evidence we would desperately need if Jim was not convicted in the criminal suit and our hope for justice therefore hinged on the civil suit. But fortunately the judge ruled in our favor: in early December, he announced that the civil suit could go forward despite the unfinished criminal investigation and the lack of an arrest.[3] This setback did not prevent Jim's lawyers, however, from continuing to try to delay the trial. They would ultimately succeed in getting it postponed three times, pushing the originally scheduled date back by almost a year and a half.

Throughout 1998, the discovery phases of both the civil and the criminal cases were ongoing. To the extent permitted by the court, Carey Deeley kept us abreast of findings in the civil suit's discovery, but the state attorney general's office was being taciturn about their progress. We were perplexed as to why Jim hadn't been arrested yet, especially after we learned that an arrest had recently occurred in a similar case in nearby Howard County. That case involved an Ellicott City woman, Sandra Lee Taylor, who had been missing for ten and a half years when her remains were found in August 1995. In November 1997, the state medical examiner's office declared the death a homicide, and shortly thereafter, on November 25, Kenneth Allen White, a mechanic whom Taylor had met at a bar the night she disappeared, was arrested and charged with first-degree murder. The evidence? Patrons and employees saw Taylor talking to two men and later leaving the bar with them. One of these men was subsequently identified as White; police questioned him right after the disappearance and at other points during the next two years. They became suspicious because of inconsistencies and changes in his story, and therefore as soon as the case was declared a homicide, they applied for and obtained an arrest warrant for him.[4]

We felt that our case had at least as much, if not more, circumstantial evidence—enough, we believed, to convince a jury that Jim was guilty. There was, to begin with, the spate of early evidence: he was allegedly the last person to have seen Susan alive; the utility lineman working in the cherry picker above Jim's house the night she disappeared saw a car leave Jim's driveway around 4:00 A.M.; Jim's accounts of his activities and whereabouts for the twenty-four hours following Susan's disappearance—including his claim that he'd gotten up the morning after Susan's visit and gone for a jog and then, becoming tired, had hopped onto the Light Rail and ridden into downtown Baltimore for the rest of the day—were inconsistent and improbable; his downstairs bathroom was filled with dirt when the maid came to clean a few days later, and Jim asked the woman that suspicious question about how often she emptied her vacuum cleaner bag; he failed the polygraph he took a few months after Susan disappeared. In addition, there was the accumulated evidence that Jim was prone to violence—not just the three assaults on police officers in the last couple of years but hearsay evidence from former acquaintances and colleagues who claimed to have seen Jim become enraged at various times—and that Jim had a pattern of lying and evading, as, for example, when he claimed that Susan had caused the injury to his foot, when he denied assaulting an officer in one of his arrests, and when he insisted that the polygraph was faulty. Furthermore, the discovery of Susan's body in a remote place strongly suggested, according to criminal profile theory, that Susan had been killed by someone close to her, not a stranger. And the hypothesis that that person was probably Jim had been strengthened by recent testimony that, contrary to his claim, Jim was familiar with Wolfsville, where Susan's body had been left: Frank Napfel had located a witness prepared to testify to this effect. She was the cashier at the general store a short distance from the gravesite. When Frank showed her a photo of Susan and Jim, she recognized them, saying they had stopped at the store one time; Jim had come in to purchase something, and the woman remembered seeing Susan sitting out in the car. She was struck by Susan's stylish appearance and by the expensive car, which she described exactly. According to Frank, this woman was a credible witness and was willing to testify under oath. Another woman, a frequent customer at the store, also recalled seeing Susan and Jim there, but she did not want to give her name or testify.

Additional suggestion of Jim's guilt was that he had made no real effort to try to find Susan, despite his claim to be a grieving husband who dearly loved his wife. The most compelling evidence, though, was the history of domestic abuse. Police records and medical records, as well as police officers and doctors, would attest to the numerous injuries Susan had allegedly suffered at the hands of Jim over the years, including a broken arm, fractured ribs, cut tongue and lips, pulled-out hair, lacerations, welts, bruises, swellings, and black eyes. The photograph of Susan taken by Jonathan in July 1993 could be displayed, and hopefully a medical expert would point out to the jury how unusual it is for a hematoma on one side of the forehead to affect not only the eye on that side but also the other eye; this phenomenon, we'd been told, suggests an unusually severe blow. Susan's most recent psychiatrist, Dr. Ellen McDaniel, would probably be willing to testify that in her opinion, Susan had suffered from battered wife syndrome during her relationship with Jim.[5]

Finally, we believe there were indications that Jim may have had a financial motive for killing Susan and hiding her body. Over the years, Jim had built up a sizable portfolio from investments in the stock market and in real estate; then in 1993 he added approximately $4 million to this already accumulated wealth by collecting two pension funds from McCormick.[6] Thus, by the time Susan separated from him and began talking about divorce, Jim was a millionaire several times over. As I have indicated, we had always had the impression that Jim's identity was closely tied to his wealth and his financial independence; he therefore probably began to feel threatened by the prospect of losing control over this wealth in a divorce situation.[7] One solution, of course, was to persuade Susan not to divorce him, which we know he tried to do via his wooing and his blackmailing. But as the marital troubles worsened in late 1993, divorce must have seemed more and more of a possibility, and so, it appears, he began secretly to take steps to assert control over his financial resources.

Of the two pension plans Jim collected in the fall of 1993, one was a qualified plan that automatically names the employee's spouse as beneficiary. The only way Jim could maintain control of this fund was to get Susan to sign a release, in effect giving up her beneficiary privilege. She was reluctant to do this, but Jim promised it would make no difference because he would name her sole beneficiary anyway. However, she later discovered that he had on the sly allocated just half the fund to her and had named his six children by his former wife co-beneficiaries. She was furious when she found out he had lied to her. In addition, Jim kept from her the fact that he had withdrawn from McCormick his other pension, a nonqualified fund that did not require the spouse's signature for release. This fund was tax deferred as long as it remained in control of McCormick; by withdrawing it, Jim incurred $400,000 in combined federal and state taxes. He paid the taxes, keeping Susan ignorant of the transaction. (Apparently Jim got Susan to sign without reading that year's joint tax returns.) She only learned of it when it came to light during the exchange of interrogatories that resulted from her filing for separate maintenance in early 1994. She also discovered that Jim had without consulting her transferred certain assets from joint accounts into individual accounts held solely in his name. Jim was so evasive in his answers to the interrogatories that Susan's divorce lawyer, Ann Turnbull, found it difficult to arrive at a conclusive assessment of his net worth.[8]

Jim must have realized that if Susan were to go through with a divorce, he would be forced to give a full disclosure of his assets. And by the summer of 1994, divorce looked to be inevitable, especially after Nicholas issued his ultimatum to Susan about distancing himself from her if she did not sever all ties with Jim. If Susan died before she divorced him, of course, Jim would not have to part with any of his money, but the probate proceedings that would follow from the death of his wife would involve the airing of his financial situation. For whatever reasons, Jim appears to have been uneasy about the prospect of full financial disclosure—suggested by his evasiveness with Ann Turnbull and his choosing to take complete control of his pension funds, in essence removing them from the public record by taking funds out of McCormick, even though removing the nonqualified plan meant that he had to pay a large amount of money in taxes. Fearful of disclosure, Jim may have realized that the only scenario in which his financial situation would remain unaccounted for by outside parties would be if Susan disappeared and her body was never found, or not found for a very long time. A skillful prosecutor, we felt, could have argued that this thought had crossed Jim's mind and that if he did kill her in a fight that got out of control—we didn't go so far as to believe her murder was premeditated—the thought re-occurred to him as he panicked about what to do in the aftermath. I stress that this is all speculation and that in and of itself the theory would not make a case against Jim, but it added to the body of what we considered to be compelling circumstantial evidence.

Given this array of evidence, we didn't understand why Carolyn Henneman still felt the case was not strong enough to prosecute. We kept hoping she had good reasons for stalling; maybe, we thought, the police were secretly working on some strategy they were certain was going to yield the hard evidence needed to clinch the case. And then, in early May 1999, Ms. Henneman quietly dropped a bomb: she announced that the attorney general's office had decided to call off the investigation because of a lack of "evidence sufficient to support a criminal prosecution."[9] We were stunned. Our reading and research over the years had shown us that numerous cases like ours with *less* compelling evidence had been successfully prosecuted. We suspected that Ms. Henneman's real reason for calling off the investigation might have been to save face: we understood that Ms. Henneman had on a previous occasion been gotten the better of in court by Steve Allen, the aggressive lawyer Jim had hired, and we suspected she might be gun-shy about going up against him again. Now, because of what we considered her in part self-serving move, we were left with little hope that a criminal prosecution would ever take place. Although a murder case is never closed, the chance of new evidence coming to light on its own, without an active investigation trying to unearth it, was slim. Justice for Susan in the criminal court system had, it appeared to us, been sacrificed for face-saving.

The prognosis for the civil suit had also turned grim by the spring of 1999. The previous fall, Steve Allen had started making noises about how his client's mental condition was deteriorating. Then in November, he filed court documents stating that Jim had recently been diagnosed with "organic brain disorder and dementia." Because this condition affected his ability to recall, Allen argued, it precluded him from being deposed in a civil law suit.[10] If Jim could not testify, Jonathan and Nicholas's case against him would probably be severely weakened. The judge appointed to the civil suit trial might decide that none of the spousal abuse charges could be included if the alleged perpetrator could not be present to defend himself or answer questions. Furthermore, the jury might be more sympathetic to Jim if they knew he was suffering mental decline, whereas if he were present, he would probably alienate jurors by his arrogant, odd behavior.

Given this inauspicious development, Carey Deeley had increasingly been advising Jonathan and Nicholas to reconsider the offer to settle out of court, which Jim's lawyers had proposed the previous winter and Jonathan and Nick had rejected. Carey pointed out additional reasons, besides Jim's inability to testify, why it might make sense to settle. One of these was the way Jim's lawyers would no doubt drag Susan's name through the mud at the trial, digging up any dirt they could find in an effort to make the jury less sympathetic to her. It would be emotionally wrenching to have to sit through this be-smirching of their mother's character. In answer to Jonathan and Nicholas's objection that a settlement might be construed as a mer-cenary act on their part, Carey rebutted that more likely it would be construed as a tacit admission of guilt on Jim's part. Further, argued Carey, the end result of a settlement would be virtually the same as a verdict of guilty in a civil trial: Jim would be required to part with some of his wealth, which he jealously guarded and which was the sole thing he seemed to have going for him now.

Jonathan and Nicholas took these arguments seriously into con-sideration. They were worn down by all the stalling and delays that had gone on in both cases. For the past five years, they had spent every day consumed with this case, trying to achieve justice for their mother. They were exhausted, and now they were facing the very real possi-bility that their case might be lost in a civil court because of Jim's (supposed) inability to testify. If they lost the case, they would have to go through life haunted by the knowledge that they had failed to achieve justice for their beloved mother. As the summer wore on and the trial date (September 13) grew closer, they constantly wrestled with the question of whether to settle. Then in late August, they were required to attend a pre-trial settlement conference, a routine pro-cedure in which a settlement judge tries to talk the parties into set-tling out of court. The outcome of this conference was that the case was resolved and dismissed.

The judge put a gag order on those privy to the details; they were not to discuss the reason for the dismissal or to state whether there had been a financial settlement. My brothers and I were each faxed a confidentiality agreement to sign if we wanted access to these de-tails. We all declined to sign it, because we did not want our ability to speak freely about our sister's murder to be inhibited in any way. In particular, I wanted to be free to express my suspicions in this book, and my brother Bill wanted to voice his criticism of the state's handling of the criminal suit. To this end, Bill has been composing an article, which will probably eventually take the form of a letter to the *Baltimore Sun,* in which he raises a number of questions concerning the validity of Jim Harrison's "dementia" and the role this excuse has played in preventing justice from being achieved for our sister. With Bill's permission, I quote an excerpt from his draft here:

> Conveniently, this newfound incompetence not only precludes Mr. Harrison from being deposed in a civil law suit; it also (presumably) would render him unable to understand criminal charges against himself, making a criminal proceeding difficult. It certainly seems an abrupt change in mental capacity for a relatively young (62 years old at the time the diagnosis of dementia was made) former Chief Financial Officer of McCormick & Co. In *Baltimore Magazine*'s October 1995 article about Susan's disappearance, Margaret Guroff reported, "Jim was known as a brilliant businessman. But some say he could play the fool when it served him." . . . Why was no arrest made before Mr. Harrison's "dementia" became a factor? . . . In deciding to call off the investigation, how much weight did the Attorney General's Office give to Mr. Harrison's "markedly deteriorated" mental condition? Where is Jim Harrison now (I'm told his Lutherville home appears unoccupied) and what treatment is he receiving for his illness? Will the Attorney General's Office monitor Mr. Harrison's activities and if he recovers, will the investigation of Susan's murder be re-opened?

It has now been three years since the state called off its investigation. My family's bitterness about the prosecutor's handling of the case remains. In fact, our bitterness has deepened, because during this time we have had brought to our attention numerous missing person cases in Maryland and elsewhere that have been prosecuted even *without* a body and, to our knowledge, with circumstantial evidence no stronger than in Susan's case. In November 2001, a Howard County man named Paul Stephen Riggins was convicted of killing his long-missing (since July 1996) wife, whose body has never been found, and sentenced to life in prison.[11] In 1989 in Montgomery County, prosecutor John McCarthy won a conviction against Gregory Tu in the murder trial of Tu's missing wife, Lisa.[12] In another 1980s no-body case in Montgomery County, former prosecutor Eric E. Wright convicted William Hurley (no relation to our family) of manslaughter in the death of his estranged wife, Catherine (two and a half years after the conviction, her body was found and Hurley confessed).[13] One of the most famous of such cases in recent times is the October 2000 murder conviction in New York of plastic surgeon Dr. Robert Bierenbaum, whose wife, Gail, disappeared in 1985. Prosecutors built their case on evidence that Bierenbaum was capable of murder, had a motive, and tried to hide his tracks. Among this circumstantial evidence were the facts that "he was violent and angry about his wife's desire to leave the marriage; he did little to look for her and appeared relieved after she vanished; he sent a rug in their apartment out for cleaning. . . ."[14] These details sound hauntingly familiar.

New developments in our case continue to crop up occasionally. For example, a Baltimore area woman who belatedly learned of the case, after the civil suit had been dismissed, contacted Tom to tell him that one of Jim's sons had been a classmate of her son at Gilman years earlier and had come to live with them for a couple of weeks to escape his violent father. We always turn such information over to Carey Deeley, but we do so halfheartedly, for we know that no matter how much new evidence accumulates, and no matter how compelling it is, it is probably useless as long as the state is willing to allow Jim's mental condition to bar him from testifying.

And so our family is left in limbo, albeit a different kind of limbo from that which we inhabited during the missing person phase. We at least have the comfort of knowing where Susan is now—lying in the ground next to her parents—but we do not have the comfort of knowing that justice has been served. We must live with the excruciating knowledge that Susan's killer has gotten away with murder.

As these pages have indicated, I strongly suspect that Jim Harrison is that killer. But because the state will not prosecute, I do not know this for a fact. If I am wrong, and if Jim Harrison is reading this book, I offer a sincere apology for the pain my suspicions have caused him and his family. But if I am right, I implore him, as one human being to another, to do the right thing, the decent thing, the honest thing: confess, and end this torture for our family.

Epilogue

$\mathcal{A}$lmost eight years have now passed since Susan was murdered. As happens with any death, time has eased the pain for the survivors. Months, rather than days, now go by when I don't break down at the sight of something that reminds me of Susan. Childhood photographs that I had to remove from my sight for the first two or three years are now back in their places on my living room mantel. Christmas and Susan's birthday are no longer days I have to steel myself to get through. And my brothers and nephews and I can now say Susan's name and refer to her death, and even utter the phrases "the body" and "the remains," without wincing or without tears welling up.

But the sadness is always there, and the anger. They are the undercurrent of every joyous or hilarious extended-family gathering. Jonathan got married last summer, and toward the end of the rehearsal dinner, when all the riotous toasts by the groom's and bride's friends were concluded, Katie, Jonathan's soon-to-be-wife, stood up and made a serious toast, an eloquent tribute to the mother-in-law she wished she could have known and whom she would keenly feel the absence of down through the years. As Katie spoke, I felt pulled between tears and rage: tears at the thought of how Susan would have loved having this wonderful young woman as a daughter-in-law, and rage at the injustice of Susan's having been cheated of this experience. I glanced around the room at my brothers and nephews, and the moist eyes and clenched jaws I witnessed told me that they were gripped by the same thoughts.

As time has passed, such onslaughts of emotion have gradually lessened in frequency and duration. But it has been a struggle for each of us:

For Bill, the hardest thing has been the knowledge that he wasn't able to protect his little sister. His big-brother role toward Susan was forged in early childhood. A scenario my parents used to repeat and chuckle over sticks in my memory as an emblem, at once touching and humorous, of this relationship: One afternoon, some boys new to the neighborhood came upon Susan playing in our front yard and began bullying her, trying to get her to tell them her name, when Bill suddenly rounded the corner, marched across the lawn, and putting a protective arm around his sister said, "You don't have to tell them, Susan." When Susan was a freshman at Taunton High School, the Tabor Academy Glee Club, of which Bill was a member, came to perform at an assembly. Susan was thrilled when the director suddenly stepped forward and announced, "This next song is dedicated to Susan Hurley"—a surprise cooked up by Bill for the benefit of his little sister.

It was Bill who took the most strenuous steps to help Susan as she spiraled downward during her years with Jim: dropping everything to fly down to Baltimore on a few occasions when she was particularly upset, pleading with her to come up to Massachusetts to stay at his house every time she called in hysterics, arranging for her to get medical and psychiatric workups. A man who had achieved success in his career and in almost everything he had applied his efforts to, Bill was dismayed by his inability to save his sister. Following her murder, he applied the same kind of energy to trying to resolve the case that he had applied to trying to get her to leave Jim. He spearheaded the family's efforts and for the first few years was almost daily on the phone with the various professionals involved in the case. When those efforts proved fruitless, with the dissolution of the criminal and civil suits, in his frustration he channeled his energies into composing the article mentioned in the last chapter. Counseled to wait to publish it until matters involving the resolution of the civil suit were completed, he put this project on hold. Now he feels free to publish it and has been honing it into a letter, waiting for an opportune time to submit it to the Baltimore media, perhaps on the next anniversary of Susan's disappearance. Fueling Bill's urge to see some kind of justice done for his little sister is the photograph he keeps above the desk where he works at home, a snapshot of Susan and him, aged seven and ten, playing together on the swingset in our childhood backyard.

My brother John also suffered keenly from the knowledge that he hadn't been able to save Susan. The two had been especially close. They shared an interest in art—although a veterinarian by career, John is a talented amateur sculptor and painter—and John was very sensitive to Susan's problems. Whereas Bob and I would become exasperated when we seemed to be getting nowhere reasoning with Susan, John would patiently counsel her for hours over the phone during her low periods. He had been looking forward to her August 1994 visit to Massachusetts because he thought it would give him the opportunity to encourage her in the steps she was taking toward a new life. With this plan in mind, he had lined up an excursion to a custom lampshade shop in the Boston area, hoping the visit might give her some ideas for her own budding business and keep her inspired about her fledgling independence. Although he normally would have stayed on the phone with her when she called in a depressed mood, he cut her call short on the afternoon of August 5 because he knew he'd be seeing her the next day and so didn't see any need to forgo his scheduled softball game for this conversation. But something in the tone of her voice troubled him, and so when he returned home around 7:00 P.M. he called her back, leaving the message on the machine that she would never receive: she had already left for Jim's. In the days and weeks and months that followed, John had to live with the haunting question of whether he could have saved Susan if only he'd stayed on the phone with her.

John was gripped by regrets for a long time—not just the regret about having cut short the phone conversation but also the general regret that he hadn't fully realized the danger Susan was in that summer and hence hadn't done enough to try to steer her away from it. At the time the tragedy struck, John had been at a fork in his career, having recently made the decision to switch from pathology research to clinical work. But when Susan disappeared, his career plans suddenly paled into insignificance, and he put them on hold. For almost a year, he spent virtually all his waking hours in the effort to find

Susan, and even after he started back to work, in a demanding clinical practice, he devoted most of his non-work hours to the case. It took him longer than it took the rest of us to develop a thick skin regarding the tragedy: he couldn't bear to read newspaper articles about the finding of her remains, and only in recent weeks has he felt he might finally have the emotional fortitude to get through the manuscript of this book.

My brother Bob has had an additional struggle to contend with, besides the regret and sadness we all have suffered. At the time Susan disappeared, his two daughters were very young, just five and seven years old. It would have been hard enough to tell them that their aunt had died a conventional death, never mind tell them that she had disappeared and probably been murdered. He and his wife, Cyndy, therefore decided to say nothing about the situation at first, thinking Susan might soon be found and then they would tell the girls she had died in some kind of accident. Throughout the first year, Bob was under the stress of having to edit his end of crisis-related phone conversations whenever his daughters were in the room and to fabricate reasons for flying down to Baltimore for family meetings with police and media. Finally in June, when it became clear that Susan might never be found and when the memorial service was pending, Bob and Cyndy told the girls that Susan had died of an illness and that they—the parents—had to travel down to Baltimore for the funeral. They could get away with pretending that the reason they weren't taking the girls with them was that the latter were too young to attend a funeral and, besides, the long trip to Baltimore would be tiring for them.

But then after Susan's remains were discovered and her real funeral was planned, Bob and Cyndy found themselves in the predicament created by their well-intentioned deceit: now there would be no reason not to take the girls to a family funeral, for they were older and also the funeral was going to take place in Hingham, the town where they resided. So this time Bob and Cyndy told them that the funeral was a memorial service and that since such services are less of a big deal than funerals, there was no reason for them to miss school that day to attend (school had just started up following the

Christmas–New Year's vacation). For the next four-plus years, Bob and Cyndy struggled with the question of how and when to tell their daughters the truth. There never seemed to be a right time: the lurid details that would have been too horrific for small children to hear would be equally disturbing to adolescent girls. Finally, just before Jonathan's wedding last summer, Bob and Cyndy sat their daughters down and told them the whole story, for they knew that with all Susan's old friends in attendance at the wedding, references were bound to be made that would cause the girls to suspect the truth. To the parents' relief, they took it fairly well, and so Bob can now talk openly with his daughters about what happened to their aunt. Although it was stressful for him to have to repress his grief, the preoccupation with protecting his children gave him a shield of sorts against the kind of raw pain John was experiencing.

As for Jonathan and Nicholas, they have suffered mightily, but they have come through the tragedy intact. I have been amazed at their bravery and their grace. While other young men their age had nothing more to worry about than passing exams and performing well in sports, these two were living a nightmare. For over two years, they had to go about their daily business of being students while all the time wondering where their mother was, what kind of end she had met, whether they would ever find her body. When her remains were finally discovered, that nightmare was supplanted by another one: knowing their mother had been murdered and her murder would probably go unavenged. Added to the strains on Jonathan's life were all the duties and responsibilities he had to carry out as guardian of his mother's estate.

And yet the two carried on in a dignified and productive manner. They stayed in school; they continued to excel at sports and to maintain strong friendships; they graduated on time, Jonathan from Cornell University Law School and Nicholas from Middlebury College; and they both moved to the Boston area and began promising careers. How have they managed to maintain such equilibrium in a situation that would have caused many young men to fall apart psychologically? I think part of the answer lies in the closeness they share, a bond from which they have each derived deep comfort. But I also attribute their strength to the influence of their dad. Tom is a model of stability and sanity, perhaps the result of having weathered a rocky childhood. His parents divorced when he was small, each went on to marry and divorce and remarry, he had a variety of stepparents and step- and half-siblings growing up, and his young adulthood was punctuated by frequent long-distance phone calls from his incoherent mother, whose alcoholism eroded her once-respectable life and eventually claimed her at the age of fifty-two. In the face of all this tumult, Tom developed a strong will to survive and succeed. He was an excellent student and a dedicated Boy Scout, eventually an Eagle Scout; he went on to Harvard, then to naval officer candidate school, and then to law school. It was this same equanimity and determination that enabled him to serve as a beacon of stability for his sons during the surreal years following Susan's disappearance. Despite his own no-doubt complicated feelings—lingering bitterness about the divorce now overlaid by pity and sadness—he tried to make life as normal as possible for the boys, encouraging them to stay in school when they first wavered about going back, attending Parents' Weekends and the boys' sports events, inviting them to bring their girlfriends home to his house for vacations. The stability Tom provides for them has in recent years been enhanced by his marriage to Leslie, an exceptionally kind and understanding woman whom Jonathan and Nicholas have grown to love.

But I think an additional source of strength for Jonathan and Nicholas is the love of life and the warmth and humor they inherited from Susan. Through all the tragedy, they never lost their ability to laugh or to care about how other people were doing. Even in the early months, they'd get a twinkle in their eyes when they would affectionately recall some funny anecdote about their mom. And despite their own great suffering, they were sensitive to the suffering of others. A friend of Jonathan's committed suicide a few years ago, and I was touched when I met the young man's mother at Jonathan's wedding last summer and she told me that every Mother's Day since her son's death, Jonathan has sent her flowers. When I mentioned this later to a friend of Susan's, she said, "Jonathan gets that from his mother," and I nodded, remembering again how Susan had had all the boys on Jonathan's college lacrosse team send a Mother's Day card to the mother of their teammate who had recently died.

The good hearts and solid characters of Jonathan and Nicholas are perhaps most tellingly reflected in their choices of wives: Katie, Jonathan's new wife, and Sarah, Nicholas's fiancée, are kind, sensitive, intelligent young women. They both respect the important role Susan's memory plays in Jonathan's and Nicholas's lives. Katie hungrily read the manuscript of my book last fall, and she loves listening to Jonathan's childhood recollections about his mom. Sarah was moved when Nicholas chose what would have been Susan's sixtieth birthday, this past March 2, to propose to her. He called me the next day to announce the engagement, and he told me that when they went out for their celebratory dinner the night before, Sarah asked him what his mother's favorite dessert was, saying she wanted to order that in honor of Susan. Then, with a chuckle, Nick proceeded to tell me that he had no idea what Susan's favorite dessert was, but noticing how Sarah was wistfully eyeing the apple pie à la mode on the menu, he said, "My mom loved apple pie." Hearing the humor and affection in Nick's voice as he related this tale, I couldn't help but think to myself, "He's Susan's boy, all right," and a smile spread over my face at the same time that tears came into my eyes.

It is this type of gentle weeping, rather than the disconsolate sobbing of a few years back, that more often characterizes my bouts of sadness today. I weep for all the beauty and joy of life my sister has been robbed of, for all the family laughter she cannot share in. How she would have loved the scene at Jonathan's wedding reception last summer: her whole family—siblings, siblings-in-law, sons, nieces, new daughter-in-law—and scores of her old friends rock-and-rolling the night away in high spirits beneath a star-studded Vermont sky. At times like those, the thought always knifes through me, "How unnecessary her death was."

This thought is perhaps the key insight my attempt to find Susan has yielded me. I began my exploration of her life in guilt, wondering why I have fared well while she spiraled downward, why our lives took such different courses despite our sharing the same genes and background and many of the same personality traits. And what my reflections have concluded is that a few key circumstances account for our different destinies. As the first daughter, she was more vulnerable to my parents' influence than I was, specifically to my mother's sense of social inferiority and her destructive ways of coping with it, and to my father's drive to enter the upper-class patrician world that had traditionally snubbed the Boston Irish. Then there was the historical circumstance of the modern feminist movement's being launched just after Susan's formative, young-adult years had occurred and just as mine were occurring. This timing meant that Susan entered adulthood believing that a woman achieved security and happiness by being pretty and ladylike and by "marrying well," whereas my generation, of course, rebelled against these notions.

The combination of the 1950s image of womanhood, the complicated feelings about class Susan derived from my parents, perhaps a genetic predisposition to alcoholism, and the tendency she unwittingly learned from my mother to use alcohol as a method of escaping emotional problems resulted in Susan's making the disastrous choice to become involved with Jim Harrison. This misguided step proved fateful, for the cycles of violence-and-denial and the role alcohol played in the couple's dynamic made the relationship almost impossible for Susan to extricate herself from. Susan had such a strong need to appear a "lady" and to portray herself as the opposite of my mother that she catapulted into despair every time she let this image lapse. So strong were both her need and her shame that she would latch onto denial after such a lapse; she couldn't bear for the world to know that she got drunk and that she and her husband had violent, degrading fights. Her denial was so extreme that it blinded her to the danger she was putting herself in.

But—and here's the tragic rub—she almost did extricate herself. I really believe that the strength and self-confidence Susan was beginning to feel after finally moving out, following the December 1993 fight, could have saved her, if only she had been able to stay away from Jim and from alcohol completely. I keep recalling the clarity and sanity I heard in her voice in our January and February 1994 phone calls; I remember thinking that this was the real Susan, the strong person stripped of the misguided notions that had influenced her for much of her life. But her strength flagged and faltered in the coming months; she would take two steps forward, by meeting with her divorce lawyer or lining up another business contract, and then one step backward, by seeing Jim again or turning to alcohol following an argument with him.

One of those steps backward was taken on August 5. If only she hadn't gone over to Jim's house that night. If only she had stayed home and waited for Nicholas, eaten the Chinese takeout with him that he brought back for supper, gone to bed early as planned, and taken their scheduled flight to Boston the next morning. If only she'd had those five days with the family, a visit that could have given her the encouragement she needed to stay the course. If only she'd been able to hold on to the new life she had embarked on.

That's the real tragedy: that Susan died just as she was beginning to live.

Appendixes

Notes

Appendix A
Chronicle of Alleged and Suspected Abuse of Susan by Jim

The following material is based on reports from the Baltimore County police and medical records provided to me by my brother John Hurley, who obtained them from Susan's internist, Dr. Ruth Kantor, in the fall of 1994.

12/14/87, Report No. F-421-547. Susan called 911 alleging spousal abuse. But when the police arrived, she would not answer the door, so they entered through an open garage door. Susan was intoxicated and had a bruised eye and scratches on her knees. She claimed that while Jim (whom she was living with but not yet married to) was out of the house, she'd received an anonymous phone call saying he was not going through with his divorce. When Jim returned home, drunk, she complained to him about the call, and he proceeded to hit her in the left eye with his fist. He then pushed her to the floor and left the house. Questioned about the history of their relationship, Susan reported that she had been living with Jim Harrison at this address for about four years and that they had had problems in the past. (This was a mistake on someone's part because at this time, Susan and Jim had been living together about three years.) She said he had broken her arm during an argument one and a half years earlier, but this had not been reported to police. The warrant/summons procedure was explained to Susan, who stated she would prosecute. (She apparently did not follow through on this.)

12/27/87, Report No. F-433845. Police responded to Susan's call alleging spousal assault and battery. Susan stated that she and Jim had argued about going to church; he did not want to go and threw water on her. Susan claimed that Jim had physically hit her in the past.

7/31/88, Report No. G-211199. Police were called to the house by Susan twice on this date. The first time was for a domestic dispute: Jim had accused Susan of letting her children run her life and an argument had ensued; Susan feared he would become violent, because of his violence in the past, so she called 911. The responding officer advised Susan to go someplace else until she could see the commissioner to file charges on the earlier assaults. She said she was going to prosecute on the earlier assaults and she would leave the house in a little while. The officer left the house and then was called back five minutes later after 911 received a second call from Susan saying that after the officer had left, Jim had begun arguing again and had struck her in the mouth with his hand, causing a cut to the inside of her lower lip. The police officer upgraded the report from a domestic to a spousal assault. The officer stayed at the house until the victim left for the commissioner's. (There is no indication as to whether she actually filed charges.)

2/18/90, Report No. I-045034. Susan called the police during a domestic dispute, claiming Jim had begun arguing with her over her not wanting him to talk to her or put his arm around her while she was trying to sleep the night before; he called her a "bitch, whore, and slut" and then took her purse and hid it from her. Jim told the officer that no such argument had taken place and that his wife was under psychiatric care. When police asked Susan if she wanted to leave, she first said yes, but then changed her mind and said she did not need the police.

7/9/90, Report No. I-188062. Police responded to Susan's call claiming that she and Jim had gotten into an argument while they were out to dinner, the argument had flared up again after they got home, and Susan had then left the house and gone for a walk to get away from him. Upon her return home, she found the doors locked and began pounding on a door; Jim came out and pushed her to the ground. Susan further stated that Jim had told her *she would be dead by July 15* (emphasis added). It was noted that both parties had been drinking. The procedure to prosecute and to seek an ex parte order was explained to Susan; she stated that she would not prosecute at this time. She was advised to seek shelter at another location, but she declined. The police attempted to contact Susan between July 19 and July 23, with negative results.

9/3/90, Report No. I-251702. Police responded to Susan's call alleging spousal assault. Jim had come home intoxicated, and Susan had pretended she was asleep as he went through the house turning on the lights and throwing things around, until he started throwing some of her important documents. She then got up, at which point Jim started yelling at her, put his hand over her face—even though he was aware that she had just had surgery done above her lip—and shoved her. The ex parte order procedure was explained to Susan.

3/9/91, Report No. J-063709. When police responded to Susan's call, Susan stated that her husband was having an affair and that when he arrived home, they began fighting, at which point he grabbed her and threw her down to the ground. Jim countered that his wife had begun arguing with him and had picked up a plastic cup and begun hitting him on the head with it. Jim agreed to leave the house and went to stay in a hotel. The ex parte order procedure was explained to Susan, and she was referred to a counseling agency. The police attempted to follow up with Susan on March 14, 15, and 18, with negative results.

6/20/91. Susan went to the Greater Baltimore Medical Center emergency room complaining of pain and tenderness in her left rib area; she claimed to have received the injury when she had fallen down on June 17. The report states, "The patient is not very informative about her condition at this time. . . . [T]he patient appears to be confused at this time and appears to be in acute distress. She wanted to leave the ER right away and wanted to have the x-rays right away." The x-rays showed a fracture of the third left rib.

7/3/91. Susan made a follow-up visit to her internist, Dr. Ruth Kantor, who noted that the rib was healing well but that Susan seemed "hurried, anxious, distressed" and had lost weight. Dr. Kantor wrote that she suspected "family discord." She noted the existence of some old bruises on Susan's left upper arm.

11/28/91, Report No. J-378351. Police responded to Susan's call reporting that Jim had pulled out some of her hair and struck her in the back with his hands. She had a red mark on her back. Jim stated that nothing had happened. Both parties were intoxicated. Jim was arrested. The ex parte order procedure was explained to Susan, and she was referred to a counseling agency. (She apparently did not follow up on the referral.)

4/26/92, Report No. K-113457. Susan called police for a spousal assault. She reported that Jim had thrown her down the steps of the house from the second floor, causing an abrasion to her left knee. When the police arrived, Jim was in the master bathroom shaving. He reported that Susan had assaulted him by grabbing his sweater off of his back. A report was filed for assault against both parties. Susan refused to prosecute. Approximately half an hour later, Susan called a second time, stating that Jim had assaulted her and caused a bruise to her buttock. The injury was verified, and Jim was placed under arrest. At the time, Jim stated that he had injuries himself that he had failed to mention previously on the officer's first arrival. He stated that Susan had scratched his back. However, there were no signs of injuries. He then stated that Susan had stomped on his foot with her shoes on, causing a bruise, approximately two hours prior to the police officer's arrival. He said he wanted her arrested for assault based on these injuries. Susan indicated that the bruise on Jim's foot had been caused by his doctor during a physical examination four days earlier, on April 22. Contact with the doctor verified that the doctor had caused a rather large bruise to the top of Jim's left foot. The police noted that the bruise was dark purple in color with signs of yellowing on the outer edge, indicating that the bruise was not just received. Jim refused to allow his injuries to be photographed. While being processed by police, Jim refused to answer all questions, claiming he had been falsely arrested. After he was released on his own recognizance, Jim counted his money and claimed that a police officer had stolen a $100 bill. When Jim recounted his money with the police officer, the "missing" $100 bill was discovered by Jim.

5/1/92. Susan saw Dr. Kantor for injuries sustained in the April 26 incident. Dr. Kantor noted, "Pt. has been abused by her husband for many years—most recently thrown down the stairs by her husband. L. leg is bruised, L. knee is badly bruised. . . . A lot of hair was also pulled out."

11/29/92, Report No. 92-335-0028. Police responded to Susan's call stating that she and Jim had been sleeping when Jim jumped out of bed and started hitting her and breaking things. When the police arrived, Jim was outside of the house and stated that his wife was a manic depressive and that she freaked out and broke things around the house. He said he did not hit his wife. Police noted dried blood on Susan and a cut on her tongue. Jim left the residence for the night. The ex parte order procedure and county family violence counseling were explained to Susan. She said she did not want to charge Jim.

12/4/92. Susan saw Dr. Kantor for injuries sustained in the November 29 incident. Dr. Kantor noted that Susan had a "lumpy, sore r. anterior 5th rib," "bruises along r. side x 3, extending from iliac crest to r. lat. thigh," and a "tongue bite l. tip of tongue." X-rays revealed that Susan had a "fractured r. 5th rib ant/lat and possibly 6th & 7th ribs as well." Dr. Kantor also wrote that Susan "[h]as been in tremendous pain . . . Taken nothing for pain, can't sleep. Has been drinking a lot lately, esp. when she's upset. In fact, drank heavily Sat. nite at a party before she started fighting w/ her husband. Can't get herself to stop drinking. Quite worried about it."

2/16/93, Report No. 93-047-042. Police responded to Susan's call stating that on February 12–13, Jim had held her against her will. During this time, he pushed her fully clothed into a bathtub full of water. She changed into a bathrobe, at which point he locked her in a bedroom. Then he periodically entered the room and threw water, urine, and soda on her. At another point during these two days, he pulled her off the bed by her ankles several times, allowing her head to hit the floor. Susan said that at some point during the pushing, he elbowed her ribs, breaking one. She explained that the reason for the assault was that her husband accused her of having an affair with her ex-husband and returning home late from her son's basketball game. Follow-up contact was made with Susan on March 2 by telephone. Susan stated that she did not wish to go ahead and continue. The officer did not fully understand her statement, so asked, "Is the suspect there with you?" She replied, "Yes." The officer then asked, "Would he get upset if he knew who you were talking to?" She again replied, "Yes." The officer next asked, "Do you plan on filing charges?" She replied, "No." The officer made a note to contact the victim at another time to attempt a better conversation about the assault. (There was no indication as to whether this follow-up occurred.)

2/18/93. Susan saw Dr. Kantor for injuries sustained in the February 16 incident. X-rays revealed acute fractures to the left fourth and sixth ribs. Dr. Kantor noted that "Pt. detoxed from alcohol btwn. 12/4/92 and 12/9/92, had nothing alcoholic until 2/10 or 2/11/93 when she had a fight w/ her husband. Fight started over minor matter, escalated and husband became unreasonable Thurs. 2/11/93." Dr. Kantor describes the same allegations included in the police report with one additional one: "Husband threw bottles at her, missed her head but put some dents in the wall." Dr. Kantor also includes in her notes, "Husband is convinced that pt. is a crazy manic depressive and deserves these outbursts" and that he "decided he didn't need to see anyone (i.e., a psychologist, at Susan's urging), the problem was w/ the wife." The notes also state, "3rd episode of ribs fractured by husband since 6/17/91" and "(patient) will detox w/ Librium for next 5 days."

6/1/93. Susan had a phone consultation with Dr. Kantor about her drinking problems. Dr. Kantor's notes state, "Pt. is having increas-

ing marital problems, husband is more verbally abusive. . . . had
a terrible fight with husband last eve., started to drink again."
Susan told Dr. Kantor she had had two bottles of wine that day
and didn't think she could stop drinking. Dr. Kantor noted that
she was putting Susan immediately back on a course of Librium
as well as starting her on Xanax for anxiety.

7/25/93, Report No. 93-206-1313. Susan called police alleging that
Jim had become enraged, had hit her on the head, shoved her
into walls, and locked her out of the house. When police arrived,
they pried open the side garage door to enter the house. Once inside, they found Jim sleeping in the master bedroom. He claimed
he had no idea how Susan had received her injuries. Susan collected her personal belongings and left to go to a friend's house.

7/27/93, District Court Document, Case No. 1714-93SP/T. Susan
filed an Ex Parte Order for Protection from Abuse, Application
for Statement of Charges, and Petition for Protection from Domestic Violence. Jim was charged with battery. He gathered his
clothing and vacated the home.

7/27/93. Susan saw Dr. Kantor for what the latter noted as an "urgent visit" following Susan's visit to the emergency room. Dr.
Kantor described her as having a "massive hematoma on r. forehead w/ blood tracking down subcutaneously under skin into r.
orbital region, creating huge swollen black eye. L. periorbital area
is also starting to swell now but not yet discolored—r. forehead
is *very* tender, 5–6 cm. area of soft tissue swelling w/ minor abrasion." Kantor then goes on to describe the incident (described
in July 25 police report) that caused the injuries, adding, "Both
knees became scraped up & sore, r. wrist was twisted. Pt. was
able to get out of the house, as usual—began drinking heavily
as she does when *very* upset and with nowhere to go and no one
to turn to. . . . Today, smells of [alcohol] altho' last drink was
last night. *Not* clinically intoxicated, very coherent & lucid but
shaky & visibly upset. . . . Told to keep head *elevated* at all times,
son will stay close."

9/19/93, Report No. 93-262-0955. Police responded to Susan's call
stating that Jim was tearing up the house. When they arrived,
Susan was gone; Jim stated they had had an argument and Su-

san had left the house on foot. He said that earlier in the day, Susan had been abusing him, and he'd begun to follow her around the house for fear that she might break some valuable items. While he was following her around, she attacked him, striking him to the ground. Then she left the house, took some property from his car (his camera and medication), and drove away in her car. He followed her in his car, blocking her car in at a construction site and getting out and retrieving his property. Minutes later, he claimed, she followed him home and rammed his car with hers. He approached the driver's side of her car; she forcefully opened the door, striking him on his left leg. Then she got out and left on foot.

Two hours later, Susan called the same officer back and asked him to come to the house. She then gave the officer her version of the incident that had occurred earlier in the day: She said that Jim had been belittling her, and when she went to take a shower, he grabbed her by the hair in an attempt to pull her out of the shower. She said she decided to leave in her car because she couldn't tolerate the abuse; he followed her, blocked her car, entered it, and took her purse. She said she drove back home to retrieve her purse, and when she pulled into the driveway, Jim pulled her from her car, slamming her to the ground. She then went into the house to look for her purse. After not finding it there, she left on foot and went to a neighbor's residence.

Police noted that there were some scratches on the rear bumper of Jim's vehicle, but there was no damage to the front end of Susan's vehicle.

Follow-up contact concerning this incident was made with Susan on October 19. She was advised of further assistance, and other procedures were explained. She said she did not want to file charges, stating that "things are going too good" to file charges.

9/30/93. Susan saw Dr. Kantor because her knee was still hurting, but there was no swelling. Dr. Kantor noted that Susan was taking Zocor and Prozac but was not drinking at all or craving it. She said that her husband was also off alcohol. She was eating healthy foods and had a good appetite and was exercising.

10/25/93, Report No. 93-298-0525. Police responded to Susan's call claiming she and Jim had begun arguing and he'd pushed her and caused her to fall against the dresser, bruising her left knee. Susan said Jim then packed some of his clothing and left. She said her husband had a drinking problem, but she could not tell if he had been drinking prior to this incident. She said she did not know of his whereabouts. Warrant/summons and ex parte procedures were explained; she said she did not want to press charges.

11/22/93, Report No. 93-326-0668. Police responded to Susan's call alleging spousal assault. She said that Jim had been upset since his daughter had failed the bar exam the previous week. He had been out of the house all day on November 21, and when he returned home, under the influence of alcohol, he stated that he was going to destroy everything in the house. He began destroying items and struck Susan numerous times, threw her down on the floor, and kicked her. The argument continued until Susan went down into the basement, at which time Jim attempted to lock her into the basement but was unsuccessful. Eventually Jim and Susan went to sleep. When they awoke, the argument resumed, with Jim striking and kicking her numerous more times. Jim then packed several items and left for an unknown location, at which point Susan called the police.

Police noted that the house was in disarray. Susan was strongly advised to prosecute and was fully explained the ex parte procedures; counseling was recommended. (She apparently did not prosecute, file for an ex parte order, or follow through on counseling.)

12/29/93, Report No. 93-63-0125. Susan called police from a friend's home claiming that Jim had beaten her up at their home and held her against her will for eleven hours, on December 28–29. She claimed he had punched her several times and thrown her into the Christmas tree and that she suffered small cuts on her arms and forehead and thought she might have a broken rib. The Pikesville Volunteer Medic Unit 325 was contacted and responded, but Susan refused treatment. The officer noted the strong odor of alcohol on her breath. Susan denied she had been drinking.

12/29/93, Report No. 93-363-0782. Susan called police late that same afternoon claiming that Jim had tried to drive over her on the front lawn of their house with her Saab. (I do not know why Susan went back to the house that afternoon, possibly to retrieve some possessions.) Jim countered that Susan had driven the Saab at him on the lawn. The officer observed tire tracks in the snow on the lawn as well as both large and small footprints around the tracks, and he saw several bushes and shrubs torn up. Susan was reluctant to follow through with prosecution.

5/8/94, Report No. 94-128-0271. Susan called police and stated that Jim had come to her home on three occasions the night before, beating her up on each occasion. (They were separated by this time, and Susan was living in Ruxton.) When advised that a car would be dispatched, Susan vehemently objected and said she didn't want an officer to come to her home. Susan would not give any further information about the incidents except that Jim had taken her car keys and she wanted them back. The officer offered to send a car to transport her to the commissioner's office for prosecution, but she refused. She said she was familiar with the court system and felt they would not believe her. She hung up after it was suggested she contact a shelter or organization for battered women.

7/31/94, Report No. 94-212-0945. Susan called police reporting spousal abuse. She said that Jim had shown up at her home and asked her to go out to dinner. When she refused, because it was late and she was tired, Jim got mad and grabbed both her hands and twisted her fingers. He then left the location. Susan explained to the officer that she had been separated from Jim since December because of his being abusive to her. Warrant/summons and ex parte procedures were explained to her. She stated that she would press charges. (She apparently did not follow through.)

Appendix B
Advice to Victims of Domestic Violence

I am not trained as a counselor, so it is not in a professional capacity that I offer the following advice. Rather, it is in the capacity of one who realized too late that a close relative was caught in the web of domestic violence. My wisdom is, tragically, the wisdom of hindsight.

Many of you reading this book may be women like my sister. That is, you may be women who remain in a violent relationship because you know that you are at least partly to blame for the violence. I suspect that one of the main reasons Susan continually retracted her allegations and dropped charges against Jim was the guilty knowledge that she had initiated or exacerbated many of the fights; the fact that she had often done so when inebriated probably increased her belief in her culpability, for she already felt extremely guilty about her drinking. I also suspect that my sister didn't identify with the label "battered wife" because she saw it as applying only to those she considered totally innocent victims: women whose husbands turned on them without any provocation on the women's part. Susan probably saw these women as saintly, and she knew that she was no saint: she had, admittedly, hurled verbal abuse at Jim when drunk, hit and shoved him during their fights, and burned or cut up his clothes on at least two occasions. Her guilt about her role in the violence probably increased in the aftermath of an episode, especially if Jim either was behaving exceedingly lovingly toward her or was chastising her for the bad things she had done during the fight. Inevitably, then, she would feel compelled to revise her view of what had happened and convince herself that if she could only behave better—not get drunk, not begin to rage—such episodes would cease.

But she was being deeply unrealistic. She was not recognizing that while her behavior did play a role in causing the fights, that same behavior was a product of her relationship with Jim. It was the unhealthy dynamic between the two of them that caused her to get drunk and to act destructively; it was wishful thinking on her part to imagine that she could straighten herself out while remaining in that relationship. Things were too far gone. While she was right in thinking that she needed to change some of her behavior—especially to get help with her drinking—she was wrong in thinking that doing so would magically make the relationship right.

And so my advice to women who are blaming themselves for the violence in their spousal relationship is this: regardless of the extent of your responsibility for the violence, you are not going to be able to change yourself as long as you remain in the relationship. Yes, you may need to change yourself—you may have unhealthy, destructive tendencies—but it is well-nigh impossible to do so while mired in the dysfunctional patterns you and your partner have created. Get out of the relationship first; then commit yourself to seeking help.

Another reason many of you might be remaining in such a relationship is that you are deeply ashamed. Like Susan, you may put a lot of stock in the image of being a gracious, successful wife and mother. To have the world know about the sickness of your marriage, possibly about your own out-of-control behavior or drinking, would, you believe, rob you of your esteem and your identity. But, I tell you, you are letting false pride and groundless fears keep you in a dangerous position. In getting to know several friends and acquaintances of my sister's since her death, I have learned that most people knew or sensed what was going on—the fighting, the drinking, the calls to police—and none of them thought any the less of Susan for these skeletons in her closet. It turns out that some of the very people she wanted desperately to hide these skeletons from—for example, her well-bred friend Helen Lamberton, whom Susan implored me, in our

last phone conversation together, not to mention her drinking to—
were aware of and unfazed by them. Perhaps there were a few snooty
people who would have no longer wanted to associate with Susan
had they known the full extent of her problems, but all the friends
of hers I have spoken with loved her for who she was, warts and all.
In an interview with the *Baltimore Sun* following the finding of Susan's remains, Helen stated, "The only bad thing you can say about
Susan is she got mixed up with the wrong man" (Suzanne Loudermilk and Kris Antonelli, "Discovery of Body Brings Relief to Family," *Baltimore Sun,* Dec. 8, 1996, final ed., 5B).

And even if letting the world know you are a "failure" as a wife
will be humiliating and disorienting for you, wouldn't it, after all,
be better to be alive and a failure than to be dead as a result of trying
to hide your failure? Because that's what your choice may come down
to. If some prescient person had been able to get Susan to see that
she was facing this choice, of course she would have chosen life. Of
course she would rather have been alive for her sons and eventual
grandchildren, even if her lot was to be that of a single woman living in reduced economic and social circumstances, than to be dead,
never to hug her sons again, never to know her daughters-in-law and
grandchildren.

The choice put starkly to her in this way, Susan of course would
have chosen life. But she didn't see the life-and-death nature of her
choice. She didn't realize the danger she was in. If she did, she would
not have slipped back into seeing Jim again after she had separated
from him and would not have allowed the cycle of violence to start
up again. The fact that someone as physically timid as Susan could
become caught in such a cycle drives home to me its insidious nature: Susan seems to have become almost used to the bruises and cuts
and fractures. To think that she shook her head dismissively when
Jonathan pointed out to her, just six weeks before her own murder,
how close she was to having happen to her what had just happened
to Nicole Brown Simpson!

And you, some of you women reading this book, you may be
thinking the same thing about the difference between your situation
and Susan Hurley Harrison's. But stop and think again. If you cher-

ish life, if you have children and siblings and friends you love, think about what it would mean to lose all this. My sister lost all this because, I believe, she would not realistically face her situation. My advice is, sadly, too late for her, but it is not too late for you: Don't make any more excuses; *get out of your abusive relationship now.*

Appendix C
Domestic Violence Hot Lines

The following information is from the website for the National Coalition Against Domestic Violence: http://www.ncadv.org/resources/state.htm. (I am indebted to Andra Whitworth for notifying me of this resource.) To get help or give help, call the state coalition office to find the nearest program offering shelter and support.

Alabama Coalition Against Domestic Violence: 334-832-4842

Alaska Network on Domestic Violence and Sexual Assault: 907-586-3650

Arizona Coalition Against Domestic Violence: 602-279-2900

Arkansas Coalition Against Violence to Women and Children: 501-812-0571

California Alliance Against Domestic Violence: 916-444-7163

Statewide California Coalition for Battered Women: 888-722-2952

Colorado Coalition Against Domestic Violence: 303-831-9632

Connecticut Coalition Against Domestic Violence: 860-282-7899

Delaware Coalition Against Domestic Violence: 302-658-2958

D.C. Coalition Against Domestic Violence: 202-299-1181

Florida Coalition Against Domestic Violence: 850-425-2749

Georgia Advocates for Battered Women and Children: 404-524-3847

Georgia Coalition on Family Violence: 770-984-0085

Hawaii State Coalition Against Domestic Violence: 808-486-5072

Idaho Coalition Against Sexual and Domestic Violence: 208-384-0419

Illinois Coalition Against Domestic Violence: 217-789-2830
Indiana Coalition Against Domestic Violence: 317-543-3908
Iowa Coalition Against Domestic Violence: 515-244-8028
Kansas Coalition Against Sexual and Domestic Violence: 785-232-9784
Kentucky Domestic Violence Association: 502-695-2444
Louisiana Coalition Against Domestic Violence: 504-752-1296
Maine Coalition for Family Crisis Services: 207-941-1194
Maryland Network Against Domestic Violence: 301-352-4574
Massachusetts Coalition of Battered Women's Service Groups: 617-248-0922
Michigan Coalition Against Domestic Violence: 517-347-7000
Minnesota Coalition for Battered Women: 612-646-6177
Mississippi Coalition Against Domestic Violence: 601-981-9196
Missouri Coalition Against Domestic Violence: 573-634-4161
Montana Coalition Against Domestic Violence: 406-443-7794
Nebraska Domestic Violence and Sexual Assault Coalition: 402-476-6256
Nevada Network Against Domestic Violence: 702-828-1115
New Hampshire Coalition Against Domestic and Sexual Violence: 603-224-8893
New Jersey Coalition for Battered Women: 609-584-8107
New Mexico State Coalition Against Domestic Violence: 505-246-9240
New York State Coalition Against Domestic Violence: 518-432-4864
North Carolina Coalition Against Domestic Violence: 919-956-9124
North Dakota Council on Abused Women's Services: 701-255-6240
Action Ohio Coalition for Battered Women: 614-221-1255
Ohio Domestic Violence Network: 614-784-0023
Oklahoma Coalition on Domestic Violence and Sexual Assault: 405-848-1815
Oregon Coalition Against Domestic and Sexual Violence: 503-365-9644
Pennsylvania Coalition Against Domestic Violence: 717-545-6400
Comision Para Los Asuntos De La Mujer, Puerto Rico: 787-722-2907

Rhode Island Council on Domestic Violence: 401-467-9940

South Carolina Coalition Against Domestic Violence and Sexual Assault: 803-256-2900

South Dakota Coalition Against Domestic Violence and Sexual Assault: 605-945-0869

Tennessee Task Force Against Family Violence: 615-386-9406

Texas Council on Family Violence: 512-794-1133

Utah Domestic Violence Advisory Council: 801-538-9886

Vermont Network Against Domestic Violence and Sexual Assault: 802-223-1302

Virginians Against Domestic Violence: 757-221-0990

Washington State Coalition Against Domestic Violence: 360-407-0756

West Virginia Coalition Against Domestic Violence: 304-965-3552

Wisconsin Coalition Against Domestic Violence: 608-255-0539

Wyoming Coalition Against Domestic Violence and Sexual Assault: 307-755-5481

Women's Resource Center, Virgin Islands: 809-776-3966

Women's Coalition of St. Croix, Virgin Islands: 340-773-9272

Appendix D
Selected Readings

Books on and about Domestic Violence

Asher, Alexis. *Don't Let Him Hurt Me Anymore: A Self-Help Guide for Women in Abusive Relationships.* Los Angeles: Burning Gate Press, 1994.

Berry, Dawn Bradley. *The Domestic Violence Sourcebook: Everything You Need to Know.* Los Angeles: Lowell House, 1998.

Brownmiller, Susan. *Waverly Place.* New York: Grove Press, 1989.

Decker, David J. *Stopping the Violence: A Group Model to Change Men's Abusive Attitudes and Behaviors.* New York: Haworth Maltreatment and Trauma, 1999.

Evans, Patricia M. *Verbal Abuse Survivors Speak Out: On Relationship and Recovery.* Holbrook, MA: Bob Adams, 1993.

———. *The Verbally Abusive Relationship: How to Recognize It and How to Respond.* Expanded 2d ed. Holbrook, MA: Adams Media, 1996.

Fedders, Charlotte O'Donnell. *Shattered Dreams: The Story of Charlotte Fedders.* New York: Harper and Row, 1987.

Fortune, Marie. *Keeping the Faith: Questions and Answers for the Abused Woman.* San Francisco: Harper and Row, 1987.

Gondolf, Edward W. *Batterer Intervention Systems: Issues, Outcomes, and Recommendations.* Thousand Oaks, CA: Sage, 2002.

———. *Man Against Woman: What Every Woman Should Know about Violent Men.* Brandenton, FL: Human Services Institute, 1989.

———. *Men Who Batter: An Integrated Approach for Stopping Wife Abuse.* Holmes Beach, FL: Learning, 1985.

Goodman, Marilyn Shear. *Pattern Changing for Abused Women: An Educational Program.* Thousand Oaks, CA: Sage, 1995.

Jones, Ann. *Next Time She'll Be Dead: Battering and How to Stop It.* Rev. and updated ed. Boston: Beacon, 2000.

Jones, Ann, and Susan Schechter. *When Love Goes Wrong: What to Do When You Can't Do Anything Right.* New York: HarperCollins, 1992.

Klein, Ethel. *Ending Domestic Violence: Changing Public Perceptions/Halting the Epidemic.* Thousand Oaks, CA: Sage, 1997.

LaViolette, Alyce D., and Ola W. Barnett. *It Could Happen to Anyone: Why Battered Women Stay.* Thousand Oaks, CA: Sage, 2000.

Mariani, Cliff. *Domestic Violence Survival Guide.* Flushing, NY: Looseleaf Law, 1996.

Nicarthy, Ginny. *Getting Free: You Can End Abuse and Take Back Your Life.* 15th anniversary ed. Seattle: Seal, 1997.

——. *The Ones Who Got Away: Women Who Left Abusive Partners.* Seattle: Seal, 1987.

Nicarthy, Ginny, Karen Merriam, and Sandra Coffman. *Talking It Out: A Guide to Groups for Abused Women.* Seattle: Seal, 1984.

Quindlen, Anna. *Black and Blue: A Novel.* New York: Random House, 1998.

Schechter, Susan. *Women and Male Violence: The Vision and Struggles of the Battered Women's Movement.* Boston: South End, 1982.

Sonkin, Daniel Jay, Del Martin, and Lenore E. Auerbach Walker. *The Male Batterer: A Treatment Approach.* New York: Springer, 1985.

Walker, Lenore E. *The Battered Woman Syndrome.* 2d ed. New York: Springer, 2000.

Weiss, Elaine. *Surviving Domestic Violence: Voices of Women Who Broke Free.* Sandy, UT: Agreka, 2000.

Woititz, Janet Geringer. *Struggle for Intimacy.* Pompano Beach, FL: Health Communications, 1985.

Books on and about Alcoholism in Women

Beck, Sandy. *Alcoholic's Guide to Sobriety and Recovery.* Hollywood, CA: Ermine Publishers, 1977.

Blume, Sheila B. *Alcohol/Drug Dependent Women: New Insights into Their Special Problems, Treatment, Recovery.* Minneapolis: Johnson Institute, 1988.

Cary, Sylvia. *10+ Women with Long-Term Sobriety Talk about Life, Love, Family, Work, and Money.* Los Angeles: Lowell House, 1993.

Cheever, Susan. *Note Found in a Bottle: My Life as a Drinker.* New York: Simon and Schuster, 1999.

Corrigan, Eileen M. *Alcoholic Women in Treatment.* New York: Oxford University Press, 1980.

Costales, Claire. *Staying Dry: A Workable Solution to the Problem of Alcohol Abuse.* Ventura, CA: Regal, 1980.

Ettorre, Elizabeth. *Women and Alcohol: A Private Pleasure or a Public Problem?* London: Women's Press, 1997.

Ford, Betty. *A Glad Awakening.* Garden City, NY: Doubleday, 1987.

Hafner, Sarah. *Nice Girls Don't Drink: Stories of Recovery.* New York: Bergin and Garvey, 1992.

Jersild, Devon. *Happy Hours: Alcohol in a Woman's Life.* New York: Cliff Street, 2001.

Kent, Patricia. *An American Woman and Alcohol.* New York: Holt, Rinehart and Winston, 1967.

Knapp, Caroline. *Drinking: A Love Story.* New York: Dial, 1996.

McConville, Brigid. *Women under the Influence: Alcohol and Its Impact.* London: Virago, 1983.

McGovern, George S. *Terry: My Daughter's Life-and-Death Struggle with Alcoholism.* New York: Villard, 1996.

National Center for Alcohol Education. *Services for Alcoholic Women: Foundations for Change: Resource Book.* Rockville, MD: Department of Health, Education, and Welfare, 1979.

Sandmaier, Marian. *Alcohol Programs and Women: Issues, Strategies and Resources.* Rockville, MD: Department of Health, Education, and Welfare, 1977.

Stammer, M. Ellen. *Women and Alcohol: The Journey Back.* New York: Gardner, 1991.

W., Bill. *Alcoholics Anonymous: The Story of How Many Thousands of Men and Women Have Recovered from Alcoholism.* 3d ed. New York: Alcoholics Anonymous World Services, 1976.

Wallace, Patricia F., and Sister Mary Winifred. *A Guide for Women: Using the Twelve Steps to Grow Spiritually.* Denville, NJ: Dimension, 1992.

Ward, Yvonne. *A Bottle in the Cupboard: Women and Alcohol.* Dublin, Ireland: Attic, 1993.

Notes

2. The Early Years of Susan and Jim's Relationship, Mid-1980s

1. Susan's close friend Mary Jo Gordon describes how Jim insistently and insidiously pursued Susan: He "didn't push sex. . . . He just told her he wanted to be with her. He hung on her every word. He broke her down in the tiniest steps until he knew she would be receptive" (Loni Ingraham, "In Search of Susan," *Towson Times,* May 24, 1995, 17). Tom makes similar observations: "He showered her with attention. . . . He knew how to put on the big push" (Margaret Guroff, "Susan's Choice," *Baltimore Magazine,* Oct. 1995, 65).

2. Reporter Laura Lippman, who interviewed Tom in 1995 for an article she was writing about the case, describes his reaction to Jim's announcement: "Tom Owsley, looking back across 11 years to that night, says dryly, 'It was something of a show stopper.' Then he asks to change the subject" ("The Mystery of Susan Harrison," *Baltimore Sun,* Aug. 20, 1995, final ed., 4K).

3. Molly Harrison sums it up this way: "All hell broke loose" (Guroff 65).

3. The Search Begins, August–September 1994

1. Michael Ollove and Dan Thanh Dang, "Missing Ruxton Woman's Marriage Was Troubled," *Baltimore Sun,* Aug. 22, 1994, final ed., 1B+.

4. Mounting Suspicions about Jim, Autumn 1994

1. Reporter Margaret Guroff would comment on this lack of effort on Jim's part in her late 1995 article: "Jim has cooperated with investigators and reporters, against his lawyers' advice. But unlike Susan's siblings, who hired a private investigator and who call police several times a week for progress reports, Jim Harrison has hired no one to look for Susan. And in the 15 months since her disappearance, he has called police just a handful of times" (62).

2. Baltimore County Police Report No. K-113457. This incident is mentioned in several newspaper and magazine articles, including Ollove and Dang 10B; Guroff 66; and Ingraham, "In Search of Susan," 18.

3. Guroff quotes Jim as saying to her, "'A lot of people, including Jim, figured that Jim was going to be the successor to the McCormick [company]'" (brackets hers) (66). Lippman writes, "He speaks of himself in the third person, showing off a series of photographs of him with his grandchildren. 'Jim likes to read.' 'Jim gives kisses.' 'Jim likes to hug, too'" (4K). And Ingraham quotes Jim's explanation to her of his children's reaction to his divorcing their mother for Susan: "[S]ome of the children realized from Jim's point of view that Susan was prettier and better" ("In Search of Susan," 17).

4. This is quoted in Guroff's article (64), but I had heard this description of Jim's reputation before I read the article. Lippman, in the same section of her article in which she describes Jim's childlike behavior and speech, makes a similar observation: "He is 58, almost 59, and until four years ago, he was the chief financial officer of one of Baltimore's most successful and visible companies. Before his early retirement from McCormick, his reputation was for playing the bumpkin, allowing his adversaries to think themselves smarter than he" (4K). Similarly, Ingraham comments that in business, Jim "had a habit of excelling at whatever he undertook. His unassuming manner masked a shrewd mind, according to some business acquaintances" ("In Search of Susan," 17).

5. Jim told reporter Lippman, "The police said I failed it, but I looked at the chart and all the lines were the same" (4K). Reporter Ingraham states, "Then there was the lie detector test he took for the FBI last winter [actually, he took it in the autumn] when he was asked if he was responsible for Susan's disappearance. He was told that he failed it, he said. But he could plainly observe his reaction to sensitive questions was the same as his reaction to crucial queries" ("In Search of Susan," 19). Reporter Guroff writes, "Jim took a lie-detector test. Police told him he failed, but he's sticking to his story" (62).

6. Jim used this expression in virtually every interview he had with police and reporters concerning Susan's disappearance. Most of the articles cited in this book quote him using it or a variation of it.

7. Guroff comments, "To Cockeysville police, this [Susan's "going manic-depressive"] was a familiar description. It was how Jim usually explained the fights that had made the Harrisons' home a frequent destination for their blue-and-white squad cars" (62).

5. Frustrations with the Investigation, Autumn 1994

1. John McPhee, "The Gravel Page," *New Yorker,* 71, no. 46 (Jan. 29, 1996): 44–52.

2. Steve Weinberg, "Missing and Presumed Murdered," *ABA Journal* 81 (Sept. 1995): 62–68.

3. George McMullen, letter to the author, Dec. 1994.

7. Cleaning Out Susan's Cottage, November 1994

1. The more I heard about Susan and Jim's relationship from Susan's friends in the months and years following her disappearance, the more convinced I was that Susan was caught in this syndrome. Her close friend Mary Jo Gordon is quoted in Laura Lippman's article as saying, "She kept thinking if she could change herself, it would never happen. She thought it was something she did. He could be so good to her. He admired her. At the same time, he thought maybe she was better than him. He put her up on a pedestal, then resented her for being higher than him" (4K). To Loni Ingraham, Mary Jo said, "He was so good to her when he was good to her and that was the hook. She told him she would never see him again but no matter what she said she would see him again" ("In Search of Susan," 18). Mary Jo wrote to me in an e-mail, "For some unknown reason she always ended up doing what he asked eventually . . . he would wear her down with sweet talk or gifts, or simply her addiction to him. He had power over her. . . ." (May 14, 2002). Another friend, Gretel White, told Ingraham that Jim "brought a lot of excitement into Susan's life" and that "Susan really didn't want to face the world alone. She didn't know who she was, how talented she was. That was the sad thing" ("In Search of Susan," 18).

8. Growing Suspicions about Domestic Abuse, Mid-1980s–July 1993

1. Susan didn't tell anyone in the family about the wedding until after the fact, but she apparently did invite her long-time close friend Terry MacMillan, as I learned in one of the first newspaper articles that came out after Susan's disappearance. This article quotes Terry as saying that she didn't go to the wedding as a form of protest, for she knew that Jim had been abusing Susan for years. She told the interviewer that "after an altercation

at a San Francisco hotel in the mid 1980s, Susan spent the night with her [Terry was living in California at the time]. Although Susan called police, she refused to prosecute Mr. Harrison, said Ms. MacMillan. It was a pattern she repeated" (Ollove and Dang 10B).

2. As Guroff observes, "Each claimed the other was the attacker, though Susan is the only one whose bones were ever broken" (66).

3. Jonathan apparently felt the same way. Laura Lippman, who interviewed him for her article, describes his feelings when he was photographing his mother's injuries: "He looked through a viewfinder at the bruise on his mother's forehead, at the blackened right eye almost swollen shut, and tried to ignore the bile rising in his throat. He told himself: *This is rock bottom. This is the beginning of the climb out*" (5K).

9. Susan Hits Bottom, Autumn 1993

1. This incident is described in Lippman 5K.

2. This incident is also described in Lippman 5K.

3. Margaret Guroff describes Jonathan and Nicholas's affectionate, humorous attitude toward their mom's overtures: "She overwhelmed the boys with handmade gifts. 'She'd make us sweaters, mittens, lamp shades, everything,' recalls Nick, now a junior at Middlebury College. 'Sometimes you'd just mention something offhand, just admire it, and she'd make you one. You had to be careful what you said,' he jokes" (63).

10. Hopeful Beginning and Tragic Ending, January–August 1994

1. Susan's friends shared my impression: "Friends saw positive changes in her after the separation. 'She was spunky again for the first time in years,' Ms. Gordon said" (Ollove and Dang 10B). After interviewing several of Susan's friends, Lieutenant Sam Bowerman concluded, "She was a woman finally gaining her independence, at a major turning point in her life, perhaps for the first time having to know who she was and finding a sense of her own self worth. From the people I talked to, she had a zest for life probably more so at the time of her disappearance than ever before" (Ingraham, "In Search of Susan," 19).

2. A telephone answering machine tape that we found in Susan's cottage contains a conversation with Mary Jo Gordon, which Susan must have unknowingly recorded, in which Susan says such things as, "I had a horrible dream about all the things he was going to do to me," "I was going to be left with nothing," "He has all this stuff against me."

3. Mary Jo Gordon, e-mail letter to author, April 4, 2002.

4. Gordon, e-mail letter to author, May 14, 2002.

5. Ingraham, "In Search of Susan," 19; Guroff 131.

6. This conversation is described in Lippman 5K.

12. Childhood

1. I am indebted to my Irish friends Mary Kelly, Mark Cooney, and Aisling Maguire for furnishing me with the proper spelling and the etymology of this word.

13. Prep School, College, and Early Adult Years

1. A word of explanation about my name: I was baptized "Mary" and the name on my birth certificate is "Mary Hurley," but when I was a few months old my father decided he liked the name "Mary Ellen," so the family began calling me that. My parents had a friend who often told them they ought to call me "Molly," which in those days was a diminutive of "Mary" (as was "Polly"), but they preferred to stick with "Mary Ellen." When I was about to start Dana Hall and was brainstorming for a nickname, I recalled this story about my parents' friend and hence hit upon "Molly." A few of my relatives still call me "Mary Ellen" or "Mary," but most people today know me as "Molly," which is why I decided to use that name on the title page of this book. (I used "Mary" on the title page of my first two books because many of the people who called me that were still alive when I published them.)

14. The Search Continues, January–May 1995: Appeals to Jim and His Family

1. Ingraham, "In Search of Susan," 19.

2. Guroff 132.

3. Lippman 4K.

4. Christy Harrison, "Family Tries to Cope, Seeks Closure One Year after Melendi Disappearance," *Atlanta Constitution,* Mar. 26, 1995, G7.

5. *Atlanta Constitution,* May 9, 1995, A14.

6. Sergio R. Bustos, "Killer on Bus Was Lonely, Jobless, Mentally Troubled," *Sun-Sentinel* (Fort Lauderdale), May 10, 1995, final ed., 1A.

7. Cindy Elmore, "Slaying-Suicide on Bus Ended a Solitary Life of Rejected Opportunity," *Sun-Sentinel* (Fort Lauderdale), May 17, 1985, final ed., 1A+.

8. Bustos.

9. Guroff 133.

10. Elmore 10A.

15. The Memorial Service, June 1995

1. James Joyce, "The Dead," in *Dubliners* (1916; reprint, New York: Viking, 1968), 223.

16. *Unsolved Mysteries* and Other Desperate Measures, Summer 1995–Autumn 1996

1. Both of these incidents are described in Lippman (4K) and Guroff (132–33).

2. Loni Ingraham, "Woes Continue for James Harrison," *Towson Times,* July 2, 1996, 5.

17. The Search Ends, November 1996–January 1997

1. This reaction of Jim's is described in Suzanne Loudermilk and Kris Antonelli, "Discovery of Body Brings Relief to Family," *Baltimore Sun,* Dec. 8, 1996, final ed., 1B.

2. Kris Antonelli and Jay Apperson, "Snow Impedes Harrison Probe," *Baltimore Sun,* Dec. 7, 1996, final ed., 1A+.

3. Frank D. Roylance, "Forensic Scientists Listen to What Bones Have to Say," *Baltimore Sun,* Dec. 8, 1996, final ed., 7A.

4. Guroff 134.

5. Ingraham, "In Search of Susan," 17.

18. Justice Pursued and Justice Denied, January 1997–August 1999

1. This incident is described in Consella A. Lee, "Slain Woman's Spouse Charged after Altercation at Airport," *Baltimore Sun,* Aug. 14, 1997, final ed., 3B.

2. The filing of this motion is reported in Joan Jacobson, "Harrison's Lawyers Angered by Civil Suit," *Baltimore Sun,* Sept. 12, 1997, final ed., 1B+.

3. This ruling is reported in Joan Jacobson, "Suit Blaming Harrison in Death of Wife May Proceed, Judge Says," *Baltimore Sun,* Dec. 5, 1997, final ed., 3B.

4. This case is reported in Jim Hudson, "Arrest Made in Slaying from 1985," *Baltimore Sun,* Nov. 26, 1997, final ed., 1B.

5. The family had the impression that Dr. McDaniel would be willing to testify in a criminal suit, an impression that was strengthened in February 1999 when she wrote a letter to Carey Deeley stating that she would be willing to testify in the civil suit. McDaniel's intended testimony was discussed in a newspaper article following the settling of the civil suit:

> Records filed in the case show the Owsley brothers' lawyers had intended to bring Dr. Ellen McDaniel, a forensic psychiatrist, to testify that Mrs. Harrison suffered from "battered spouse syndrome" during her relationship with Harrison.
>
> "She suffered physical injuries as a direct result of Jim Harrison's abuse," wrote McDaniel in a letter to Deeley in February.
>
> "Like many abused spouses, her emotional ties to Mr. Harrison remained. She tried to find a balance between maintaining her physical safety and reestablishing some level of emotional contact but she ultimately failed," McDaniel wrote. (Joan Jacobson, "Lawsuit Against Husband Dropped," Baltimore Sun, Aug. 28, 1999, final ed., 1B)

6. The source of this information is Joan Jacobson, "Lawsuit Against Husband Dropped," and *Harrison v. Harrison,* Civil No. 94CV366/71/50 (the exchange of interrogatories in the suit Susan filed for separate maintenance in January 1994).

7. Jacobson writes in "Lawsuit Against Husband Dropped," "When Mrs. Harrison separated from her husband in December 1993, she created a 'threat to J. Harrison's complete control over his newly acquired wealth,' wrote Terry L. Musika, of PENTA Advisory Services LLC."

8. The source of the information in this paragraph is phone conversations Susan had with me and the exchange of interrogatories, Civil No. 94CV366/71/50.

9. Joan Jacobson, "Case Closed on Woman's Homicide," *Baltimore Sun,* May 4, 1999, final ed., 1B.

10. Steve Allen's statements are quoted in Jacobson, "Lawsuit Against Husband Dropped."

11. Approximately sixty-nine articles about this case appeared in the *Baltimore Sun,* all by Lisa Goldberg, between July 8, 1996, and Nov. 30, 2001, some in the Howard edition and some in the final city edition.

12. Lisa Goldberg, "Missing Victims Test Courts," *Baltimore Sun,* Oct. 1, 2000, Howard ed., 1B.

13. Goldberg.

14. Katherine E. Finkelstein, "Surgeon Convicted of Murdering Wife," *New York Times,* Oct. 25, 2000, late ed., B3. This case was closely followed by Finkelstein in the *New York Times* that autumn, with articles appearing on Oct. 13, Oct. 17, Oct. 19, and Oct. 24, all in the late ed., B3. Also, a lengthy article about the case was published in the *New Yorker* by Tad Friend ("The Harriet-the-Spy Club," 76, no. 21 [July 31, 2000]: 36–43).

Molly Hurley Moran grew up in Massachusetts, graduated from Brown University, and received her M.A. and Ph.D. from the University of New Mexico. She is an associate professor of writing in the Division of Academic Enhancement at the University of Georgia and is the author of *Margaret Drabble: Existing Within Structures* and *Penelope Lively,* as well as of numerous articles and book chapters on composition and rhetoric, technical writing, and twentieth-century British literature (all of which she published under the name of Mary Hurley Moran). She resides in Athens, Georgia, with her husband and daughter.